DECISION MAKING UNDER RISK IN ORGANISATIONS

Decision Making Under Risk in Organisations
The Case of German Waste Management

ECKARD KÄMPER
ISO Institute, Cologne

LONDON AND NEW YORK

First published 2000 by Ashgate Publishing

Reissued 2018 by Routledge
2 Park Square, Milton Park, Abingdon, Oxon OX14 4RN
711 Third Avenue, New York, NY 10017, USA

Routledge is an imprint of the Taylor & Francis Group, an informa business

Copyright © Eckard Kämper 2000

All rights reserved. No part of this book may be reprinted or reproduced or utilised in any form or by any electronic, mechanical, or other means, now known or hereafter invented, including photocopying and recording, or in any informativon storage or retrieval system, without permission in writing from the publishers.

Notice:
Product or corporate names may be trademarks or registered trademarks, and are used only for identification and explanation without intent to infringe.

Publisher's Note
The publisher has gone to great lengths to ensure the quality of this reprint but points out that some imperfections in the original copies may be apparent.

Disclaimer
The publisher has made every effort to trace copyright holders and welcomes correspondence from those they have been unable to contact.

A Library of Congress record exists under LC control number: 00109127

ISBN 13: 978-1-138-73960-4 (hbk)
ISBN 13: 978-1-138-73957-4 (pbk)
ISBN 13: 978-1-315-18408-1 (ebk)

Contents

Preface vi
Acknowledgements vii

1 Decision Making under Risk 1

2 Risk and Organisations 22

3 Risks of Waste Management 46

4 Risk and Participation 81

5 Risk and Routines 128

6 Summary and Conclusions 159

Bibliography *184*

Preface

This study analyses how organisations make decisions in situations characterised by risk. The empirical field to be studied is that of local waste management in Germany. The case of waste management has been chosen because, as will be argued in the following chapters, the management of household waste confronts administrative organisations with high amounts of risk and uncertainty. A typical feature of risk situations is that the organisation cannot avoid the problem by simply making no decision. To do this would be a decision in itself and would therefore also entail the taking if risks.

How do organisations behave in such a situation? The answer to this question will be given by a sociological analysis of decision making processes in two organisations. The study will be organised as follows: Chapter one is dedicated to sociological theories of decision making and of risk. The second chapter presents the application of this general framework to the level of formal organisations. The conclusion of the two theoretical chapters will be that organisations have to organise for uncertainty absorption in order to be able to take risks. In chapter three the two case studies will be prepared by an analysis of the legal, political, and organisational conditions in German waste management. The first case study, presented in chapter four, analyses the decision making process in an organisation that attempted to resolve its decision problems by increased efforts towards participation and anticipatory analysis. The second case study will be reported in chapter five and shows an organisation that handled the problems of risk and ambiguity by relying on established routines that were considered appropriate to the situation. Chapter six presents a summary and the conclusions of the study.

Acknowledgements

Many persons and institutions have made invaluable contributions to my work during the past few years. Special thanks go to the following persons: Prof Adrienne Héritier and Prof Wolfgang Krohn who gave me the opportunity to do the research for this study and provided me with support and encouragement; Markus Timmermeister for his co-operation and making important data available; Volker Vorwerk and Ralf Herbold for inspiring collaboration in Bielefeld; Petra Hiller and Veronika Tacke for helpful discussions of the theoretical framework; Prof Helmut Willke for indispensable support in the final phase of the work; David Geary for his careful correction of a former version of the text. The necessary infrastructure and financial support was provided by the following institutions: The European University Institute (Florence), the Institute for Science and Technology Studies (Bielefeld), the Centre for Technology Assessment (Stuttgart), the German Council of Environmental Advisors (Wiesbaden) and the Volkswagen Foundation.

1 Decision Making under Risk

The present study tries to analyse organisational processes of decision making under conditions of risk. The challenge for a sociological analysis of decision making under risk is, however, that the long tradition of theorising about problems of risk in decision making has taken place under the auspices of economic concepts of decision, risk, and uncertainty. Only in recent years, social theorists have put emphasis on developing genuinely sociological concepts of decision making, and of risk. These theoretical developments suggest that the classic conceptions of risk, rooted in economic theory, were not appropriate to guide empirical analyses of the social conflicts concerning risk (cf. e.g. Douglas 1985; Perrow 1984; Wynne 1987; Short 1984; 1989). Thus, for sociological analyses, it is necessary to develop concepts that deviate in almost all relevant aspects from the economic tradition.

In the following chapter, I will try to highlight the main characteristics of a sociological account of decision making under risk. This is necessary in order to clarify the deviations from the economic concepts. The economic tradition describes decision making as an action performed by individual or corporate actors who, on the basis of given preferences choose a course of action out of a given range of alternatives. In a sociological concept, decision making is an activity generated by behavioural expectations. The main consequence of this concept is that preferences lose their central theoretical position in explaining decision making processes. More important for the analysis of decision making are the expectations the decision reacts to.

The development toward this sociological approach will be sketched in the following sections (1.1, 1.2, 1.3). This general framework will then be applied to problems of decision making under risk (1.4).

1.1 Risk: The Initial Formulation

The initial formulation of a concept of risk was made by Frank Knight (1921). The context for the concept is provided by the framework of neoclassical economics. Within this framework, a decision situation can be characterised as follows: An actor is facing a situation with a range of decision alternatives. The actor is equipped with preferences, that are stable, exogenous, and transitive. Furthermore, the actor is characterised by maximising behaviour, i.e. he seeks to choose the alternative that serves his preferences best. The actor then makes his decision by evaluating the possible future consequences connected with the available alternatives. With the help of his preferences, the actor chooses the alternative that leads to the best consequences in terms of the actor's preferences. The interesting question for research on decision making processes is then the *degree of rationality* the decision maker achieves with his choice. Rationality is defined as the degree to which the decision maker manages to choose the alternative that serves his preferences best (Elster 1989; Luhmann 1988: 276).

Within this general framework, Knight places his concept of risk (1921: 197ff.). Risk is then to be distinguished from uncertainty. The actor finds himself in a situation of uncertainty if he cannot know whether the available alternatives really lead to the consequences he expects. This uncertainty is not measurable, because the actor does not know which factors influence the decision outcome. Risk, on the contrary, refers to measurable uncertainty. The actors thus know all of the possible decision outcomes, and the remaining problem is the calculation of the probability of their occurrence (cf. Bonß 1995: 98pp.). For Knight, only situations of risk can be subject to scientific analysis. The problem is how to turn uncertainties into risk which in turn is considered to be an information problem.

This basic concept of decision making under risk has been highly influential. It has mainly guided economic research (e.g. Arrow 1970; Anand 1993; Dickinson et al. 1994; Hey 1997). Since the sixties, when social conflicts about the risks of large technical systems arose, the concept has also been the basis for the theories of scientific risk assessment. In these theories, risk is defined as the product of the magnitude of a possible harm times the probability of its occurrence. The result is a quantifiable, one-dimensional, and probabilistic measure of risk that allows the comparison of different risks such as the use of nuclear energy, smoking, car driving, etc. This approach has proven to be extremely useful in improving the safety of complex technologies (cf. Bechmann 1993; Renn 1992).

However, from a sociological perspective, the approach to risk based on economic theorising has its deficits. First of all, one can easily see that situations of risk, as defined by Knight, will appear extremely seldom, since normally the decision makers will not be able to identify all the factors that influence the probability that certain decision outcomes will occur (Bonß 1995: 100). Second, the concept of a rational, maximising decision maker has been criticised, not only in the context of risk (e.g. Smelser 1992). For an organisational analysis, the concept requires that organisations be conceived as actors - a difficult demand (Hannan 1992; Jansen 1997; Kappelhoff 1997). Third, empirical research on risk taking behaviour has shown that probabilistic calculations are without any relevance for decision making under risk (March / Shapira 1988). Finally, the theories of risk assessment, based on Knight's concepts, have proved to be counterproductive in social conflicts about risky technologies. It has turned out to be impossible to fix a universal, objective measure of risk that is accepted independently from the social context (Renn 1992; Douglas 1985; Wynne 1987).

Accounts of risk within the economic tradition are therefore inappropriate for a sociological analysis of decision making under risk. In order to outline the sociological concepts that have been developed in the eighties and the early nineties, I will precede as follows in the coming sections. Firstly, I will concentrate on possible alternatives to the *general concept of decision making* (1.2). This will lead to the substitution of preference by behavioural expectation as the basic concept in a theory of choice (1.3). The starting point for this line of argument will be the behavioural theory of decision making, which contains many important elements of a sociological approach to decision making. In the last step, I will sketch the application of this general account of decision making to problems of decisions under risk (1.4).

1.2 Toward a Sociological Concept of Decision Making

The emergence of a specific sociological approach to problems of decision making can best be traced by examining the development of the behavioural theory of decision making, a branch of theory that is mainly connected with the names of Herbert Simon and James March (Simon 1957; March and Simon 1958; cf. Berger / Bernhard-Mehlich 1993). The key terms that characterise the development of the behavioural theory of decision making are bounded rationality (1.2.1), ambiguity (1.2.2), and decision making as rule following (1.2.3). This step-by-step rejection of the economic theory of decision making will be analysed in the following sections.

1.2.1 Bounded Rationality

The first important modification of the pure economic approach is the concept of bounded rationality. Exactly what this concept implies can be exemplified by the basic decision situation as sketched above. In contrast to a model of perfect rationality, the notion of bounded rationality introduces several limitations to a rational choice within this model. Firstly, the decision maker cannot know all possible alternatives that an external observer might identify for instance. Second, the decision maker has incomplete knowledge with respect to the consequences of each alternative. Third, it is very difficult to evaluate future events correctly, even if one has a consistent preference function.

These cognitive limitations in the process of decision making lead to the phenomenon that, in general, satisfactory instead of optimal decisions are made. This means that not all possible alternatives are examined, but only the first one that promises satisfactory results according to the underlying preferences.

For the central research question, the degree of rationality that is achieved by the decision, this means the following. Although an external observer might judge the behaviour of the decision maker as slightly irrational, the decision maker in his specific context at least intends to act rationally (March / Simon 1958; Smelser 1992: 388). If one takes into account the idiosyncratic conditions of the decision situation (complexity of the environment, structure of the organisation), one might even state that the decision maker achieves the highest degree of rationality possible under the given circumstances. Therefore, for the analysis of rationality in decision making behaviour, it is necessary to analyse the structural context in which the decision takes place.

March and Simon (1958) argue that there is no objective rationality. One can only speak of rationality in relation to a certain frame of reference. This is what is meant by the term bounded rationality. In contrast to the pure economic model the ability of the decision maker to know all of the available consequences and to anticipate all of the consequences connected with the alternatives is questioned. The modifications are thus modest, with the problem of rationality remaining in the centre of interest.

1.2.2 Ambiguity

In his later works, especially in collaboration with Johan Olsen, James March formulated a more radical concept of decision making in organisations, that rejects assumptions of rationality to a very large extent.

The basic concept of these studies (Cohen et al. 1972; March / Olsen 1976; March 1988) is the notion of ambiguity. The main consequence of this concept is that preferences lose their central position in explaining choices. Since rationality in the economic theories of choice is defined in relation to the decision maker's preferences, the notion of ambiguity makes it difficult to speak of rational decision making.

Ambiguity in organisations refers to three factors. *Firstly*, the organisational technologies are unclear. Organisational technology in this context means knowledge of how to transform an input into an output. There are organisations with clear technologies, for example a producer of cars who transforms delivered parts into automobiles, and there are organisations with extremely unclear technologies, for example a university who has to transform young people into scientists. Organisations facing completely new tasks, for instance parts of public administration implementing a new political programme, also suffer from this lack of knowledge of what they are actually doing. The *second* aspect of ambiguity is that the goals and preferences are ill-defined, inconsistent and unstable. *Third*, there is no stable participation of decision makers in the decision process and the attention of the participants to the decision fluctuates.

These three factors generate conditions of ambiguity. The existence of unclear technologies and preferences and the fluctuating attention of the participants to the situation have serious impacts on the nature of the decision process and on the achievable level of rationality.

In order to demonstrate the consequences of conditions of ambiguity for organisational decision processes, March and Olsen assume a four-step cycle of choice: (1) Individual cognitions and preferences, (2) individual action and participation in organisational decisions, (3) organisational choices, (4) events in the environment of the organisation. (March / Olsen 1976: 13) A complete cycle of choice would imply that individual preferences are the basis for individual actions in the organisation, which then lead to organisational choices. The environmental consequences of the organisational choices are then observed by the decision makers and change or confirm their preferences, that are then the basis for further actions. This complete cycle of choice would suggest a certain degree of rationality as it allows the organisation to decide, to observe the consequences of the decision and then to react by improved actions. The result would be an adaptive rationality as suggested by Cyert and March (1963: 117): The organisation would not necessarily act rationally in the classical sense, but it would be able to learn from experience.

However, the above mentioned conditions of ambiguity inhibit the cycle of choice on each of its stages. First of all, due to the fluctuating attention and participation of the members in decision processes, the individual cognitions are not always the basis for the actions they contribute to the organisational processes. There are actions in organisations which are not based on individual preferences, and many preferences are not transformed into actions. Second, the coupling between individual actions and organisational choices is quite loose. Third, the connection between actions and environmental events is far from being clear. This is due to the fact that environments of organisations are complex and that the organisational technologies are often not well understood. 'As a result, the same organisational action will have different responses at different times; different organisational actions will have the same response.' (March / Olsen 1976: 17) Finally, the connection between events in the environment and the cognitions of the individual member is a complex one. Observed events have to be interpreted, causal relationships are not easy to identify.

After introducing the concept of ambiguity, the theory allows a more radical critique of concepts of rational decision making. The concept of bounded rationality questioned the possibility of knowing all *alternatives* and of anticipating the future *consequences* of the alternatives correctly. The notion of decision making under ambiguity goes even further: The *preferences* in organisational choice are inconsistent, contested, and unstable. Often, they cannot guide the decision making and learning behaviour in the organisation. The evaluation of future consequences in decision making, for which preferences are the basis, becomes highly ambiguous and even the correct interpretation of past events, the essential precondition of learning from experience, becomes very difficult. The modification of the concept of preferences enables the behavioural theory of organisational decision making to deconstruct expectations of rational choice in a very serious way. If it is correct that preferences are unclear, unstable and endogenous, i.e. that they change during the process of deciding and of evaluating the consequences (March 1988), some basic assumptions of theories of rational choice are challenged.

As the preferences of the decision makers lose their position as the central explaining factor for choice, it is difficult to define rationality in this context. Decisions often take place without clear underlying preferences, thus it is difficult to analyse whether the decision maker has chosen the alternative that serves his preferences best, or in other words, whether he has acted in a rational manner.

The question is, however, which concept could substitute that of preference in a non-economic theory of decision making. If one takes seriously the problems of ambiguity in organisations, one cannot keep 'preferences' as the basic variable to explain decision making behaviour.

Conditions of ambiguity de-couple preferences and choices; thus preferences cannot explain the decisions that can be observed.

An answer is prepared by the development of the behavioural theory of decision making toward an institutional approach, which is mainly applied to political decisions. This perspective has been outlined by March and Olsen (1989; 1995) and suggests the concept of institutions as the central one for a theory of decisions in organisations. This approach will be sketched in the following section. Since the term 'institution' is however quite ambiguous, I will argue for modifications in the concept of institutions. These modifications, borrowed from the systems theory of Niklas Luhmann, allow for a framework for the analysis of decision making that does not need preferences as a basic concept. The new central term is that of behavioural expectations.

1.2.3 Decision Making as Rule Following

March and Olsen (1989; 1995; cf. March 1994) argue that there are two possible logics of action that underlie processes of decision making. They call them logic of consequences and logic of appropriateness. To argue, as March and Olsen do, that decisions take place according to a logic of appropriateness and not to a logic of consequences, implies a further rejection of expectations of rationality, as defined in economic theory.

Conceiving of actions and decisions as determined by a *logic of consequences* implies the following aspects: Decision alternatives are chosen by evaluating their perceived consequences according to the preferences of the decision maker. This logic of action is directed towards the future and it is characterised by anticipation, calculation, and analysis.

The *logic of appropriateness* is a rule-based one. Decisions take place by matching situations to existing rules of the organisation. As this logic of action refers to organisational rules that have been developed for past events, it is more directed to the past. It is not a logic of anticipation but one of recognising certain situations and classifying them as familiar or as new.

It is not only theories of decision making working with a concept of rational choice, which at least implicitly work with the assumption that decisions follow a logic of consequences, but also the behavioural theories of organised decision making, especially the contributions of March and Simon (1958) and Cyert and March (1963). Although these theories assume serious restrictions to anticipatory actions, actors still try to choose a course of action by anticipating its possible consequences. If one assumes that actions mainly are chosen by their appropriateness to the situation, the picture of decision making in organisations becomes different.

March and Olsen (1989: 21; 1995: 28) argue that political decisions in particular are made by referring to the logic of appropriateness. Political organisations are particularly prone to conflicting demands and expectations, and these contradictions can best be handled by the symbolic power of appropriate rules (March / Olsen 1989). It is this point in the theory, where the notion of an *institutional* perspective on decision making becomes important. What is appropriate to a given situation is predetermined by institutionalised structures, procedures, routines, identities, and role expectations. March and Olsen use the term institution as follows: 'We use the term in a more general sense to refer not only to legislatures, executives, and judiciaries but also to systems of law, social organization (such as the media, markets, or the family), and identities or roles (such as 'citizen', 'official', or 'individual').' (March / Olsen 1995: 27)

The notion that the decision situation is structured by institutions in the above sense has important consequences for a concept of decision making. For example uncertainty in decision making does not refer to uncertainty about future consequences or about the own preferences; decision makers face uncertainty about what their role, their identity, e.g. as a politician, requires.

However, March and Olsen have been criticised for the ambiguous use of the term institution (e.g. Dowding 1994). This is a serious critique since, as I argue, the concept is supposed to substitute the concept of preference as the core notion in a theory of decision making. However, although the term institution is used widely in the recent literature on organisation, decisions, and in political theory (cf. eg. Powell / DiMaggio 1991), its meaning is still ambiguous. It is therefore necessary to dedicate a short section to the discussion of what "institution" can refer to in a non-economic theory of decision making. I will suggest conceiving of institutions as behavioural expectations. On this basis, it will be possible to connect the institutional approach with a sociological perspective of decision making that substitutes "preferences" by "behavioural expectations" as the central concept of a theory of decision making.

1.3 Behavioural Expectations as the Basic Concept in Decision Theory

For the following considerations, it is important to note that the term institution will be used in a constitutive rather than in a regulative sense (cf. Scott/Meyer 1994). If one conceives of institutions as having a regulative function, actors with their preferences keep their central theoretical position. This concept of institutions that shape, channel, and restrict individual preferences is used by many scholars in political science (e.g. Dowding 1991; Dowding / King 1995; Hechter et al. 1990; Mayntz / Scharpf 1995; Scharpf 1997). In the present study, I will try to stress the constitutive function of institutionalised behavioural expectations. It will be argued that institutions as a special form of behavioural expectations constitute situations of choice and therefore deserve considerable theoretical attention. In order to shed some light on the relationship between expectations and decisions, some arguments of Luhmann will be used.

1.3.1 Behavioural Expectations as the Structure of Social Systems

The social theory that is necessary to clarify the concept of institutions and their role in processes of decision making uses a concept of action that deviates in important aspects from conventional approaches. The underlying concept of action does not take the ideas of classic action theories such as subject, intention etc as its point of departure. Action is conceived of as an *event*. This implies that it has almost no duration in time (Allport 1954: 292; Allport 1955: 615; MacCorquodale / Meehl 1953: 56). The question is then, how a system of actions can arise out of these events. How can events without duration be connected to processes?

This question can be answered with the help of the second important feature of an action: An action is not only an event, it is a *selective event* (Luhmann 1981: 137). The action selects one specific alternative from the innumerable possible courses of action. The selective character of an action implies that it suggests specific follow-up events: After someone has entered a bar, only a constrained number of meaningful connecting actions is possible. Therefore, by its selective character, any action creates *expectations* towards follow-up action. On this simple basis, actions connect themselves to systems of action. These systems consist only of actions and expectations, or, in the words of Floyd Allport: of events and structures (Allport 1940; 1962). This concept of structures consisting of events has proven to be useful especially for the empirical analysis of organisations (cf. Katz / Kahn 1966; Weick 1979). Furthermore, the perspective shows similarities to Giddens' (1984) theory of structuration (cf. Cohen 1989), since in the structure-event theory structures and actions also reproduce each other. Neither of the two concepts determines the other. One important implication is, of course, that structures do not just constrain action, but they also enable action, indeed they are an indispensable precondition for action. 'A structured system increases the area of freedom for its members.' (Stogdill 1959: 25).

The type of structure that can perform this function of connecting selective events in social systems are *expectations* (Luhmann 1995: 96, 278pp.). The concept of expectation as it is used here calls for further explanation. As expectations also play a crucial role in economic theory (Shackle 1949; Muth 1961; Simon 1981), it is important to clarify what the sociological concept of expectations, which serve as a structure for action, means. *Expectations can only structure action, if they become reflexive.* Only in the form of expected expectations ('Erwartungserwartungen'), is a structure for social action provided. For example, actor A expects the expectations that another actor, B, has of A's actions. Only if B's expectations of A's actions are expected by A, do these expectations have a structuring effect on the selection of A's actions (Parsons et al. 1951; Kelly 1955: 94; Galtung 1959: 220; Luhmann 1995: 303pp.).

The creation of structures by selective action can be called time binding (Luhmann 1981: 50pp.; 101pp.; 126pp.). The notion refers to the fact that the creation of behavioural expectations, or structures, resolves the problem that the action is only an event without any duration in time. At this point, an important problem arises. The selective character of an action does not only imply the creation of an expectation by suggesting a specific follow-up connecting action but action as a selective event also carries the message that the selection could have been made differently - there were other possibilities. As a result, the selection can be questioned. The creation of structuring expectations does not determine future actions in the system, it only suggests certain future events, but also runs the risk of being questioned. These two contrasting features of time binding both result from the selective character of action.

These considerations about the time binding effect of the generation of structures in social systems are of crucial importance for the theory of decision making under risk, which will be sketched in the final sections of this chapter. The making of risky decisions is prone to the paradoxical effects of time binding in a very serious manner, since, for reasons to be explained later, decision making reinforces the selectivity of action. Thus, both the creation of structures and the risk of being rejected appear in a much stronger version if risky decisions are made.

At this most general point of the theoretical considerations, it is important to clarify the basic problem that social systems have to solve in this perspective. The problem is to connect the events and structures to larger processes. This problem arises because of the selectivity of actions: they suggest connecting actions but, due to their contingency, they can also be questioned. Their selectivity stresses their contingency and thus, their acceptance can be refused. The problem is thus one of *providing for expectational certainty*. A prerequisite for social action is the assumption of a considerable degree of certainty (cf. Bonß 1995: 88, 90). Certain expectations allow the follow up actions to take the preceding action as a premise, as a starting point. Certainty in expectations allows for the contingency of actions to be neglected by hiding their selectivity. This challenge of connecting selective actions by providing for expectations of certainty is the basic problem that comes into attention in the theoretical perspective suggested here. This problem will also be of crucial importance when considering decision making (1.3.4), decision making under risk (1.4), and decision making under risk in organisations (chapter 2).

1.3.2 Sets of Generalised Behavioural Expectations

The concept of behavioural expectations sketched so far is very abstract but it is the basis to reformulate many important concepts of sociological theory. The basic concepts of such a social theory are actions as events and expectations as structure (Luhmann 1988: 293). Everything else can be reformulated in terms of these two concepts. Norms, values, roles, persons, rules, rituals etc. are then no longer basic concepts of social theory, but can be reformulated as sets of behavioural expectations (Parsons 1951: 24pp.; Stogdill 1959: 78; Luhmann 1988: 292).

This is the point where the notion of institution can be put into the theory of behavioural expectations. Institutions are then *sets of generalised behavioural expectations*. They are generalised in the sense that they are shared by the participants of the system (Luhmann 1964: 68; cf. Stogdill 1959). Thus, a participant has to take into account that any other participant of the group / organisation has the same expectations (Luhmann 1970). Institutions are thus a special case of behavioural expectations in the sense outlined above (cf. Hasse / Krücken 1996). This view of institutions - or, more exactly, institutionalised behavioural expectations - is consistent with the use of the term by March and Olsen (1989; 1995). I therefore suggest this clarification of the concept of institution which will be of considerable help when identifying a counter-concept to the economic account of decision making. This counter-concept, based on behavioural expectations as its basic term, will be outlined in the following section. This sociological approach to decision making behaviour will be applied to a special decision problem in section 1.4: decision making under risk.

1.3.3 Decisions and Behavioural Expectations

After this excursion to general social theory, it is possible to suggest a concept of decision that works without reference to preferences. Since decision making without prior preferences is a well-documented phenomenon (e.g. Weick 1979), a sociological approach that claims to be applicable to all kinds of decision making behaviour needs such a different account of decision making. A suggestion in this direction was made by Luhmann (1995: 294pp.; 1988). Luhmann proposes to speak of a decision if an action is observed as a reaction towards an expectation. This means that a decision occurs if the relationship between action and expectation becomes reflexive, i.e. if the expectation is taken into account by the action (cf. Kaube 1996). This taking into account can take place by the actor himself or by an observer. Furthermore, the expectations can be directed to one's own behaviour or towards the behaviour of someone else (cf. Foschi 1972).

Thus, the argument is that situations of choice occur when an actor is confronted with the expectation - by himself or by someone else - of behaving in a certain way. This leads to the alternative of concurring or deviant behaviour - a choice.

With such a conceptualisation, the basic question for the analysis of decision making becomes different. The interesting point is no longer whether the decision maker manages to choose the alternative that is the best one according to his preferences. Or in other words, the degree of rationality that is achieved by the decision is not in the focus of analysis. The first important question for an analysis working with the expectation-based concept of decision is: How do decision situations occur? By which structures is the decision pressure directed to the action? How can the decision situation - in terms of the expectations to be fulfilled - be characterised? For the decision maker, the main problem is not to choose the optimal or satisfying alternative, but to get rid of the pressure, to be able to justify his behaviour as a decision (Luhmann 1988), and to keep his identity as a decision maker (March / Olsen 1995). Generally speaking, the problem is to make sure that decisions can be connected to each other.

Ever with the option for expectations as a core concept, it is still possible to analyse preference-based decision making. If a decision maker *expects* himself to choose the best alternative, he does decide on the basis of preferences. But this remains a special case. The major part of decisions take place without preferences, or maybe even against preferences. With a theory of decision making that does not rely on preferences as central concept, it is then possible to analyse the conditions under which preference-based decision making is possible. Whether preferences do provide the basis for a decision or not is an empirical question.

Finally, it is important to avoid one common misunderstanding. The emphasis on expectations in explaining decision making behaviour does not imply at all that the actions are causally determined by social structures This suspicion is often cited against theories that stress the role of structures in bringing about action (e.g. Schimank 1992; Wiesenthal 1987; Hechter 1987). The emphasis on structures would imply a one-way causal determination of actions only if one assumed given actors that find themselves in structures that connect them with other actors and thus constrain their possible ways of action. Generally speaking, structure would thus denote the relation of the parts of a whole (Hechter 1987; Dowding 1991; Dowding / King 1995; Schneider 1997). The concept of structure presented in the preceding sections opens up a different perspective. It does not distinguish structure from actors, but from actions. The concept of selective actions structured by expectations implies that enabling and constraining are one and the same phenomenon: structures (expectations) suggest a certain range of alternative actions and thus bring about follow-up actions, which would not be possible without the pre-selection of preceding expectations.

Three additional arguments make clear that actions cannot be determined by structures. *First*, it is always possible to deviate from expectations. The above sketched concept of expectations does not imply any tendency of conformity in social action. It implies that expectations create the possibility for identifying concurring or deviant behaviour. Whether the actions confirm or deviate from the expectation is an empirical question and is not predetermined by the theory (Luhmann 1995: 278pp.). *Second*, expectations are ambiguous. Only in exceptional cases do expectations clearly demand only one course of action. Thus, structures cannot determine actions because often it is far from clear which behaviour they suggest (Weick 1979). *Third*, in most empirical situations we will find not only one structure, but several ones, that will often be in contradiction to each other. This is one of the factors crucial to creating a decision situation: the decision maker has to choose which expectation he wants to follow - if he wants to show concurring behaviour at all.

These arguments clarify the important point that a structure-based approach to decision making does not imply a one-way causal determination of actions by structures. Only structures can create situations in which someone has to make a decision, only structures create freedom to choose. Only the analysis of structures as behavioural expectations allows a specific sociological approach to decision making.

If the central problem of decision making is not the realisation of individual preferences in a rational choice, what *is* the problem according to the perspective sketched here? I argued above (1.3.2) that in a structure-event-theory the challenge for social systems is the generation of expectational certainty in order to provide for the connection of selective events. The same is true for decision making behaviour. However, in this case the problem becomes reinforced. The central variable in this respect is the *selectivity* of actions: if actions are observed as decisions, their selectivity, and thus contingency, is stressed: Since it becomes obvious that the decision could have been made differently, it is difficult to use is as a premise for following actions. An action that is observed as a decision therefore runs into a fundamental dilemma. Since the action is supposed to be a decision, the decision maker is expected to justify his selection. This description of the action as a choice, however, stresses its contingency, the acceptance of the selection as a premise for further action is endangered (Luhmann 1993b). This is the basic problem of decision making, and in the empirical part of this study I will analyse how organisations handle this fundamental dilemma.

In the second part of this chapter, I will outline the application of this sociological concept of decision making to the issue of decisions under risk. In this context, an argument which has already been suggested by the general sociological concept of decision making will gain importance: the modern society creates more and more situations in which the decision makers have to make decisions with long-term consequences. This creation of more decision pressure is, however, not counter-balanced with the provision of more opportunities to make rational choices (Luhmann 1988). The decision situations that are created by larger structural developments in the society force organisations in particular to make decisions under time pressure, under incomplete information, and under high loads of responsibility.

1.4 Risk: A Sociological Perspective

Since the beginning of the eighties, sociologists have tried to develop theories of risk. The turning of social theory towards problems of risk has mainly been inspired by the ongoing social conflicts about the contested acceptability of large technological systems, especially of nuclear energy. In the centre of these conflicts were the hazards for environment and health stemming from the use of complex technologies.

The issue of risk has been put on the agenda of the social sciences by Mary Douglas and Aaron Wildavsky (1982) and by the influential 'Risk Society' by Ulrich Beck (1986).

The approach of Beck has been criticised for its lack of theoretical coherence, and thus its inability to provide for a guideline for the formulation of a sociological theory of risk in modern society (Krücken 1997a; Dean 1998). In particular, the basic assumption of objectively increasing hazards as a characteristic of risk society has led many scholars to reject Beck's conceptual suggestions (Krohn / Krücken 1993). As Beck's approach is coupled too tightly to the problems of environmental and technological risks, it is not able to develop a general theoretical perspective on problems of risk taking and risk avoidance under conditions of modernity.

On the basis of theoretical work by Mary Douglas (1966), Douglas and Wildavsky (1982) developed a framework designed to explain differing risk preferences in society. The basic assumption of the cultural approach in risk research is that the perception of risks is connected to institutionalised patterns of social organisation. Conflicts about technological and environmental risks are thus conflicts about forms of social organisation (Douglas / Wildavsky 1982: 187). The critique of this approach concentrates on the fact that the framework provided by cultural theory (Thompson et al. 1990) cannot account for the complex structure of modern society. Furthermore, the analysis of risk taking behaviour in organisations overburdens the theoretical instruments of cultural theory (Douglas 1992: 60pp.). Efforts to apply cultural theory to organisations, such as Coyle (1997), do not lead to insights additional to the broad literature on organisation theory.

The systems theoretic approach by Luhmann (1990a; 1993a) promises to allow the analysis of the social construction of risk at the societal level (Japp 1996; Krücken 1997a; 1997b; Schmidt 1997) and in formal organisations (Hiller 1993). In developing a general framework of decision making under risk, Luhmann abstracts from issues of environmental and technological risks. The underlying concept of decision making has been sketched in the first part of the present chapter. In the following sections, I will outline the application of this general framework to the problems of risk society.

1.4.1 The Concept of Risk: Risk and Danger

In order to elaborate the sociological theory of risk suggested by Luhmann, it is firstly necessary to explain the underlying concept of risk. In a sociological perspective, conventional concepts of risk limit the scope of analysis. The most influential contribution to conceptual issues in risk research is still the work of Frank Knight (1921). Knights distinction between calculable risk and incalculable uncertainty reduces risk to a problem of insufficient information. It should therefore be possible to resolve it by more information. This conceptualisation has been highly influential in research on decision making in general and on risk topics. Not only the approach of technical risk assessment deals with risk as an information problem, also the psychological studies on risk perception (e.g. Jungermann / Slovic 1993) work, more implicitly, with the assumption that lay attitudes towards risks are irrational, ill-informed deviations from expert rationality (Douglas 1985).

In trying to establish a sociological perspective on problems of risk, Luhmann proposes a different conceptualisation. According to Luhmann, risk is a concept to be distinguished from the concept of danger. An observer speaks of a risk, when a potential future damage is due to his own decisions. Danger relates to the possibility of a damage not caused by a decision or by someone else's decision. (Luhmann 1993a: 21f.) This conceptualisation has important implications for a sociological approach. (Luhmann 1993a: 25)

Firstly, in distinguishing risk from danger the concept of *attribution* comes into the focus (cf. Jones et al. 1987). Whether the possibility of a future damage is described as a risk or as a danger is a result of attributing possible future events to a decision and to a decision maker (a person or an organisation). A sociological observer will therefore concentrate on the factors controlling these processes of attribution. In the second chapter, I will try to elaborate a framework which allows an analysis of processes of attribution in organisations. All of this implies that risk is no longer an objective concept, but a concept dependent on an observer: '[T]he concept does not indicate a fact existing independently of whether and by whom it is observed.' (Luhmann 1993a: 26p.)

Secondly, it becomes evident that risk is a problem closely related to decision making. This means that the analysis is no longer confined to ecological problems or to problems of technological safety. Every decision can be observed as risky (by the decision maker) or as dangerous (by those affected). This shift to a more general level of analysis, together with the notion of the construction of risk, opens up the possibility of a sociological analysis of the transformation of risk within the society and especially within the political system.

Thirdly, risk is no longer considered a problem of lacking information. If one starts the analysis with the distinction of risk and danger, the problem of decision making under risk is the *time binding* with social costs. The binding of time means the creation of structures in social systems (Luhmann 1993a: 52). This means in the context of risk problems: with a decision one commits oneself to a certain future course of action with implications for others. In the language of systems theory this phenomenon is called time binding with social costs. Thus, risk is not an information problem, but a problem of making dispositions about the future that affect others in society. After a decision there will be people affected who in turn will have a different attitude towards the consequences of the decision because these have been opposed on them by a decision made by others. As a result, the possibilities to achieve a consensus on risk issues decrease significantly. More information or moral appeals cannot resolve conflicts about risks, they even tend to increase them, because the decision makers and those affected are not talking about the same phenomenon.

1.4.2 Decision Making in the Risk Society

The framework outlined above provides us with important concepts which should allow us to describe how situations of risk emerge, how decision makers choose risks, and how the accountable actors are identified in cases of damages. Taken with the idea that decisions take place on the basis of behavioural expectations, and not of preferences, the following perspective on decision making in the risk society emerges.

The emergence of risk as one of the dominant problems in modern society is explained by Luhmann with his thesis that the general mechanisms of attribution have changed due to changes in the semantics of time (Luhmann 1993a: 33pp). The future is no longer determined by the past, but it can be shaped by *decisions in the present*.

The result of this development is the fact that surprising damages and deviant events (i.e. disappointments of expectations) are attributed to decisions. The attribution of harmful events to decisions leads to the increased use of the 'risk'-semantic. In traditional forms of society such deviant, unexpected events were ascribed to fate, to God's will or to other factors which were not influenced by decisions. During the development towards modern society a steady transformation of dangers into risks can be observed. The attribution of damages and unforeseen developments to human decisions in turn leads to increased expectations towards decision making: the belief that the future can be shaped by decisions in the present increases the general pressure to make decisions, and to make them in a rational way that anticipates the consequences of present action.

This general growth of the pressure to make decisions with respect to the future becomes especially manifest in those parts of society which are considered to be responsible for decision making anyway: the political system and formal organisations in general. Organisations and their members find themselves under a steady pressure to make rational decisions in order to bring about positive effects and to avoid possible harmful outcomes. By the process of transforming dangers into risks, this expectation to decide is reinforced. This is especially true of organisations of the political system. Decison making in political organisations is therefore in the focus of attention in the empirical chapters of the present study.

When making decisions in the face of risks, the problem of time binding arises (cf. above, section 1.3.2). Decisions communicate new expectations, thus they create structures. This generation of structures is a disposal about the future. It is risky because the future is unknown in the present. The implications are as follows:

First, through decisions, to a certain degree one commits oneself to a certain course of action. A decision implies the expectation that other actors take the decision as point of departure for their own actions. This would be a confirmation of the expectation communicated by the decision.

Second, because it is a choice out of a range of alternatives, at the same time any decision communicates its own contingency. There are other possible decisions, which could turn out to be better in the future. Therefore, the acceptance of the decision is endangered. The more selective the decision is, the more this mechanism is reinforced.

Third, a decision as a time-binding event has effects in the social dimension. The disposal about the future affects others as it constrains them in their possible future actions. In the case of risk, they have to fear damages, imposed on them due to decisions made by others. Their expectations of the future will differ from those of the decision makers. They expect different damages than the decision makers do, and they may not be willing to accept these possible burdens imposed on them by others. The people affected do not feel the pressure to decide in view of an uncertain future as the decision makers do. Therefore, the possibilities of arriving at a consensus about risk issues decrease significantly.

The differing expectations of decision makers and affected actors are relevant for the choice of risks as well as for the allocation of accountability in the case of damages. The differing expectations lead to differing modes of attribution. Decision makers attribute decision outcomes differently than affected people, thus there will be conflicts about the risks and dangers which one has to face, as well as about what behaviour is adequate when something goes wrong.

It will be useful to further clarify the proposed framework by stating that conventional suggestions to solve problems of risk taking by increased endeavours towards more rationality, more information, and more participation seem to miss the very core of the problem. These suggestions are still inclined to a preference-oriented perspective on risk issues. This can be explained by three points.

First of all, within the proposed framework, the society generates constant pressure, especially on organisations, to make decisions with respect to the future. This happens by special modes of attribution, which connect unforeseen events and damages to past decisions, and by corresponding expectations regarding the making decisions. With the underlying expectation-related concept of decisions, one can see that this increased pressure to decide stems from increased expectations, and not from increased possibilities of rationality (Luhmann 1988: 297).

Second, the systems theoretical framework suggests that risk is not a problem of lack of information. The problem is that, due to constant structural pressure, decision makers have to commit themselves despite an unknown future and that other people, who do not feel these pressures, will be affected by this. This implies that more information about possible alternative courses of action and about the possible future consequences of the alternatives at hand will not solve the problem. It is even likely that more information will increase the problem because more information is connected with more communication and therefore with an increased likelihood of rejection. The contingency of a decision becomes more apparent by increased information (Luhmann 1993a: 101pp).

Third, as differing attitudes towards risks are due to differing positions within the decision making process, the possibility of consensus with respect to risk issues is decreased. The nearby solution of transforming those affected into decision makers by participatory procedures (cf. e.g. Rehmann-Sutter et al. 1998) does not promise success. The experience of participation is not encouraging. It seems to be impossible to identify and to organise all of the actors potentially affected, and after any decision, despite participation efforts, there will be (new) people affected (Luhmann 1993a: 152pp).

1.5 Conclusions and Implications for the Research Design

The conclusion that can be drawn from this sketch of a sociological perspective on decision making under risk is that conditions of risk aggravate the general problem of establishing expectational certainty in social systems. The structural pressures of the risk society turn more actions into decisions. Thus, more actions face the dilemma of providing for certain expectations under conditions of high selectivity and contingency. More actions are expected to make commitments for the future, and this has to take place under massive uncertainty. The present study tries to analyse how *organisations* handle these problems. In accordance with a perspective that puts behavioural expectations in the focus of attention, the starting point for such an analysis is presumed to be found in the specific expectational structure of organisations. As will be analysed in detail in the second chapter, the special form of behavioural expectations in organisations generate a constant decision pressure. Additionally, by allocating responsibility for uncertain future events, these expectations generate conditions of risk.

Thus, the question that will be addressed in this study is the following: How do organisations provide for expectational certainty under these structural conditions? The central notion for this aspect will be uncertainty absorption. Uncertainty absorption denotes exactly the problem of generating certainty before and after the decision that in the preceding sections has been identified as a basic challenge to social systems.

This implies the following questions: How do behavioural expectations generate decision pressure and risk in organisations? Which possibilities do organisations have to minimise uncertainty that is generated by vague, ambiguous and contradictory expectations? How do they *absorb* this uncertainty? These issues will be addressed in the second chapter.

The empirical case chosen for the analysis of decision making under risk in organisations is the one of local waste management in Germany. As will be analysed in chapter three, the decision situation for local administration in waste management is characterised by responsibilities for uncertain future events, and by ambiguous decision premises. It is therefore a classical case of risk. In order to analyse organisational processes of uncertainty absorption under risk, two case studies of local decision making processes were conducted. With the help of interviews, and the analysis of local newspapers and official documents, the decision making procedures in these case are reconstructed with respect to the central research question: How do these organisations provide for certain expectations under conditions of risk?

For the empirical analysis, the first implication of the theoretical basis is that a considerable amount of attention has to be devoted to the description of the decision situation, the structural context in which the organisations analysed here find themselves. The analysis of the structural context for the empirical case studies is done in chapter three. How can the decision situation for local administration in German waste management be characterised? Which kind of decision pressure is generated by the structural context in which the organisations find themselves? Which risks do they face? Which uncertainty absorbing capacity do the external demands have for these organisations? The answers to these questions prepare the case studies that analyse the efforts of the organisations to make acceptable decisions, i.e. to absorb uncertainty.

The empirical analysis must, however, be placed in context by a second theoretical step: the application of the framework sketched in this chapter to decision making processes in organisations. This will be done in the second chapter. According to the general theoretical perspective, the central questions will be the following: How do organisations get under pressure to make risky decisions? Which structures direct decision pressure to and within organisations? How can organisations deal with the pressure? The key to possible answers lies in the concept of behavioural expectations: the expectations that structure organisations can be conceptualised as institutionalised decision premises. These premises fix the conditions that have to be taken for granted by the decision maker in an organisation. They construct the organisational risks in terms of uncertainty and responsibility, and at the same time they provide the organisations with options for dealing with risks. They constrain and enable organisations in their efforts to make decisions.

2 Risk and Organisations

The first chapter was dedicated to the discussion of general concepts of risk and decision making. Starting with the influential formulation of Knight (1921), I argued that economic theories of decision making under risk neglect too many empirical phenomena which are relevant from a sociological perspective. Therefore I considered it necessary to use genuinely sociological concepts of decision making, and of risk, in order to analyse processes of decision making under risk in organisations. These concepts are provided by neo-institutional and systems theoretic accounts of organised decision making. The basic notion is that decisions do not take place on the basis of preferences, but as a reaction to behavioural expectations. As far as future events are attributed to present decisions, one can speak of risk.

In the present chapter, I will apply this framework to the example of decision processes in formal organisations. In order to develop a framework which can analyse processes of risk taking in organisations, the concept of decision making developed in the first chapter will be applied to formal organisations in the following sections (2.1). The specific form of behavioural expectations in the context of formal organisations will then be developed. In formal organisations, behavioural expectations take the form of decision premises (2.2). Behavioural expectations are the structure of social systems. So the concept of decision premises allows the structure of formal organisations to be described in detail. Decision premises can take the form of programmes (2.3), channels of communication (2.4), and personnel (2.5).

The important questions that structure the analysis of decision making and decision premises in organisation are: Which kinds of risk do these premises impose on the organisation? How do they allocate responsibility? What is their time orientation? Since structures do not only restrict but also enable action, one must also ask which possibilities of action are made available for the organisation by its particular arrangement of structures. With the help of the concepts to be developed in this chapter, it will be possible to characterise the decision situation for German public administration in implementing the waste legislation of recent years. This application of the framework will be done in the third chapter.

2.1 Decision Making and the Absorption of Uncertainty

At the very heart of the framework of organised decision making utilised in the present analysis lies the concept of uncertainty absorption. *The general problem of expectational certainty takes the form of uncertainty absorption at the level of organisations.* The concept was coined by March and Simon (1958: 176). However, only the theory of organisations proposed by Luhmann (2000) puts this concept at the centre of attention. In its most general form, absorption of uncertainty takes place when a decision made under uncertainty provides the basis for another decision. In the words of March and Simon (1958: 186): 'Uncertainty absorption takes place when inferences are drawn from a body of evidence and the inferences, instead of the evidence itself, are then communicated.' A decision draws conclusions from the information at hand; the follow-up decision does not consider the information that was the basis for the first decision, but takes the inferences drawn by the first decision for granted. By this combination of decisions made under uncertainty, the organisation *absorbs* uncertainty. Any decision made under uncertainty does not communicate its uncertainty, but only its certainty. The information processing on which the first decision was based is not repeated. To consider organisations as systems that steadily connect decisions with decisions and thereby neglect and absorb the uncertainty involved in every decision has important implications for a theory of organisations.

Firstly, it should be made clear that uncertainty absorption within the proposed framework is considered a precondition for organised decision making. The mechanism relieves the decision maker of uncertainty and of responsibility as he can take for granted a decision made by someone else in the organisation. If this mechanism did not work, the organisation could not make decisions. The most important precondition for a 'smooth' functioning of uncertainty absorption is the presence of a certain degree of trust in the organisation. For a person in a position to accept a decision as a premise for a decision of his own, he has to trust in the information processing capacities of the position that made the first decision (Luhmann 1964: 172ff.). A lack of trust therefore undermines the ability of the organisation to make decisions.

Another factor that influences the working of uncertainty absorption, and thereby the fundamental ability of the organisation to make decisions on the basis of its own decisions, is the amount of uncertainty that is communicated together with the decision. If it is too obvious that the first decision was made under uncertainty, it does not fulfil its function of absorbing uncertainty for the following decision. It is this point where the general considerations in chapter one about selectivity of actions and decisions can be concretised. It becomes clear that the decision could have been made differently, that it is contingent. Therefore, its acceptability is contested and the organisation is burdened with too much uncertainty. Brunsson (1985) identifies decision rationality as the most important factor that can block the organisation in this way. This surprising statement makes sense if one accepts the fact that procedural rationality in decision making implies the assessment of all possible alternatives and their consequences. According to Brunsson this type of rationality heightens the degree of uncertainty as observers recognise that there were other possible alternatives. The selectivity, and thus contingency, of the decision is stressed. The organisation will therefore hesitate to make further decisions on this basis. This role of decision rationality in processes of organised decision making will be of great importance in the case studies in chapters 4 and 5.

Secondly, by relying on the mechanism of uncertainty absorption, the organisation systematically produces risks for itself and dangers for its environment. This is because every decision takes place under conditions of uncertainty. Complete information is not possible. But the organisation, in order to continue making decisions, has to treat any decision as certain. This leads to a certain closure with respect to the real uncertainty in the world outside the organisation. The organisation becomes susceptible to postdecisional surprises and disappointments (Harrison and March 1988). Therefore, uncertainty absorption does not mean elimination, but rather a neglect of uncertainty. In other words, certainty and uncertainty are processed simultaneously. By this mechanism, the organisation enables itself to decide in a certain way on the basis of uncertain information but at the same time runs the risk of being surprised (Japp 1996). The absorbed uncertainty can reappear in the form of surprising consequences. Such surprising consequences of one's own past decisions might be described as damages.

On the other hand, if the organisation is too aware of possible negative consequences, again its ability to make decisions under uncertainty is blocked. The organisation can become aware of future threats after a rational process of decision making, or when the past is characterised by the experience of failure. At this point, the argument of Brunsson (1985) on the role of rationality in organised decision making reappears, as well as the statement of March and Olsen (1995: 200) that negative experiences in the past affect the risk preferences in organisations.

This argument clarifies the fundamental dilemma of organisations with respect to risk issues: The ability to decide in a certain way in view of uncertainty is the precondition of organised decision making. On the one hand, this leads to the susceptibility of surprises. Thus, the organisations produces risks and dangers (Japp 1996). On the other hand, the lack of this ability can lead to paralysis within the organisation as it is too aware of possible negative outcomes and of the uncertainty connected with the decision and therefore hesitates to make decisions. As will be illustrated later in the empirical chapters of the present analysis, this can lead as well to risks for the organisation, since there is no escape from the dilemma in the direction of non-deciding and thereby avoiding risks: it is an important feature of decision situations under conditions of risk that the option not to decide is attributed as a decision as well. Potential damages and losses in the future can therefore be ascribed to this decision and the organisation must take responsibility for these (cf. Hiller 1993; Luhmann 1993a).

A *third* important implication of the proposed concept of decision making is the fact that the absorption of uncertainty is identical with the taking of responsibility. The position that draws inferences from incomplete information and communicates these inferences in the form of a decision, has to take responsibility for the accuracy of the conclusions drawn from the information. With respect to the functioning of the organisation, this means that responsibility substitutes lacking information (Luhmann 1964: 175). The other parts of the organisation, which decide on the basis of this decision, are thereby relieved of some responsibility. Of course, they would also have to take responsibility when their own decision is used as a basis for a further decision within the organisation. But responsibility for the conclusions that provided the basis for their decision is taken by the position that made the first decision.

Here too we can identify possible paralyses of decision making processes. If for some reasons the mechanism of uncertainty absorption does not work, the responsibility to be taken for the follow-up decisions can be too high. The organisation becomes blocked and must find a way of reducing the burden of responsibility. The identification of possible ways to reduce heavy burdens of responsibility will be an important aspect of the case studies reported in chapters four and five.

Having applied the concept of decision making prepared in the first chapter to decision processes in organisations, let us now turn to the application of the proposed general concept of behavioural expectations as the structure of social systems to the special case of organisations.

2.2 Decision Premises

Decision premises are behavioural expectations that have to be taken into account when a decision is made (Luhmann 2000). In accordance with the framework developed in the first chapter, decision premises constitute the structure of organised social systems. Institutionalised decision premises generate and structure the decision situations the organisation faces. They are themselves results of decisions of the organisation and can also be changed by decisions of the organisation. They are formalised, i.e. their fulfilment is obligatory for the members of the organisations; they are generalised, i.e. they are fixed for a wide range of situations and not only for one single decision; and they are institutionalised in the sense that they are shared by most of the organisation's members. This leads to an enormous, and constant, pressure on members of the organisation to decide, or to take into account that their behaviour will be considered a decision.

The concept of decision premises refers to the aspects that are taken for granted when the decision is made (Simon 1957). According to Luhmann (1976; 2000) there are three different types of decision premises. First, there are premises that fix conditions for the correctness of the decision. These tell the organisation which decision outcome can be considered a success, and which is a failure. This type of premise is called *decision programme*. Second, we have premises that fix which part of the organisation has to participate in the decision and which are the contributions to the decision. This distribution of competencies within the organisation will hereinafter be called *channels of communication*. Third, *personal* decision premises can be identified. These imply the skills, education, and motivation of the persons who participate in the decision making process.

Decision premises therefore fix the conditions under which the decision will be considered correct, who has to participate in which way, and which personal orientations will become important within the decision process. They define which factors have to be considered in the decision and which ones can be left aside. The interesting point then becomes the question of how precisely the premises fix the conditions for the decision, if they create contradictory demands and to which aspects they direct the attention of the decision makers. This argument will be further developed in the following sections in which I will describe the three types of decision premises in detail.

Against the background of the previous section, one can say that the function of decision premises is the *absorption of uncertainty*. Possible organisational paralyses therefore come into the focus of attention. If the premises fix the conditions for the decisions too imprecisely, or if they create contradictory demands, they fail to absorb uncertainty for the decision to be made. The decision process is burdened with high loads of uncertainty that must be absorbed in order to make the decision acceptable to other parts of the organisation or to the environment. As was seen above, this leads to heavy burdens of responsibility to be taken. The organisation will therefore either refuse to make a decision, or will look at other possibilities to reduce uncertainty and responsibility.

The concept of decision premises is in close proximity to the concept of institutions as it is used by March and Olsen (1989; 1995). March and Olsen use the notion of institutions to refer to all the factors that create decision situations (March / Olsen 1995: 27). In the case of organisations, in addition they are generalised and formalised and thus take the form of decision premises. Decision premises are therefore institutionalised behavioural expectations that are fixed for a certain number of cases and situations (generalisation) and the fulfilment of which is the precondition to gain and hold membership in an organisation (formalisation).

I will use the concept of decision premises to describe the structure of organisations. The advantage of this approach lies in its ability to account for the relationship between different structural features of organisations. One can identify tensions and contradictions between the three aspects of organisational structure. This is a major determinant of decision situations in organisations. Moreover, with respect to their function, the absorption of uncertainty, one can clarify the conditions under which one type of premise can become more important than the other two. This can be the case when e.g. the programmes of the organisation, because of their inaccuracy, are not able to absorb enough uncertainty for the decision. The importance of personal factors like motivation and personal commitment to a course of action will then become more important with respect to the function of uncertainty absorption.

In the following sections I will turn to the description of the three types of decision premises in more detail. The task is to identify their role in creating decision situations in organisations. Important issues to be considered are their contribution in the building of decision pressures, the allocation of attention within the organisation, the allocation of responsibility, the types of uncertainty they impose on the organisation, and the possibilities for organisational action they create.

2.3 Programmes

The concept of decision programmes has a long tradition in organisation theory. Initially coined by Simon (1957) and March and Simon (1958), it was put more precisely by Eckhoff and Jacobsen (1960) and further elaborated in writings by Luhmann (1964; 1971, 1976). As will be argued below, also the two possible logics of decision making identified by March and Olsen (1989; 1995), the logic of consequences and the logic of appropriateness, refer to the same issue. Regarding risk-taking behaviour in organisations, decision programmes play a key role. This is because programmes regulate the allocation of responsibility and of attention, and they define the time orientation of the decision to be made. Thus, the concept touches all of the important questions raised in a sociological theory of risk-taking.

Before outlining briefly the main features of decision programmes, it is important to stress the fact that, in reality, most decision programmes will be a mixture of both conditional and goal programmes. The pure form of eihter will appear very rarely. However, in order to analyse processes of attribution of responsibility in organisations, it is important to clarify the basic mechanisms of the two programmes.

According to Luhmann (1971), decision programmes fix the conditions for the correctness of a decision. They contain rules that have to be followed in making the decision, including rules for the application of these rules. They can take two basic forms. Either they prescribe triggering conditions for a fixed set of decisions. Or they prescribe a goal that has to be reached with the decision.

The first type of decision programme has the form 'If A (conditions) then B (a certain decision)'. This means that the decision maker has to recognise a certain situation and then trigger off the course of action that is prescribed by the program for this situation. The decision maker has to match a situation to certain rules and then to decide in a prescribed way.

The typical example of this way of decision making are legal decisions (cf. March / Olsen 1989: 25). This form of programme has been called performance programme (March / Simon 1958) or subsuming programme (Eckhoff / Jacobsen 1960). However, in order to maintain a conceptual continuity, I prefer to accept the term used by Luhmann and will therefore refer to this type of programme as a *conditional programme*.

The second type of programme prescribes an end that has to be achieved by the decision, a time limitation, and a certain pool of allowed means to reach the end. Thus, the programme does not define triggering conditions but desirable outcomes that have to be achieved by the decision. In accordance with the terminology suggested by Luhmann, this programme will be referred to as a *goal programme*.

The differing orientations of the two types programmes - input-oriented versus output-oriented - have important implications for an analysis of organisational decision making under risk. First of all, the two programmes have different time orientations. The conditional programme is strictly past-oriented. It requires the matching of present decision situations with rules and routines that are based on past experiences. On the contrary, the goal programme provides for an orientation towards the future. It prescribes the desired future effects of the decision and requires an anticipatory calculation of possible consequences.

This insight leads us to another important issue in the context of decision programmes. The conditional programme produces a certain blindness with respect to the consequences of the decision. The decision maker has to identify present facts and to subsume them under rules that have been built in the past. The consequences of the decision do not make any difference with respect to the correctness of the decision: it has been performed correctly when the identification of the facts and their matching with existing rules have been done accurately. On the contrary, a decision programmed towards the reaching of an end is performed correctly when a) the end has been reached, b) the unintended consequences do not outweigh the positive outcomes, and c) the employed means did not lead to excessive costs or were not in contrast to legal rules.

These arguments suggest that a goal programme leads to more demanding requirements for the decision maker than a conditional programme. This point is stressed if one turns to the question of responsibility. In the case of a conditionally programmed decision, the decision maker is responsible for the correct identification of the situation and for the accurate matching of this situation with the appropriate decision. He is *not responsible for the consequences* of the decision. If the decision is contested because of its results the decision maker can pass the responsibility for undesired outcomes to that part of the organisation that designed the decision programme. The decision maker can only be held accountable for mistakes that he made in the matching of the situation with the rules.

In the case of a decision programmed towards the reaching of a goal, the decision maker has to take full responsibility for the consequences of the action. His decision will be considered a failure if the desired end has not been reached, if the decision has many negative side effects or if the means used were too expensive or were not in accordance with legal rules. Thus, the decision maker has to take responsibility for events in the future that are uncertain when the decision has to be made. At this point, a decision becomes risky as only when the decision maker has to take responsibility for uncertain outcomes, i.e. in the case of goal programmes, the organisation becomes sensitive to risks (cf. Brunsson 1985). In contrast, when decisions are programmed on a conditional basis, i.e. when the decision is blind for its consequences, there will be no risk for the decision maker (Hiller 1993). Moreover and particularly in the case of public administration, goal programmes can lead to contradictory demands with respect to responsibility. The decision maker has to act in order to achieve the goals prescribed by the programme, and he has to act according to the law, which can imply a contradiction. The decision has to be lawful and effective.

Regarding the function of decision premises, the absorption of uncertainty, one can say that conditional programmes absorb more uncertainty than goal programmes. They direct the attention of the organisation to events that took place in the past. Uncertainty about future events is not considered. The decision process is therefore relieved of uncertainty. Or in other words: the uncertainty is absorbed by the decision programme, by the formalised behavioural expectation to decide by matching a situation with a rule. A goal programme absorbs less uncertainty, as future events, the occurrence of which is uncertain, have to be considered. Moreover, the attention of the decision maker is also directed to conditional restrictions when the organisation has to decide within the framework of legal rules. The results are contradictory demands and a high level of uncertainty. Given it is not possible for the organisation not to make a decision, as this would mean the failure to fulfil the programme, the uncertainty has to be absorbed by the other decision premises. This could take place by personal commitment and motivation of the participating decision makers (Brunsson 1985), or for example by integrating other parts of the organisation or of the environment into the process of decision making.

To sum up, decision programmes are the key concept for analysing risk taking behaviour in organisations. According to the framework developed in chapter one, risk is the result of a process of attribution: negative events are attributed to a decision. It should be clear now that at the level of formal organisations this attribution is mainly performed by decision programmes. The linking concept is responsibility: a goal programme ascribes responsibility for negative consequences to the decision maker, a conditional programme attributes the responsibility to the level that enacted the programme. Thus decision programmes help identifying the decision that is considered the cause for the negative event.

2.4 Channels of Communication

In many theories of organisations, the channels of communication are considered the decisive point with respect to organisational structure (Burns and Stalker 1961; Lawrence and Lorsch 1967). This concept of organisational structure, confined to communication channels, has especially been used to analyse the information processing capacity of organisations (Lawrence and Lorsch 1967; Galbraith 1973). Within the framework used in the present analysis, channels of communication are only one aspect of organisational structure, besides programmatic and personal decision premises. Channels of communication absorb the uncertainty for the decision in two different ways.

First, the communication channels of an organisation are defined by the distribution of opportunities and duties to participate in a decision. The positions of the organisation that participate in a decision process will normally make contributions on the basis of specialisation. For a decision about a product innovation, for example, a producer of chemical products will rely on the contributions of the departments of marketing, research and development, and of production (Lawrence and Lorsch 1967). Similarly, for a local administration unit, trying to plan a waste incinerator, the participation of the professional staff in the administration, of the local politicians, and of external experts are necessary to absorb a certain amount of the uncertainty connected with such a decision. In this process, every organisational unit that contributes to the decision, has to take responsibility for that part of the task falling within its competency. The marketing department is responsible for the correct estimation of client demands, the R&D department has to take responsibility for the scientific and technological aspects of the new product, the production department has to guarantee efficient and faultless production.

The *second* aspect of communication channels as a decision premise is the nature of the contribution the position or department has to make for the decision process. The contributions can, for example, be consultation, preparation of the decision, taking note of the decision, making the final decision. This is a decisive point with respect to the sharing of responsibility. The expert makes his consultation on the basis of the assumption that the politician makes the final decision. This relieves much of the burden of responsibility from him. The politician is relieved of responsibility because he can rely on the accuracy of the expert's advice. This mechanism of uncertainty absorption is disturbed when, for example, the expert's competence is contested, or when political decision makers refuse to take responsibility and justify their decision only by the expert's vote. This places too much responsibility on the expert who, in the future, will tend not to commit himself to a decision with his advice.

To sum up, channels of communication absorb uncertainty by allowing a reliance on contributions of *specialised departments* of the organisation or of external experts which are considered correct. The means of absorbing uncertainty is a division of labour (Simon 1981: 51). When preparing a decision, a decision maker does not have to consider the opinion of everyone else in the organisation, but only a restricted number of positions. This reduces the amount of information that has to be considered.

Whether the division of labour within the organisation takes more hierarchical or more segmented forms, determines the capability of the organisation to absorb uncertainty (Burns and Stalker 1961). In the economic sector in particular, organisations have in recent years tended to bring channels of communication into a less hierarchical form. The result seems to be that this part of the organisational structure absorbs less uncertainty (Baecker 1993), and therefore pressurises the other decision premises.

The literature that concentrates on this aspect of organisational structure suggests that the main problem of this mechanism of uncertainty absorption is the dilemma of differentiation and integration (Lawrence and Lorsch 1967; Cyert and March 1963). Only when the departments of an organisation really specialise in their task, can they take responsibility for their contribution to a decision. On the other hand, over specialisation endangers the capability of the departments to communicate with each other. In this case, the departments cannot absorb uncertainty for each other because their specialisation leads to differing outlooks that block their ability to make contributions to the decisions of the other departments (Lawrence and Lorsch 1967).

In addition to their uncertainty absorbing effect, channels of communication can of course also introduce uncertainty into the decision making process. For example, many formal decision making procedures in public administration prescribe the participation of citizens in the decision. From the perspective of the organisation theory used here, this can be seen as a factor of additional uncertainty. However, when referring to decision situations under risk, one should conceive of channels of communication as a possibility for an organisation to react to problems of responsibility, uncertainty, and ambiguity.

2.5 Personnel

The idea of considering individuals as something external to the organisation has a long tradition in organisation theory and probably goes back to Barnard (1938). Herbert Simon used this idea, for his theory of decision making in organisations, to conceptualise personal traits as premises for the decisions to be made in organisations (Simon 1967). Simon therefore sees the skills and the knowledge of the members as a premise for the decisions of an organisation (Simon 1960: 10). One could also add personal traits such as motivation or personal commitment to the respective task, etc. All these factors serve as a premise for the decision as they absorb uncertainty. They are thus a part of the organisational structure (cf. Becker 1970; Böhret 1982). For example, if a decision maker, such as a technical expert, commits himself strongly to the realisation of a technical solution to an organisational problem, this personal commitment, together with the technical expertise of the person, reduces the decision alternatives the organisation will take into consideration. This is a mode of absorbing uncertainty for the organisational process of decision making.

The factors which influence these personal decision premises are mainly the professional education, the socialisation of the member inside and outside the organisation, and the career possibilities which the organisation offers its members.

The skills and the knowledge by which a person pre-structures a decision are formed during the professional education and the socialisation inside and outside the organisation. What motivates a decision maker to pursue a task is mainly influenced by the incentives provided by the promotion prospects should the decision produce positive outcomes. For German public administration, for example, it has been noted that promotion and payment are only loosely coupled with the individual performance. This is considered to hinder strong personal motivation (Mayntz 1985: 161). The degree of personal commitment to a decision making process may also depend on the professional education of the organisation members. This statement may also be illustrated with an example from public administration in Germany which is mainly staffed with lawyers, the second important professional group being engineers (Werner 1971). Both professions might differ in the degree of personal involvement in a decision making task: whereas engineers tend to commit themselves to solutions they consider technically intelligent, lawyers do not tend to identify personally with concrete decision alternatives (Luhmann 1987: 289). Both approaches imply different modes of absorbing uncertainty for a decision.

If the organisational personnel is a premise for the decision making process like programmes and channels of communication, some general considerations concerning decision premises are also true for personal premises. First of all, it has been noted above that uncertainty absorption is closely connected with the taking of responsibility. Thus, uncertainty absorption by personal factors like strong motivation and commitment leads directly to the attribution of responsibility to persons (Brunsson 1985). This allocation of responsibility takes place independently of the form and the exactness of the programme.

Secondly, as with other types of decision premises, the personnel can also introduce ambiguity into the process of decision making. This ambiguity, which results from the varying attention and participation of organisation members has been illustrated in the studies done by Cohen et al. (1972) and by March and Olsen (1976). If the organisation cannot rely on the steady personal attention to, and participation in, decision processes, the organisation will face serious problems of ambiguity.

Thirdly, if the programmes and the channels of communication do not absorb enough uncertainty to allow decisions to be made, this will put pressure on the personnel. The analysis of Burns and Stalker (1961) suggests that ambiguity about the channels of communication can lead to personal stress. Ambiguity in the programmes, especially in goal programmes, can also lead to personal stress (Becker 1970) and to more importance of the personal: if the conditions for an appropriate decision are not clearly defined, personal styles of decision making gain more importance (Luhmann 2000: 186; Koch 1992).

2.6 Uncertainty Absorption by Decision Premises

After this rough sketch of the three types of decision premises, I will now turn to their combination in structuring the organisation and in absorbing uncertainty for decision making. As a social system that is structured by formalised and generalised behavioural expectations, an organisation produces a *constant pressure to make decisions*. Normally, these decisions will have to be made under conditions of uncertainty. The members of the organisation therefore face the difficulty of constantly making decisions on the basis of incomplete information. This leads to enormous loads of responsibility and the ability of the organisation to act is challenged.

An *ideal type* organisational solution to this problem would be the following. The organisational structure transforms *responsibility* into *accountability for mistakes* (Luhmann 1964: 172pp.; Hiller 1993). This is achieved by conditional programmes and by hierarchical division of labour within the organisation. The higher level programmes the lower levels conditionally, therefore the decision making behaviour of the lower level consists of matching rules with situations; the lower level is *accountable* to the higher level for the correct application of the rules, the top of the hierarchy is *responsible* for the consequences of the decision. Responsibility is turned into accountability and both are located in different positions of the organisations. The uncertainty absorbing position is relieved of responsibility and has only to account for the correct interpretation of rules while the responsibility for the consequences of decisions is taken by the programming level. This transformation of responsibility into accountability is mainly performed by programmes.

The second important contribution to this mechanism is provided by the division of labour in the organisation. Every position makes a contribution to a decision, is only responsible for the correctness of this, possibly rather small, contribution, and can be held accountable for mistakes in this contribution. At the level of personal decision premises this requires the ability to match rules with situations. In public administration, this structure leads to the importance of professional lawyers. In an organisation structured like this, the decision premises absorb uncertainty to a very high extent. The organisation is able to constantly produce decisions, even though these decisions have to be made under uncertainty. The organisation, however, will be blind to the consequences of its decisions, the probability of unpleasant surprises is therefore quite high.

This ideal type structure of organised decision making will not, however, appear too often in reality. The factor most likely to disturb the smooth functioning of uncertainty absorption in an organisation is the programming of decisions towards the reaching of goals. As has been shown above, the main feature of goal programmes is that they allocate the responsibility for consequences to the position that makes the decision. Responsibility for the consequences cannot be shifted to higher levels in the organisation, meaning that the uncertainty absorbing position has to take full responsibility for the reaching of the goal without unintended negative side effects. This causes problems, because it requires a careful consideration of all possible alternatives, an anticipatory evaluation of the consequences of all alternatives and the choice of the alternative that fits the given preferences best. In short, it requires a decision process according to the prescriptions of classical theories of rational decision making. As the behavioural theory of decision making in particular has shown (March and Simon 1958; Cyert and March 1963), such a rational procedure of decision making is not able to absorb uncertainty about future consequences; particularly in political contexts, there is also an enormous amount of ambiguity with respect to preferences (March and Olsen 1976). The effect is that the decision making position in the organisation has to take responsibility for future events which are highly uncertain. It has to decide under risk (Brunsson 1985).

The tendency especially in political organisations to programme decision towards the reaching of goals instead of on a conditional basis has been observed by several scholars (e.g. Offe 1974; Japp 1994; March and Olsen 1995). With regard to public administration this tendency has been labelled the 'politicisation of administration'. This tendency has in the literature mainly been ascribed to dynamics of the political process. The main factors in this process are the taking over of more and more new and complex tasks by the political system (Luhmann 1990b), the process of policy formulation that creates ambiguities in the programmes for the administration (Baier et al. 1988), and the pressure on the political system, particularly regarding issues of technological and environmental risks, to consider the consequences of its own decisions (Luhmann 1993a).

As a result, political programmes have the tendency to take the form of rather ambiguous and unclear goal programmes with plenty of room for administrative discretion. For public administration, this has the consequence that the above sketched absorption of uncertainty does not work because the organisation is burdened with high loads of responsibility for achieving uncertain future events. Moreover, the organisation will have to balance conflicting values because assumptions about the occurrence of future events are highly value-loaded. Thus, the administration has to fulfil political tasks, because it must ensure that its decisions are acceptable. Thus, the organisation has to follow specific strategies in order to absorb the uncertainty. The possible organisational strategies to cope with these situations of decision making under risk will be analysed in the next section. These patterns, taken from the literature about decision making in organisations, provide us with some clues about the behaviour of the organisations which I will analyse in the case studies.

2.7 Possibilities of Reducing Risk and Uncertainty

Up to now, we have seen how decision premises in organisations absorb uncertainty in order to provide for the constant production of decisions under incomplete information. I also demonstrated how the decision premises can fail to absorb uncertainty, especially when programmes take the form of goal programmes. This leads to uncertainty, ambiguity, and high loads of responsibility in the process of decision making. In this section, I will try to identify organisational strategies to reduce these burdens on decision making.

According to the framework developed in the previous sections, situations of ambiguity, uncertainty and high responsibility appear in organisations when a) the decision premises fail to absorb enough uncertainty, or b) when the decision premises impose contradictory demands on the organisation. The organisational coping with ambiguity about premises and uncertainty about future consequences has been the main topic of several behavioural, institutional, and evolutionary theories of organisational decision making (March / Simon 1958; Cyert / March 1963; March / Olsen 1976; 1989; 1995; Weick 1979; 1995). Against the background of a concept of organisational structure based on decision premises, it is possible to classify these strategies for coping with ambiguity according to the three types of decision premises. Organisations try to reduce uncertainty and ambiguity by creating more informal decision *programmes* (2.7.1), by establishing new *channels of communication* (2.7.2), or by relying more on the *personal* motivation and commitment of their members (2.7.3).

2.7.1 Rules of Appropriateness

The most important point made in the literature on organisational coping with uncertainty and ambiguity is March and Olsen's statement that organisations, even when they are expected to reach a goal in the future, tend to decide strictly according to institutional rules of appropriateness (March and Olsen 1989; 1995). These findings are in accordance with the evolutionary concept of decision making by Karl Weick (1979; 1995), who argues that organisations always act retrospectively instead of anticipatory. They act on the basis of rules that have been developed in the past which are matched to present situations. Or, in other words, organisations that are programmed by goal programmes tend to act as if they were programmed conditionally. Goal programmes tend to overburden the structural capabilities of organisations in terms on uncertainty, and responsibility. Thus, in the face of goal programmes, organisations stick to informal conditional rules that have been developed in the past and the task thus becomes routinised (Eckhoff / Jacobsen 1960). The problem of responsibility is then handled parallel to the practice in the face of a formal conditional programme: the organisational position that has to decide is made accountable for the following of these informal rules, deviant behaviour has to be justified (Luhmann 1964: 172pp.). Decision making according to rules of appropriateness allows the organisation to transform responsibility into accountability. The decision maker is accountable for the correct application of rules (which can also be informal), instead of taking responsibility for the occurrence of uncertain future events (cf. Luhmann 1964: 172pp.). This means that the practice to make decisions according to rules of appropriateness creates a blindness with respect to future consequences of present decisions. Here we have the central organisational mechanism of transforming external expectations into internal premises.

Even if there are no rules available that seem to fit the situation at hand, the organisation refuses to act according to a logic of consequences, as would actually be required by a goal programme. The organisation begins to experiment. It makes small decisions, observes and evaluates the consequences and on this basis creates new rules of appropriateness. This mechanism of learning from experience in the face of an ambiguous present has been described in detail in the behavioural theory of the firm by Cyert and March (1963) and in the evolutionary model of organised decision making by Weick (1979); the difficulties of learning from experience have been stressed by March and Olsen (1976; 1995).

In any case, if the organisation acts according to rules of appropriateness or on the basis of experiential learning, decisions are made almost exclusively on a past-oriented basis. This is of crucial importance with respect to risk issues, when organisations are held responsible by the public for possible future consequences. The structural tendency of organisations to act on the basis of past experiences leads to the production of risks for the organisation and of dangers for the organisational environment.

2.7.2 Reduction and Extension of the Network of Communication

The second important means to cope with situations of ambiguity and uncertainty relies on the decision premise of channels of communication. In the face of risky decisions to be made, organisations will either try to reduce or to extend their internal and external networks of communication.

The *reduction* of organisational positions to include in the decision process would aim at a reduction of possible opinions to be considered in the decision. This would result firstly in a reduction of preferences, which could significantly heighten the ability of the organisation to make a decision as preferences are then less ambiguous and contested. The garbage can model by Cohen et al. (1972) includes this possibility of making a decision exactly at that point in time when only the members who support it can participate. Secondly, however, the result could be a reduction of the information that is contributed to the decision. This can minimise the uncertainty under which the decision has to be made as the organisation maintainy its ignorance, which can lead to a higher readiness to make the decision (Brunsson 1985). Of course, such a reliance on ill-informed decisions in order to reduce uncertainty can have its disadvantages.

One will more frequently observe strategies that rely on the *extension* of the number of contributions to be made to a decision. This is especially the case with political organisations, that often produce decisions with contested legitimacy. By including scientific and technical expertise, and by allowing for public participation, organisations can hope to make better informed decisions which also consider a wider range of preferences. This strategy is in accordance with prescriptions of classical models of rational decision making. One could therefore expect the production of a better informed decision, based on a balanced consideration of all preferences. In most empirical cases, however, both the inclusion of more information and of more preferences will turn out to be very difficult. Given that information is almost always contested and ambiguous, and that preferences are conflicting, the organisation will face difficulties in actually including these additional contributions in the decision. The result will therefore quite often be a symbolic action (Edelman 1967; Feldman and March 1981) or, in the words of Brunsson, 'talk' (Brunsson 1989). This point will be analysed more deeply in the empirical chapters of the present study.

2.7.3 Personal Commitment

Turning to personal decision premises, one can identify two general possibilities for organisations to react to ambiguities, uncertainties and to burdens of high responsibility. First, if a decision programme imposes tasks which are too difficult for the organisation with its given division of labour and its given personnel, it can react by changing persons. The organisations can dismiss members, it can hire new ones, or it can assign its members to new positions. By this the organisation might achieve a better fit between the demands of the task, i.e. the programme, and the skills and the motivation of the participating persons.

The second general possibility of reducing uncertainty and ambiguity is to rely on the personal commitment and motivation of the members. To a very large extent the members of the organisation can absorb uncertainty by committing themselves to a course of action which is connected with uncertainties. This strategy implies a refusal of classical concepts of rationality, as it requires the neglect of the uncertainty of the decision and the taking of personal responsibility for the course of action to be taken. Brunsson (1985) has argued that this mechanism can absorb lots of uncertainty in a decision process and therefore makes it more likely that the other parts of the organisation will also follow this course of action. Due to the personal commitment of an influential decision maker, the 'real' uncertainty of the decision does not come to the attention of the organisation, the uncertainty is absorbed by the decision premise 'personnel' and the organisation can easily make further decision on this basis (cf. Levin / Sanger 1994). Here again, the general point can be observed that uncertainty absorption produces an inability to appreciate the consequences of the decision. The organisation creates the fiction that it decides on the basis of certain information, but it *must* create this fiction because otherwise it would not be possible to make further decisions.

The general point that can be derived from the preceding discussion of organisational mechanisms of reducing ambiguity and uncertainty is that they all produce blindness with respect to future consequences. This seems to be the precondition for the making of risky decisions. Without ignoring the complexity and uncertainty of the future, the organisation cannot make decisions.

2.8 Political Organisations: The Problem of Legitimacy

In the previous sections, I developed general concepts that can account for decision making under risk in organisations. Although I made some references to special problems in political organisations, it is now necessary to further clarify an important factor that arises out of special demands for political organisations.

The general function of political organisations is to make collectively binding decisions. This means that this type of organisations, in addition to general demands of decision making under uncertainty, has to make sure that its decisions are acceptable in its environment. In accordance with the framework outlined abbove one can say that a decision is accepted if the addressee takes the decision as a premise for his own action (Luhmann 1983). Within organisations this acceptability is ensured by the mechanisms of uncertainty absorption that have been described above. If the organisation is dependent on the acceptance of its decision by non-members, the problem of making *legitimate decisions* arises.

An organisation with the function of producing decisions that are acceptable for its environment faces the problem that the production of the decision cannot be separated from its communication to outsiders (Luhmann 1964: 111). One cannot look for the 'right' decision without considering how the decision will be accepted. The *process* of decision making is then of vital importance (Brunsson 1989). The organisation will try organise its decisions in the form of legitimising procedures (Luhmann 1983). Or, when it turns out that the acceptability cannot be created for every single decision, the organisation has to rely on a general basis of trust (Luhmann 1964: 112). If the environment has a general trust in the organisation's practices of decision making, the decisions produced by the organisation will be accepted more easily. Therefore, for political organisations the existence of a certain basis of trust in its structures and processes is of vital importance for the fulfilment of its function. However, the need to create trust and legitimacy conflicts with necessities of the decision process itself. What is necessary to make the public believe that the decision is legitimate can be in conflict with what is necessary to make technically sound decisions. The public will call for anticipatory rationality, the organisation will tend to rely on its experience and its routines.

The literature suggests that organisations react to these contradictory demands by a de-coupling of formal processes and structures on the one hand and the actual decision making process on the other hand. The demand for organisations to create trust and to consider different values in the decision process may lead to symbolic actions and to a loose coupling between formal structures and the actual process of uncertainty absorption (Meyer and Rowan 1977; Brunsson 1989).

Very generally speaking, political systems have reacted to this problem by a division of labour: they become differentiated in politics and administration. The *political* task is then to consider as many preferences as possible, to balance values, and to achieve consensus for certain courses of action. The genuine political contribution to the decision is the provision of legitimacy. This is achieved by organising the process of making political decisions in formal procedures (Luhmann 1983). The task of the *administration* is then to implement these decisions. The acceptability of the political decisions should not be contested since they are based on the legitimacy provided by the political procedures. The de-coupling of the political and technical contributions to the decision outlined above is achieved by organisational differentiation.

Not only the studies about the implementation of political programmes (Pressman and Wildavsky 1973; Mayntz 1980) have made clear that this model does not work in reality. With a theory of organisational decision making that puts the uncertainty absorption into the focus of attention, one can say that this model of the administrative implementation of politically legitimised decisions can only work on the basis of conditional decision programmes. Only if the administration is programmed with if-then-conditions, is it relieved of responsibility for the consequences of its decisions, which is shifted towards the political level. The conditional programme absorbs much uncertainty for the administrative organisation, which can then concentrate on making rational decisions. In accordance with classical works in organisation theory (Thompson 1967; Meyer and Rowan 1977), Brunsson (1989) stated that politics buffer the processes of administrative decision making. In other words, political programmes *absorb uncertainty* for the decisions of the administration.

If the administration is programmed towards the reaching of goals the situation becomes different. The administration is responsible for the occurrence of uncertain future events and, if the means to reach the ends are contested, different values have to be considered in the decision process. The administration becomes 'politicised' (Offe 1974). The acceptance of the decision is not provided by the political programme because value and interest conflicts are not resolved in the process of policy formulation but are shifted to the level of implementation. The administration has to ensure the acceptance of its decision, it therefore becomes a political organisation as well. This means that the division of labour between politics and administration collapses and the administration has to fulfil genuine political functions as well. One important question therefore for the analysis of the following chapters will be how public administration provides for this buffering of its decision making behaviour that is no longer performed by prior political decisions.

2.9 Conclusion

The result of the first chapter was the assumption that risks arise by structural decision pressures which attribute future events to present decisions. This very general notion has been applied to organised social systems in the second chapter. The conclusions are the following.

Organisations are social systems that constitute themselves on the basis of formalised and generalised behavioural expectations. These expectations, which in the form of decision premises constitute the structure of the organisation, generate a constant pressure to make decisions. Thus, given that the future is unknown, organisations face the constant expectation to make decisions under uncertainty. Organisations handle this constant pressure by absorbing uncertainty. The absorption of uncertainty can be achieved processually - by constantly connecting decisions with decisions - or structurally - by making decisions on the basis of decision premises.

Uncertainty absorption is the precondition for the organisation to hold the constant pressure to make decisions on the basis of incomplete information. By absorbing uncertainty, organisations generate the fiction of deciding on a basis of certainty. An external observer, however, might identify that the uncertainty is only neglected and is not really eliminated. By this neglect of uncertainty, the organisation generates a systematic blindness for the consequences of its decisions and it becomes susceptible to surprises. The risk consists of the possibility to regret the decision at a later point in time when one has information about what has happened in the mean-time, and this information cannot be neglected as it was possible when the decision was made.

At the societal level this separation of past and future is the precondition for the emergence of risk conflicts. At the organisational level one can see that it is a consequence of the steady demand to absorb uncertainty. In order to absorb uncertainty, one has to treat the information at hand as certain. The neglected uncertainty can then return in the form of surprising consequences. It is very likely that these surprises will be judged differently by the environment and by the organisation. As far as the *environment* of the organisation did not participate in the decision, it will conceive of possible damages as dangers - as something that has been imposed on them by someone else's decision. As far as the *organisation* is responsible for the consequences of its decisions it will conceive of these consequences as a risk.

It becomes apparent that the concept of responsibility is of crucial importance for analysing conflicts about risky and dangerous decisions of organisations. Only when the organisation can be held responsible for surprising consequences, do possible post-decision surprises constitute a risk for the organisation. The key question for the analysis of risk taking behaviour in organisations is therefore: How do organisations attribute responsibility for consequences of their decisions? I argued that the allocation of responsibility is done by the decision premises, mainly by decision programmes. For the special case of political administration one can say that whether the organisational structures shift the responsibility for consequences to politics or to administration is a major determinant on form and structure of conflicts about risk.

For the empirical chapters, the following research questions arise. How can the decision situation that local administration in Germany faces when implementing the federal waste policy be described? Which responsibilities, uncertainties, and ambiguities arise out of the task of disposing household waste? These issues will be addressed in the third chapter. It focuses on the analysis of the external expectations that are directed towards the organisations of local administration. In a second step, I will address questions such as the following: Which possibilities do the organisations have to react to these tasks? How can they re-allocate responsibility, absorb uncertainty, and reduce ambiguity? What do these mechanisms imply for the ability of the organisations to handle situations of risk? Answers to these questions will be suggested in the two case studies, reported in chapters four and five. The case studies analyse one central aspect of local waste management: decisions about waste treatment plants. The risks connected with these complex decisions will be described and analysed in the next chapter.

3 Risks of Waste Management

The purpose of the following chapter is to prepare the case studies in chapters four and five. It will describe the external expectations and demands that are addressed to local administration in Germany when implementing the federal waste policy. In accordance with the general framework sketched in the preceding chapters, the description is guided by the following questions: How precise are the demands for local waste management? Are there contradictions in the expectations the administration has to fulfil? Thus, to which degree do these demands create ambiguities for the organisations? The answers to these questions lead to the *uncertainty absorbing capacity* of these external expectations. The lower this capacity, the more the organisations have to provide for certainty with their own, internal structural adaptations. This is supposed to be the precondition for decision making under risk. These structural adaptations will then be analysed in the two case studies.

The conclusion of the present chapter will be that the political reactions to the ecological dangers of waste disposal led to a policy that imposes high pressure on the local bodies of administration to make complex decisions. These decisions are characterised by highly uncertain consequences for which the local administration has to take responsibility. Or in other words: Local administration faces situations of making decisions under risk. This point will be elaborated in detail in the following sections. The result of the present chapter will be the starting point for the case studies in chapters four and five in which I will describe the ways in which the observed organisations handled these risks. This will be done in terms of the concepts developed in the second chapter.

This chapter will be organised as follows. I will begin with a brief sketch of the ecological dangers that result from the handling and disposal of household waste. German waste policy reacted to these potential hazards by mainly relying on three technical options: disposal, treatment, and avoiding / recycling (3.1). These three technical possibilities have been in the centre of waste policy in recent years in Germany. Therefore, after a description of the general institutional context in which local waste management in Germany takes place (3.2), I will turn to the analysis of the regulations of waste disposal (3.3), waste treatment (3.4), and avoiding and recycling of waste (3.5). This will lead to theoretical conclusions about the character of the decision situation in which local administration finds itself when establishing systems of waste management (3.6, 3.7). These conclusions about responsibility, uncertainty, and ambiguity in waste management provide the basis for the case studies that follow.

3.1 Waste: Ecological Dangers and Technical Responses

In the sixties, the most common way to handle household waste in Germany was to deposit it in dumps. The handling of waste was considered a public task, mainly because of aesthetic and hygienic reasons (Herbold / Wienken 1993). Without elaborated legislative foundation, this task was performed by the municipalities and communities. It consisted in the erection of a waste dump, in collecting the waste from the households and carrying it to that dump. These dumps were of modest technical sophistication: without any protection of the ground, the waste was tipped in a quite unsystematic, unordered manner. In 1972, the first federal waste act only formalised this local practice. The formal responsibility for the collection of waste was located at the municipal level, the communities were responsible for the disposal of the waste.

At about the same time, the observation of waste dumps led to first hints about potential dangers of depositing waste. Especially water seepage began to attract attention of scientific experts (Herbold / Vorwerk 1993). It became clear that the water seepage was a serious threat to the quality of the ground water. The second potential threat turned out to be the gas emissions from the dump (Martens 1990). These potential dangers were heightened by three factors that limited the possibility of scientific forecasting of the potential hazards of waste dumps. First, there is an almost complete lack of knowledge about the chemical composition of the waste (Haber et al. 1991). It is impossible to describe the composition of a waste dump in terms of chemical or biological patterns. Second, dumps change over time. New substances are constantly added, the old ones change in their features. Third, every single waste dump is specific, i.e. there are no two dumps that have the same features. These three factors lead to the conclusion that it is impossible to foresee and control the reaction of waste dumps scientifically (Krohn 1997; cf. Cord-Landwehr 1994: 182pp.). In reaction to these threats, the dumps, step by step, became more sophisticated. The waste was compressed and crushed before it was put into the dump, the dumps themselves were sealed up at the top and at the bottom. The intention was to improve the possibility to observe the dump and, if needed, to change the technical features of it (Krohn 1997).

The efforts to minimise the hazards to ground water, ground, and air due to waste disposal led to technically sophisticated landfill sites. However, the problems of uncontrolled emissions due to the unforeseeable chemical and biological reaction of the dump were not resolved. Additionally, two further aspects of waste management came to the attention of the decision makers and led to a further politicisation of the problem of waste.

The *first* aspect was the problem of scarce resources, which came to public and political attention especially after the oil crisis of the seventies. In Germany, this led to first considerations to strengthen efforts to minimise the amounts of waste that were produced by the economic dynamics after the second world war. This idea of avoiding waste by new ways of production and consumption was combined with the idea of recycling. The model of cycles emerged: waste was to be transformed into new products, so that, ideally, no waste at all would be produced. These ideas were politically approved for the first time in the Waste Management Programme of the Federal Government in 1975.

The *second* important aspect that supplemented the efforts to build safe waste dumps was the fact that the space for dumps became scarce (SRU 1991: 121). The existing dumps were almost full, the possibilities to build new ones were restricted because of the now known geological requirements for a landfill site and because of the contested acceptability of waste dumps in the public.

These two additional problems of handling waste attracted the attention in German waste management to further possibilities to handle the waste problem. To avoid waste before it arises, and to recycle the waste that was unavoidable, were the ideas that emerged at that time and led to the insight that the end-of-pipe technology of technically sophisticated landfill site was not sufficient to resolve the waste problem of Germany (Herbold / Wienken 1993). However, avoiding and recycling are goals that cannot be reached without the collaboration of producers and consumers. The *avoidance* of waste requires innovations in the production processes that lead to less waste; additionally, the behaviour of the consumers has to change. The precondition for the *recycling* of waste is the separate collection of the different types, like glass, paper, plastic, and organic waste. This requires technical and organisational efforts as well as the co-operation of the waste producers. To influence these things is an extremely difficult political task. Only in the nineties did the German political system codify avoidance and recycling efforts in concrete policies.

A further reaction to the experiences made with the hazards connected with dumps and the problems of building new dumps was the effort to put more emphasis on the treatment of waste before depositing it. This means that, before the waste is deposited in the dump, it is treated in order to reduce its volume and especially in order to reduce its biochemical reactions. The most common technical option to reach these goals is the incineration of the waste. However, in recent years, an alternative possibility to treat the waste before its deposition emerged; the option to treat the waste biologically and mechanically gained more and more interest. This led to the emergence of one of the main conflicts in German waste management: is the waste to be treated in waste incinerators or in bio-mechanical plants? Opponents of waste incineration argue that the bio-mechanical option is cheaper, more flexible, and that its emissions are less toxic. The other side argues mainly that bio-mechanical treatment does not lead to waste disposal without after-care and thus does not fulfil the requirements of waste treatment. Furthermore, it is claimed that the toxic emissions of waste incinerators are controllable by advanced filter technology. This conflict will be of crucial importance in the two case studies reported in chapters four and five.

To put emphasis on the treatment of waste meant the integration of an already known technical possibility into a larger system of waste management. The incineration of waste is only one element of the complex system of treating waste. The goals to be reached with the technical treatment of waste were a) to have dumps without after-care, i.e. without unforeseeable reactions and emissions (Haber et al. 1991), and b) to save on the scarce resource of space needed for dumps. The idea of treating the waste before depositing it, however, creates new problems, the most important of which are the emissions of a waste incinerator and the highly toxic dusts, that are filtered out of the emissions and have to be disposed. Additionally, and of specific importance for the present analysis, waste incineration sites suffer a constant lack of acceptance by the public (Haber et al. 1991). The political and legal conflicts that arise around the siting procedures can block the decision making process significantly.

3.1.1 German Waste Policy in the Nineties

Against the background of these technical possibilities, that developed step by step due to the experiences with waste management and its consequences (Krohn 1997), German waste policy developed into the direction of an extremely complicated policy field. Technical and geological requirements for waste dumps, measures to avoid and recycle waste, and regulation of waste incineration became the most important elements of the German waste policy of recent years. The implementation of this policy, which is a duty of the local administrative level, raised the issue of constructing complex socio-technical systems of waste management (Herbold et al. 1997). As will be shown below, the task of establishing these socio-technical systems confronts the decision makers at the local level with risks. The main elements of this policy will be described in the following sections.

The most important developments towards the system of waste management that we face today in Germany were done at the beginning of the nineties. The political and legal regulations of waste management as they appear at the end of the nineties, can be classified along the above mentioned three technical approaches to the waste problem: Depositing, treatment, and avoiding / recycling of waste. As will become clear in the following sections, the three aspects of waste management are highly interrelated.

Before explaining the regulations on waste management in more detail, it will be necessary to sketch the general institutional framework in which the local handling of the waste problem takes place. The important points in this context are the structure of politics and administration at the local level (3.2.1), the local responsibility for the disposal safety of the waste management system (3.2.2), and the mode of financing of the waste management system (3.2.3), that the local bodies have to follow. These three institutional characteristics touch the central theoretical aspect of the risk sociological framework that is used here: they all determine the degree of responsibility local administration has to take in waste management.

3.2 General Aspects: Local Waste Management in Germany

In Germany, the depositing and treatment of waste is a task of the communities. In order to prepare my analysis of local decision making processes in waste management, it is therefore necessary to shed some light on the general framework in which these decision processes take place.

3.2.1 Politics and Administration at the Local Level

Within the German political system, the lowest administrative level is the local one (Kommunalebene), with the state level (Länderebene) and the federal level (Bundesebene) above it. The status of the communities in the German political system is an ambiguous one.

On the one hand, the local level has to implement policies that are made at the state and federal levels. In this respect, the communities are bodies of administration that have no formal influence on the formulation of the policies they have to implement. Although many policy making initiatives go back to problems at the local level, and the policies can be shaped in implementation, the formal policy making procedures take place without the participation of the local level. This situation leads to a general tendency of task overload at the local level. The political system as a whole shows the tendency to accept more and more complex tasks (cf. e.g. Luhmann 1990b); some of these tasks are then shifted to the local level but, however, mostly without corresponding raises in financing and in equipment, especially in terms of personnel. Thus, the local level faces serious financial and organisational difficulties in fulfilling its administrative task.

On the other hand, the communities act on the basis of the constitutional principle of 'local self-administration' (cf. art. 28 of the German Basic Law). This means that, within the framework of legal prescriptions made by higher political levels, the communities have a certain autonomy to arrange and form local affairs. In order to fulfil this more political task, at the local level we also find the differentiation of politics and administration. There are elected local parliaments, whose members are part-time politicians. These local politicians are non-professionals who deal with the political affairs of the communities parallel to a usual full-time job. The administrative part of the communities is run by professionals, mostly engineers and lawyers. The division of labour between these two parts corresponds to the usual one between politics and administration: the administration prepares the decisions, the parliament makes the decision and thereby takes responsibility for it, the administration implements it on the basis of the political mandate.

These roughly sketched organisational features of the local bodies have some important implications for the character of the decisions made at this level. Firstly, the ambiguous status of the communities, between implementation of state and federal policies on the one hand and the principle of local self-administration on the other hand, leads to the fact that the differentiation between politics and administration at this level can be found in at least two forms: the communities as a whole can be considered *administration* with respect to implementation of policies made at higher political levels, that for these policies make the genuine *political* contribution of legitimacy. With respect to local self-administration, the differentiation of politics and administration corresponds to the local political bodies and the administrative part of the communities. The participation of politicians, who hope to be re-elected by the public, in local decision processes makes these decisions susceptible for political opportunism. In general, these factors may lead to situations where implementation of federal policies is in contradiction with the principle of local self-administration. This will be an important point with respect to the highly contested decisions about waste treatment facilities, which will be analysed in my case studies.

Secondly, the above mentioned characteristics of politics and administration leads to certain idiosyncrasies of local decision making processes. At this level, the politicians are laymen and the administrators are professionals. The cleavage of these two divisions of political organisations, observable at higher political levels with complete professionalisation, is even stronger at the local level. For example, the administrative professionals very often consider the local politicians as incompetent and as too emotional and opportunistic in their contributions to the decision making process. Thus, the differentiation between politics and administration is at this level reinforced by different professional orientations between these two segments. This might be especially true of small communities and municipalities.

These features of local politics and administration lead to rather complex and ambiguous conditions of responsibility and accountability. This fact will be highlighted in the case studies. The general tendency is, however, that the task of constructing complex systems of waste management and especially of planning and siting waste treatment facilities leads to an overload of responsibility to be taken, and uncertainty to be absorbed at the local level. The task of waste management, the technical, legal, and political aspects of which will be sketched in the remaining sections of this chapter, imposes risks on the communities that overtaxes the division of labour between politics and administration at this level.

3.2.2 The Goal Programme: Achieving 'Disposal Safety'

Turning to the concrete features of waste management, as it is to be performed by the German communities, the first important point is the legal and formal responsibility for the functioning of the local waste management systems. This responsibility lies with the communities. The most important legal term in this context is the disposal safety, i.e. the certainty that the community is able to take care of its waste according to the legal and technical requirements. The disposal safety has to be ensured in the long run, usually for at least ten to fifteen years. The requirement to achieve disposal safety is a *goal programme* for the local administration. Roughly speaking, the fulfilment of this goal programme implies three general, and highly interrelated, aspects.

With respect to the *technical* functioning of a waste management system, first of all it is necessary to guarantee the collection of the different types of waste. The types of waste that are to be recycled have to be collected purely, e.g. the paper collected must not be polluted with plastics, glass etc. Otherwise the recycled products are of inferior quality. The most important technical aspect, however, is to make sure that there are enough facilities to treat and to deposit the waste. Thus, the size of the facilities has to correspond with the expected amount of waste. If there is too much waste, the disposal safety is not guaranteed, i.e. the community is not able to take care of its waste in a way according to the legal prescriptions. Furthermore, of course the technical facilities have to be safe. There must be a minimal risk of accidents and the facilities have to work smoothly, i.e. without disruptive incident or malfunctioning that would endanger disposal safety.

The *legal* requirements of the functioning of waste management systems consist of regulations, especially for the depositing and treatment of waste. These legal prescriptions will be analysed in detail in the following sections. The community is responsible for the fulfilment of these regulations. Otherwise the waste management facilities are not permitted by the regulatory bodies and, again, the disposal safety is not guaranteed.

With respect to the *political* aspects that endanger the disposal safety, the most important factor is the highly contested public acceptability of waste facilities in Germany. The siting of waste disposal sites and of waste incinerators creates conflicts between decision makers, the people who live next to the planned site, and local environmental pressure groups. Resistance against these siting decisions is well-organised, and the German legal system contains many possibilities to prevent these decisions. For the administrative planning procedures, public participation is prescribed; i.e. well-informed and well-organised opponents of the waste facilities have certain possibilities to influence the decision. I will deal with the structure of the formal planning procedures in more detail in sections 3.3 and 3.4. The more important option to prevent the siting of a waste disposal site or of a waste incinerator is, however, to institute proceedings against the siting decision after the formal planning procedure. Not only can a court stop a local planning process by declaring that there have been mistakes in the formal planning procedures but even when the court gives the 'green light' to the administrative decision, the planning has to be stopped during the court proceedings. This possible, even likely, delay of the decision process can as well endanger the disposal safety.

A further aspect connected with the contested acceptability of waste sites is the fact that the conflicts about the siting decisions, of course, affect the political life of a community. As has been suggested above, especially the local politicians, without technical specialisation and with the interest of getting re-elected, tend to question decisions about the siting of waste disposal sites and waste incinerators, that have been prepared by the administration. The professionals in the administration, mostly convinced of the technical and legal appropriateness of the solution they suggested, perceive this political influence on the decision as a major disturbance. The conflicting parties are therefore not only decision makers on the one and affected citizens on the other hand, as is suggested too simplistically by Luhmann (1993a). Local politicians tend to assume the arguments of the opponents, because they are subject to serious political pressure. As a result, local politicians can also be found among the opponents to waste treatment facilities. This makes the political resolution of conflicts about waste treatment facilities more complex.

To sum up, the concept of local responsibility for the disposal safety, the most prominent aspect of the local duties in waste management, opens up a range of requirements that are often conflicting and that create many social and political conflicts. The actors in these conflicts are local pressure groups, local politicians, local administration, courts, and higher political levels.

The requirement of disposal safety is a *goal programme* for local administration. The decision programme consists of a goal to be reached by the decision: The task is to construct a waste management system that 'works' according to the technical, legal, and political requirements. The means to reach this end can be chosen quite freely, as long as they are consistent with the legal framework. As will be described in the following sections, the technical possibilities and legal constraints of waste management open up a wide range of alternative solutions to solve the decision problem, i.e. to reach the goal of a safe waste management system. The uncertainties on the way to reach this goal are immense: Will it be possible to establish a waste management system that works technically? Will it be possible to match the sometimes conflicting technical and the legal requirements? Will the necessary decisions be acceptable politically? Or will they be blocked by political or legal conflicts? Thus, we have a classical situation of risk as it has been developed in the second chapter: The consequences of the decisions to be made are highly uncertain. The decision makers, however, are accountable for the occurrence of these consequences. Whether or not the decisions are right can only be judged in the future.

A precondition for the correct fulfilment of a goal-programme is a certain degree of an established organisational technology (cf. above, chapter 2). This means, that it is necessary to have well-known cause and effect relations in order to achieve a goal prescribed by the decision programme. The decision makers have to know which decisions have which consequences, so that they know which decision to make in order to fulfil the requirements of the programme. As will be described in the remaining sections of this chapter, the situation in German waste management lacks this feature. The task to be fulfilled is new and complex, the means to achieve the end of a safe waste management system are unknown. In other words, since the legal requirements, and technical possibilities, to construct waste management systems are the result of rather recent developments, the task of establishing these systems is a rather new one for the communities. Established organisational routines, that are normally used to handle decision situations with goal programmes (March / Olsen 1995), quite often do not exist. In the case studies of the present study, I will try to analyse how the local administrations handle this complex decision problem.

3.2.3 Amplification of Risk: The Mode of Financing Waste Management

One aspect that increases the intensity of conflicts about waste management and which especially prolongs them into the period after the facilities commence operating is the mode of financing the system of waste management. This mode of financing is *legally* prescribed: Local waste management has to be financed by charges. These charges are paid by the producers of waste, i.e. the households. In contrast to taxes and duties, charges are paid for a certain service. This implies that there must be an identifiable service to which the charge can attributed (SRU 1998: 190; Siekmann 1994). The service, in our case, is the management of the household waste. The charge has to be cost-effective: This implies firstly, that no other possibility to finance the waste management system can be used and secondly that the charge must not be higher than necessary to fulfil the task (Zwehl / Kaufmann 1994; Hermann et al. 1997: 88p.).

This mode of financing has several implications that further complicate the local management of waste. The local budgets of the charges have to be balanced in quite short periods. This creates conflicts with the very long-term investments necessary for the construction of waste treatment and disposal facilities. One important effect is that cheap technical solutions can burden the charge budgets very heavily in the short run (Lemser et al. 1998).

The burdening of charge budgets by long-term financial investment has enormous political consequences in the communities. The necessity to raise the waste charges in a community is a constant source of intense political conflicts. Due to the developments of recent years in the direction of complex technical systems of waste management, waste charges have risen enormously (SRU 1998: 189). Moreover, they differ significantly between the communities. Charges for waste management have become a serious burden for individual households. Thus, people demand that the charges be calculated in a transparent manner and especially in a way that allows citizens to save money by reducing their production of waste (Fricke / Zink 1996; Lemser / Tillmann 1996). Since the communities are free to choose their system of charge calculation (Bienroth et al. 1995), changes are always possible, as long as the legal requirements for waste charges, especially the principle of cost-effectiveness, are fulfilled. Roughly speaking, the charge can be calculated on the basis of weight, of volume, or of frequency of collection (Oechler 1993). However, as practical experience shows, it is difficult, if not impossible, to create a just charge system that rewards and punishes the citizens according to their individual waste production without creating incentives to tip the waste in forests or on to the street (Ihmels 1993; SRU 1998: 193).

A further paradoxical consequence of the practice of financing local waste management by charges is the following. Today, the modern systems of waste management in Germany are to a large extent based on complex technical facilities, such as landfill sites, waste incinerators, composting plants, and the like. Additionally, the communities have to build complex organisational and technical structures in order to collect and transport the waste in an appropriate manner. To a very large extent, the running costs of the waste treatment and disposal facilities are fixed costs, i.e. the running costs arise rather independently of the amount of waste that is treated or deposited. Thus, the complex systems of waste management, including efforts to avoid and recycle waste and including large facilities to treat and deposit waste, create immense running costs, even if the amount of waste that has to be handled declines (Klockow 1995). Due to the successes of recent years to avoid and recycle waste (cf. section 3.5) the amount of waste to be processed in the 'classical' system of collection, incineration, and depositing has declined dramatically. The effect for the individual citizen is that he produces less waste and has to pay much higher charges for his waste, absolutely and relatively.

The opaque connection between complexity of the waste management system and the level of waste charges leads to immense conflicts in local waste management. The local decisions to plan and construct waste facilities touch the charge budgets immediately and with long-term effects (Lemser et al. 1998). A decision that leads to a facility that is too large for the amount of waste in the community burdens the community for years, financially and politically. The two possible solutions to escape the financial burden are: a) to raise the charges, or b) to treat or deposit waste from other communities in the facility (Wagner 1996). Both alternatives create political conflicts.

From a sociological perspective, the interesting point in this context is the fact that the *economic* decision to invest in the construction of a facility creates a *political* risk, i.e. the risk of losing political majorities at the local level. In addition to the point made in the previous section, the legal responsibility for disposal safety, the system of financing waste management by charges to be paid by the citizens sets the decision makers under political pressure. The decision about waste facilities, to be made under uncertainty and burdened by the legal responsibility for the disposal safety, becomes more pressurised by the question of political responsibility.

Finally, and most important, one has to note that the decisions about waste facilities have to be made simultaneously with the goal of disposal safety and under the principle of financing the waste management system with charges in a cost-effective manner. This creates a decision situation that offers almost no positive solution: *Either* the constructed facilities are too small. This would mean that the community is not able to handle its waste and therefore fails to achieve the goal of disposal safety. *Or* the waste facilities are too large for the amounts of waste. This would imply raising the charges or treating and depositing waste of other communities. The possibility of arriving at an appropriately sized waste management system with acceptable charges is extremely small.

In terms of the risk situation for the local administration, the mode of financing implies not only the amplification of risk in the social dimension (one's own decisions affect others), but also, in combination with the goal of disposal safety, a contradictory demand with respect to the planning of the waste management system.

3.3 Depositing of Waste

I will now turn to the analysis of the three aspects of waste management and their regulation by federal waste policy. In addition to the depositing of waste, which is the topic of this section, waste treatment (3.4.), and the avoiding and recycling of waste (3.5) are the central aspects of a waste management system that fulfils the requirement of disposal safety.

The depositing of waste confronts the decision makers with two main problems. The waste disposal site has to be sited suitably and constructed in an appropriate size; and the disposal site has to be safe with respect to emissions. The legal prescriptions for the depositing of waste can be classified with respect to these two problems.

3.3.1 Planning and Siting

The classical response of the German political system to siting problems of waste disposal facilities has been the instrument of *planning*. The idea is that administrative agencies use methods of long-term, anticipatory planning in order to achieve the optimal amount and distribution of waste disposal capacities. Two instruments of planning have been used in German waste management: The establishing of Waste Management Plans (Abfallentsorgungsplan), which is a duty of the state level (Länder); and the planning permission procedure (Planfeststellungsverfahren) (Herbold / Wienken 1993). The main features and problems of both instruments will be sketched in the following section.

The *Waste Management Plan* is a duty of the state level that can be found in all versions of the German Waste Act of 1972 until the most recent form of 1996. The idea is that the state level develops plans for the waste management in the respective state. These plans are supposed to contain locations for waste disposal sites. The plans are supposed to be binding for the local administration, i.e. they are to serve as a premise for the local decisions about waste management systems. The desired effect is a two-fold one: Firstly, the capacities to dispose waste correspond to the amount of waste that is to be handled in the respective state because the state level of administration is supposed to know the relevant data and information. Secondly, the communities are relieved of the responsibility for the extremely difficult decision of siting a waste dump, because the formal responsibility for siting lies with the states (Brückner / Wiechers 1985; Petter 1994).

In practice, however, the instrument of the Waste Management Plan never did work. The states hesitated to plan the waste disposal facilities in an anticipatory, and binding manner. On the contrary, the Waste Management Plans of the states tend to report the status quo of the stock of waste disposal sites instead of prescribing the locations of these sites in a binding and anticipatory way (Petter 1994; Wagner 1996). The instrument of Waste Management Plans has never been implemented (SRU 1991: 92).

The supposed effects of Waste Management Plans, efficient and coordinated action of the communities in one state and relief of local responsibility for siting decisions, cannot thus be observed in the reality of German waste management. In practice, the communities have to take full responsibility for the siting and planning of their waste disposal sites. The problem of contested public acceptability of waste disposal sites has already been described above. Since the states did not accept the responsibility for this part of the waste management planning, and shifted it to the communities, of course the problems of acceptability affect the local efforts to establish safe and working systems of waste management. The problem that waste disposal sites lack acceptance in the public could so far neither be resolved by the second important instrument of planning in waste management, the planning permission procedure.

The *planning permission procedure* (Planfeststellungsverfahren) is an important part of German administrative law. It is a formalised procedure to make administrative decisions. It is used in order to organise and legitimise processes of political planning. Planning permission procedures take place in all cases of public infrastructure projects.

The idea of the planning permission procedure is that projects planned by public administration such as streets, sewage plants, waste disposal sites and similar projects that contribute to public infrastructure are permitted by a higher administrative authority. In the case of projects planned at the local level, the proper authority for the permission of the plan is the district administration, which in Germany is part of the state administration. Thus, the classical constellation for a planning permission procedure is that a public authority controls and permits the plan of another public authority.

The planning permission procedure is supposed to allow a comprehensive consideration of all relevant aspects of a complex decision, such as the interests of affected citizens, the environmental impacts of a project, the compatibility with other projects, possible alternatives for the project, and the question whether the project is necessary (Rahner 1993). In order to consider and weigh up all these (and more) aspects of the planning decision, the permitting authority has considerable room for discretion in permitting the plan (Beckmann et al. 1988; Paetow 1991).

Although the planning permission procedure has a long tradition in the German legal system, it was regulated in a unitary and binding way only in 1975 with the federal Administrative Procedure Act that for the first time fixed rules for all formal administrative decision procedures (Kopp 1987). Sections 72-78 of the Administrative Procedure Act refer to the planning permission procedure. According to section 73, the procedure runs as follows. After the application for the planning permission is made, the permitting authority contacts the respective authorities that are technically responsible for the important aspects of the project. For a landfill site, the permitting authority for example would have to contact the authorities responsible for water and ground. After the opinions of the technical authorities have been considered, the application has to be published in the municipalities that are likely to be affected by the project. Within a certain period, the citizens can make written objections. These objections have to be considered publicly in the planning permission hearing. Considering the objections by the citizens, the permitting authority makes the final decision about the plan. This final decision, the planning permission resolution, arranges all relevant aspects of the respective projects. No other legal permissions are necessary (Battis 1988). The planning permission resolution can, however, be subject of subsequent legal processes, initiated especially by affected citizens.

In terms of risk and uncertainty, the planning permission procedure is a very interesting, though complex phenomenon. Generally speaking, it is a means to rationalise and legitimise goal-programmed administrative procedures. The duty to make planning decisions, like projects for streets, sewage plants, and waste disposal sites, constitutes a goal programme for the respective authority. In order to make sure that these administrative decisions be accepted by the public, i.e. in order to ensure their legitimacy, the decision making process is organised in a formalised procedure. However, as the practical problems of planning permission procedures in Germany show, it is a rather difficult task to legitimise a goal-programmed decision in a formalised procedure.

The legitimising aspect of the planning permission procedure is made obvious by the fact that public participation is allowed. This prescription of public participation - which touches the decision premise of channels of communication - affects the decision process significantly. The objections made by the public very often refer to the important points that can question projects like waste disposal sites in particular: is the project necessary? Are there alternative ways of realising the project, especially alternative locations that are more suitable? The non-consideration of justified objections would make the planning permission resolution susceptible to subsequent court decisions which could cancel it. The necessity to justify the plan to the public leads to a very tight co-operation between the applicant, the technical authorities, and the permitting authority. As a result, the impression arises that the decision is already made when it has to be justified publicly. The legitimising effect of the procedure is affected by this fact. The hearings in the planning permission procedures are thus characterised by heavy, and often very emotional, conflicts between citizens, organised pressure groups, scientific experts, and the administrative authorities (Hoffmann-Hoeppel 1994). Due to the complexity of planning decisions, the necessity to make a rather water-proof decision before it has to be justified to the public, and due to the fact that subsequent legal proceedings are very likely, the time period necessary to plan infrastructure projects has become extremely long in Germany.

From the perspective developed in chapter two of the present study, the growing importance of the planning permission procedure, and particularly its formal regulation in the Administrative Procedure Act in 1975, indicates a politicised administration. Due to general political developments, the administration has to take responsibility for complex planning decisions that are programmed towards the reaching of goals, for example the construction of an appropriately sized, suitably sited, and safe waste disposal site. In order to ensure the legitimacy of the necessary decision, the decision making process is organised in a formalised procedure that is supposed to consider all relevant aspects of the plan and that ends up with a binding decision. Therefore, in the process of administrative decision making, genuinely political tasks are to be fulfilled, like the organisation of consensus, and the weighing of values and interests.

Generally speaking, the problem of legitimising a goal-programmed decision in a procedure is due to the time orientation of a goal programme (cf. Luhmann 1983). As has been argued above, a goal-programmed decision will be considered correct, if in the future the goal has been reached. This means that the necessary facts with which the correctness of the decision can be jduged are not known when the decision is made. This implies that in the planning permission procedure, that is supposed to declare the correctness of the decision, the relevant facts also cannot be known. The planning permission resolution is based on scientific assessment and anticipation of future developments. However, a decision based on probabilistic assumptions is highly value-loaded and therefore very susceptible to conflicting preferences. The risk that the decision will be cancelled afterwards by a court decision is very high.

All these points lead to the fact that planning permission procedures suffer serious problems with respect to risk issues. In terms of decision premises, the picture is the following. The administration is programmed towards a goal (programme), and the participation of other administrative authorities and especially of the public is prescribed (channels of communication). This leads to high loads of responsibility (goal programme) and to a high uncertainty with respect to acceptability of the decision. Planning permission procedures can go on for years, and even afterwards the decision process is blocked by the risk of negative court decisions. As decision premises, the goal programme of constructing waste disposal sites together with the prescription to make the decision in a planning permission procedure, fail to absorb much uncertainty. The decision to construct a waste disposal site in accordance with legal prescriptions is burdened with high loads of responsibility for, and uncertainty about, the consequences of the decision: it is an extremely risky decision. This touches the ability of the communities to fulfil their goal programme of 'disposal safety'.

To sum up, the German instruments that were designed to allow long-term and anticipatory planning in waste management suffer serious problems. The instrument of the waste management plan has never been implemented effectively. The states hesitated to fix sites for waste disposal sites. As a result, the practical responsibility for siting waste disposal sites lies with the communities, although the states are formally supposed to take responsibility for this part of waste management. The effect is an additional burden for the communities in terms of risk.

With the example of the planning permission procedure, which is extremely time consuming and uncertain with respect to its results, one can see which amounts of uncertainty and responsibility are connected with decisions about waste disposal sites. Although the planning permission procedure continues to be an important part of German administrative law, it cannot solve all problems connected with risky planning decisions. Despite the use of waste management plans and planning permission procedures, which were supposed to relieve the communities of responsibility and of uncertainties with respect to the acceptability of siting decisions, the task of constructing waste disposal sites remains a difficult one.

3.3.2 Regulation of Emissions from Waste Disposal Sites

The most important political reaction to the problem of emissions from waste disposal sites is the Technical Instruction for Household Waste (Technische Anleitung Siedlungsabfall) of 1993. Although this administrative instruction is supposed to regulate all aspects of local waste management, it is right in the centre of recent conflicts about waste management because of its precise and rather strict prescriptions with respect to the technical features of waste disposal sites. The interesting point is that the regulations of the emissions from waste disposal sites strongly affect the decisions about another element of a waste management system, the treatment of waste. This will be made clear in the following section.

The regulations of the Technical Instruction for Household Waste react to the above mentioned problems of depositing waste. The goal is to construct waste disposal sites without the necessity of after-care and to use as little space as possible. The most important aspect of the Technical Instruction for Household Waste is the prescription of the quality of the waste that is to be deposited. In order to reduce the chemical reactions in the deposited waste, the technical instruction prescribes that the waste shall fulfil the parameter of 5% loss by combustion. The loss by combustion is a parameter that allows the degree of organic reaction taking place in the waste to be described (Leporn / Henschel 1993). The decisive point with respect to the limit of 5% loss by combustion is that the only technical possibility of reaching this limit is the *incineration* of waste. That means that, without explicit regulation, the Technical Instruction for Household

Waste prescribes waste incineration. Other technical options to treat waste, especially the bio-mechanic technology, are excluded. It is this fact that makes this technical instruction a heavily discussed and highly contested part of German waste policy. The conflicts about these implications will thus be at the centre of the case studies.

The other very important aspect of the prescriptions in the Technical Instruction for Household Waste is the fact that it contains interim regulations. At this point, ambiguity about decision premises is introduced into the requirement for the communities. The demands which it contains with respect to the technical level of waste disposal sites and with respect to the incineration of waste, oblige local administration to make sustained and long-term investments in new technical facilities, especially new waste disposal sites and new waste incineration plants. In order to give the communities enough time to realise these complex technical projects, the Technical Instruction for Household Waste contains that possibility that, if there are no alternative solutions, the communities have to implement the prescriptions only by the year 2005. Until 2005, temporary arrangements that do not fulfil the prescriptions of the technical instruction are allowed. As a result, the local decision makers have a rather long period to adapt to the prescriptions. Since the Technical Instruction for Household Waste fixes all the important aspects of waste management, the present time period can be characterised as a transition period (SRU 1998: 175). The full impact of the prescriptions contained in the technical instruction will be only observable by the year 2005.

As a decision premise for administrative decisions in waste management, the Technical Instruction for Household Waste creates many ambiguities although, or maybe because, it fixes very precise and clear prescriptions for waste management. First of all, it prescribes, albeit indirectly, the incineration of waste. Incineration is necessary to fulfil the requirements of the chemical quality of waste that is deposited in landfill sites. Waste incineration, however, is one of the most contested technologies in Germany. In certain aspects, in the public discussion it has taken the role that nuclear energy took in the seventies and eighties. The public resistance against waste incineration is carried by highly organised and well-informed pressure groups. Although many scientific experts now consider waste incineration a safe technology with respect to health and environmental effects (SRU 1998: 215pp.), the conflicts about the siting of waste incinerators create paralyses for decision processes in German waste management. Thus, the Technical Instruction for Household Waste obliges the communities to make decisions about waste incineration that create strong and constant conflicts with affected citizens and organised pressure groups. Many communities therefore tend to question the prescriptions of the Technical Instruction for Household Waste. The legal obligation in a matter which is highly contested scientifically and politically tends to create resistance in many local administrations.

Moreover, the Technical Instruction for Household Waste itself leaves much open to interpretation with respect to its imperative effects. *First* of all, the Technical Instruction for Household Waste is no legal act; it is an instruction for the implementation of the Waste Act. Formally it is supposed to be an internal guideline for the administrative authorities that permit the waste management planning of the communities (cf. Hermann et al. 1997: 56). This non-legal character of the Technical Instruction for Household Waste gives room for political conflicts at the local level. It is at this point, where the conflict between implementation and local self-administration arises: the implementation of a federal policy affects seriously the demands of local self-administration and it is highly contested whether such a serious intervention can be made on the basis of a technical instruction. The willingness to accept the Technical Instruction for Household as a premise for local decisions is thus quite low.

The tendency towards conflicts about the binding nature of the technical instruction is reinforced by a *second* important ambiguity. In clause 2.4 of the technical instruction, there is the possibility to permit exceptions from the regulations, if the respective measure is in accordance with the public welfare. The public welfare, in this case however, is defined by the technical instruction. This very ambiguous possibility to permit exceptions of course gives leeway to political discussions at the local level (e.g. U. Meyer et al. 1996). Pressure groups and local politicians, who try to avoid waste incineration, use the clause 2.4 to argue for waste management systems without waste incineration. The third source of ambiguity in the Technical Instruction for Household Waste, which was important until 1995 at least, was clause 13, which prescribed the examination of the effects of the instruction by 1995. Until 1995, this clause raised the hopes of opponents that the technical instruction might be changed and thus waste incineration would not be necessary anymore. More recently, there have been speculations about an European directive for the regulation of waste disposal sites that might relieve the strict standards of the Technical Instruction for Household Waste (SRU 1998: 229). The construction of waste incineration plants would then no longer be necessary. Due to the interim regulations until 2005 in the Technical Instruction for Household Waste, European developments might affect the local decisions about waste incineration plants. In effect, opponents to waste incineration may hope that the legal prescriptions change before 2005. This heightens the uncertainty for local decisions about waste treatment facilities (Wagner 1996).

These ambiguities of the Technical Instruction for Household Waste, together with the very long period of transition until 2005 create a very unusual situation. On the one hand, the technical instruction contains a very clear regulation: a local waste management system without waste incineration is not allowed. However, the ambiguities explained above create a difficult decision situation for the local decision makers, because the decision process becomes highly susceptible to political considerations about the binding nature of the technical instruction. Changes in political orientations at the federal and at the state level, that can lead to different interpretations of the technical instruction or to a change in the instruction itself, immediately affect the administrative decision processes at the local level.

A final important effect of the Technical Instruction for Household Waste is created by the regulation which allows exceptions until 2005. Communities which have waste disposal sites that do not fulfil the requirements of the technical instruction have an interest in filling their landfill sites until 2005. A struggle for waste has begun. Facilities for depositing waste have become extremely cheap. The same is true of facilities for waste incineration. Because it is not possible to fill the old dumps with incinerated waste (because of the enormous volume reduction) many communities do not incinerate their waste anymore. This leads to the effect that many incineration plants are not working to capacity. Due to the high fixed costs, the owners of the incineration plants seek to get more waste into their plants. As a result, the prices for waste incineration, like the prices for depositing, have sunk enormously in recent years.

Besides the negative environmental effects of depositing untreated waste in dumps that do not correspond to the best available technique, the consequence for the local decision makers is the following. During their planning of local waste management systems, including new waste disposal sites and waste incineration plants - both highly contested technologies - , they are confronted with cheap offers to treat and deposit their waste in other communities. They therefore hesitate to make the unpleasant decision to build incineration plants and tend to accept these offers. The effect is that the necessary decisions to fulfil the technical instruction household waste are not made. After 2005, capacities to treat and deposit waste are likely to be very scarce, the prices will rise again. It is very likely that many decisions at the end of the nineties were made under distorted conditions in terms of prices.

Together with the rather unclear regulations of the Technical Instruction for Household Waste, the effects of the long transition period until 2005 lead to difficulties in implementing the technical instruction. The very low prices for external depositing and treatment of waste make decisions on constructing dumps and incineration plants more difficult and politically unacceptable at the local level.

However, given that the Technical Instruction for Household Waste has a binding effect in its present form, it makes the general goal-programme to provide for disposal safety more precise, and more difficult. The instruction says that a waste management system, in order to fulfil the requirements of disposal safety, has to contain a waste incineration plant as an important and indispensable element. The programming of the local administration towards the reaching of this goal creates a situation of a politicised administration. The above mentioned ambiguities of the Technical Instruction for Household Waste make the administrative decision processes in the communities even more susceptible to political considerations. The anticipation of future political developments which might affect the form and interpretation of the technical instruction therefore becomes an important aspect to be considered by the local decision makers.

As a goal programme, the necessity to construct a waste management system in accordance with the prescriptions of the Technical Instruction for Household Waste, creates risks for the local administrations. The communities have to take responsibility for the uncertain future consequences of their decisions. This situation is accentuated by the ambiguities created by the technical instruction. Although it prescribes the use of the waste incineration technology very precisely, ambiguities about the binding effects of the instruction, together with the controversial nature of waste incineration, lead to constant and serious political conflicts about the correct interpretation of the technical instruction.

With the Technical Instruction for Household Waste, the possibility that the decision might afterwards turn out to be the wrong one, compared to alternative courses of action, rises enormously. On the one hand, an early commitment to waste incineration by a community may turn out to be a mistake if political changes at higher levels lead to different interpretations, or even to changes in the technical instruction. On the other hand, the hesitation to build an incinerating plant may lead to delay and in 2005 the respective community might not have a safe waste disposal management system. Furthermore, while the external treatment in an existing incinerating plant may be cheap in the beginning, the costs of external treatment are likely to explode after 2005.

The example of the Technical Instruction for Household Waste demonstrates how contradictory expectations create alternatives for the decision makers. The increased number of alternatives increases the risk of making a decision which will be regretted in the future.

3.4 Treatment of Waste

In principle, the technical option of treating waste before depositing it, faces the same requirements as the depositing of waste. First of all, the siting has to be organised. Second, the emissions have to be regulated. These requirements have to be considered in the context of the questionable acceptability of this technology.

3.4.1 Siting

Similar to siting of waste disposal sites, the siting of waste treatment plants in Germany has been considered a task of political planning. Thus, for a long time, the planning instruments mentioned above have been used to site waste incinerators, i.e. the waste management plan and the planning permission procedure.

The waste management plans to be made by the states are supposed to contain sites for waste incineration plants as well. However, as has been argued above (3.3.1), the instrument of waste management plans has never worked in practice. Instead of specifying sites for waste dumps and incinerators in an anticipatory and binding manner, the waste management plans report the status quo of waste management structures in the respective state. Thus, they do not relieve the communities of siting decisions.

The organisation of siting decisions for waste incinerators in the planning permission procedure has the same characteristics as the planning permission for waste disposal sites. In 1993, however, the prescriptions for the permission of waste treatment plants changed significantly. As a reaction to the political discussion about the conditions for economic investments in Germany, and in order to facilitate investments in the eastern states of Germany, the so-called Investment Facilitation Act was enacted. This act contained many measures designed to facilitate economic investments and to reduce bureaucratic obstacles for enterprises. Among the regulations of the Investment Facilitation Act was the prescription that waste treatment plants are not to be considered under the planning permission procedure but under the German Nuisance Act (Bundesimmissionsschutzgesetz). This change of the permission procedure has major implications for the siting decisions of waste treatment plants, especially of waste incinerators.

The most striking difference between the planning permission procedure and permission procedure according to the Nuisance Act is that the applicant has a right to the permission if the permission conditions, especially with respect to emissions, are complied with. This is different from the planning permission procedure, in which the permitting authority has to consider the necessity for the plant and to examine possible alternatives with respect to technology and with respect to the location of the plant (Rahner 1993). In the planning permission procedure, the permitting authority has to weigh the different aspects of the planning decision, instead of simply matching a decision (permission) with a condition (fulfilment of emission standards), as in the procedure according to the Nuisance Act. The reason for this fundamental difference in the procedural structure is that the planning permission procedure was designed to permit planning projects of public authorities by higher authorities. The purpose of the permission procedure according to the Nuisance Act is to permit private investment projects. In private investments, the necessity and possible alternatives need not be examined because economic decision makers are supposed to calculate these risks for themselves (Rahner 1993). In the case of public authorities as applicants, the necessity to plan the respective project has to be justified.

For the permitting authority, the difference between the planning permission procedure and the permission procedure according to the Nuisance Act is the one of goal and conditional programme. In the planning permission procedure, the authority has to reach the goal of a decision that is in accordance with the public welfare. It has to choose the best possible alternative out of a range of options to reach this goal. When an authority has to permit a plant according the Nuisance Act, it has to make a decision in the form 'if - then'. If the plant fulfils the requirements of the emission standards fixed in the Nuisance Act, then the permission has to be given.

The supposed effect of this new procedural requirement for the permission of waste incineration plants is obvious. The permission procedure is supposed to be relieved, in order to allow faster and more efficient decisions about waste treatment plants. The uncertainty absorbing capacity of an if-then-rule is much greater than of a goal programme in which all possible alternative options to reach the goal have to be considered. That the intention of the Investment Facilitation Act is to hasten the permission practice of German administration is not only obvious from the political debate in Germany on this issue at the beginning of the 1990s, but also because other provisions of this act point in the same direction.

First of all, and very importantly with respect to political conflicts about waste incineration plants, public participation in the procedure under the Nuisance Act is restricted compared to the planning permission procedure. It is only citizens who are immediately affected by the projects that may make objections in the procedure. The automatic participation of conservationist pressure groups, as it is prescribed in the planning permission procedure, is not part of the procedure under the Nuisance Act (Fröhlich 1994; Müllmann 1993). Furthermore, the exclusive effect of the procedure under the Nuisance Act with respect to possible subsequent legal conflicts is stronger. Only objections that have been submitted within the period stipulated can be treated in the public hearing and also in any subsequent legal process (Mayer et al. 1994; Appold / Beckmann 1990).

The effect of these efforts to relieve the formal permission procedure is that the conflicts between decision makers, those affected and environmental pressure groups are shifted into the political discussion at the local level. The question of the necessity of a plant and of possible alternative technologies and locations burden especially the political conflicts. The decision makers cannot shift these conflicts into the permission procedure by saying: 'These points will be addressed in the formal administrative procedure.' Any possible acceleration effect of this introduction of a more 'lean' permission procedure will most probably be undermined by more intensive political conflicts before the formal permission procedure.

These considerations indicate that the regulations of the Investment Facilitation Act create new uncertainties for local decision makers. It is not clear whether the decisive questions of requirement and alternatives will be treated in the formal permission procedure or whether they have to be tackled in the preceding political discussion in the communities. Opponents to waste incineration, of course, tend to demand that the requirement of a plant and the choice of the best possible alternative in technology and location be clarified in a political decision, before the formal permission of the plant begins. In the case studies we will see that pressure groups and other opponents use the argument of the now prescribed 'lean' permission procedure in order to pressurise administrative and political decision makers. The demand that the requirement for the plant be examined and alternatives be considered can thus hardly be rejected in the political discussion. The pressure to make a 'rational' decision rises.

3.4.2 Regulation of Emissions

One of the most important aspects of waste treatment, especially of waste incineration, is the question of emissions from these plants. In particular, the suspicion that waste incinerators produce large amounts of dioxane is one important argument of opponents against this technology.

The conflicts about the emissions from waste incinerators follow the typical patterns of risk conflicts. The scientific experts and many political decision makers consider the present regulations of the emissions as sufficient. The respective prescription in Germany can be found in the 17th Instruction for the Implementation of the Nuisance Act (17th BImSchV), enacted in 1990, which fixes rather strict limits for emissions from industrial plants. Environmental pressure groups and political opponents of waste incineration, however, doubt the sufficiency of the limits of the 17th BImSchV.

Technical and scientific experts claim that the limits of the 17th BImSchV guarantee safety for the environment and for health (SRU 1998: 215pp.). These arguments are often illustrated with the example that the amount of dioxanes in country regions without any industry is higher than in the immediate environment of a waste incinerator (Haltiner 1993).

The most important argument of the opponents to waste incineration is the fact the limits of the 17th BImSchV of course can only account for substances that are known. Due to the complicated and unknown chemical composition of waste, however, it is not possible to anticipate which substance will be emitted by a waste incinerator. Filter technology and legal requirements cannot react to substances which are not known. A second important point is that the German Nuisance Act controls only emissions. Such a regulative approach offers no possibility to control 'hot spots' with a high concentration of industrial and incinerating plants (Héritier et al. 1996).

Who is right in this conflict, is beyond the scope of a sociological analysis. With respect to the subject matter of the present study, administrative decisons about waste treatment facilities, it is important to note, however, that in recent years the emissions from waste incinerators have not been at the centre of conflicts about waste incineration. Although it is still an important topic, the more important issues have been the size of waste incinerators, their effects on efforts to avoid and to recycle waste, and especially the costs of waste incineration.

3.5 Avoiding and Recycling of Waste

In recent years, German waste policy has put emphasis on efforts to avoid and recycle waste. Although this part of waste management is not in the focus of the present analysis, it is necessary to highlight some of the important recent developments with respect to this issue. This is because the efforts to avoid and recycle waste affect the decisions about waste treatment facilities very seriously. To put it briefly, the successes in recent years in avoiding and recycling have minimised the amount of waste that has to be treated and deposited. This has affected decisions on waste incinerators and disposal sites because the most important information in these planning processes is the expected amount of waste.

3.5.1 Waste Management Concepts and Separate Collection

The Waste Act of 1986 was the first legal regulation that contained provisions on avoiding and recycling of waste. These prescriptions were, however, too imprecise to lead to concrete measures of avoidance and recycling. Only the waste acts of the states contained more instructive regulations, the most important of which is the demand that the communities are to establish so-called waste management concepts. These waste management concepts are supposed to describe all relevant elements of the waste management system of the respective community. These waste management concepts also have to contain measures to avoid and recycle waste. The intention was to facilitate the planning at the state level and to make decisions about waste incinerators and disposal sites more transparent.

In order to support avoidance, the communities have to organise the so-called waste avoidance advice (Abfallberatung) (Fonteyn / Pfänder 1988; Hermann et al. 1997: 67). This entails that the citizens are supposed to be informed about how to avoid waste by changing modes of consumption etc. This measure is normally supported by public campaigns in newspapers, by advertisement, or by other means of public information.

The recycling of waste, by its very nature, must be organised in a more elaborate manner. The most important precondition for recycling is the separate collection of waste types. The most important types of waste that can be collected separately and recycled are glass, paper, and biological waste. The main problem is to control the behaviour of the citizens to a certain degree with respect to the correct use of the different dustbins (cf. e.g. Jansen 1989). In order to be recyclable, the different types of waste have to be collected in a pure form (Haber et al. 1991). Otherwise recycling is impossible.

After the separate collection, the recycling itself has to be organised. The most difficult part of this task is the construction of the composting plants that are necessary to recycle biological waste. The construction of composting plants in principle faces the same problems as the construction of waste incinerators. And like waste incinerators, ill-sized composting plants also burden the local charge budgets (Scheffold 1995). Although the public acceptance of these facilities up to now is not as contested as that of waste incinerators, there is the same problem of finding the adequate size of the plant. More recently, also the potentially dangerous emissions from composting plants have come to public attention. It is likely that the discovery of this problem will lead to more serious acceptance problems in the future. However, in recent years, the efforts to avoid and recycle waste by measures at the local level have had considerable success. The effect of these efforts is, of course, that the amounts waste that has to be handled in a 'traditional' way, i.e. the combination of incineration and disposal, has been reduced significantly. This has important impacts on decisions about waste treatment plants, which are the focus of the present analysis.

3.5.2 Decree on Packaging Waste

The same effect can be observed with measures taken at the federal level to support avoidance and recycling. Section 14 of the Waste Act of 1986, and section 24 of the new Waste Act of 1996, open up the possibility for the federal government to enact decrees that impose obligations on manufacturers to take back used products (Hermann et al. 1997: 69p.). The most important decree on the basis of section 14 of the Waste Act is the Decree on Packaging Waste (Verpackungsverordnung), enacted in 1991.

The Decree on Packaging Waste contains a new instrument in German environmental policy by imposing the obligation on manufacturers of packagings to take back their used products (cf. SRU 1998: 206pp.). The only way to evade this obligation is the participation of the producers in a self-organised system of collecting and recycling packaging waste. The German Industry reacted to this decree by establishing the Duales System Deutschland GmbH (DSD), a firm that takes over this task of collecting and recycling used packagings. The implication for the consumers is a further dustbin in the households. They have to separate packaging waste from other types of waste. The packaging waste is then collected by the DSD. The implication for the communities is that, because of the considerable success of the DSD in collecting large amounts of packaging waste, the amount of waste that is to be treated and deposited by the communities is enormously reduced (Wagner 1994).

As a result, in the nineties all prognoses on the development of the amounts of waste to be handled by the communities turned out to be incorrect. This meant that the treatment and disposal capacities that were already in existence were oversized. For communities that were about to construct new facilities, this development led to a serious uncertainty in the planning process. The waste prognoses, the basic element of all planning processes for waste facilities, could not be trusted anymore. The decision processes in many communities are thus burdened by high amounts of uncertainty. This development is likely to continue because of the political intention at the federal level to enact additional decrees on the basis of section 24 of the Waste Act, for example for electronic waste, batteries, and waste from construction works (cf. SRU 1998: 199pp.).

3.5.3 Regulations on Industrial Waste in the New Waste Act of 1996

A further development towards uncertainty about the amounts of waste to be handled by the communities is initiated by the new Waste Act, enacted in 1996. Among the new regulations of this new framework for German waste management is the prescription that industrial waste can be treated and deposited by the waste producers themselves. Large firms that produce lots of industrial waste can choose whether they want this waste to be handled by the communities or whether they prefer to organise the treatment by themselves (Hölscher 1995). This opens up the possibility of looking for new and cheaper forms of treatment and disposal. Moreover, it is allowed to incinerate waste in combustion plants, that were not designed to incinerate waste, as long as they fulfil the requirements of the 17th BImSchV.

For the communities, this implies a further element of uncertainty. How much waste must be expected in the future depends on managerial decisions by the industry. The communities have no influence on these decisions (Wagner 1996; Hermann et al. 1997: 65). If, however, an industrial firm decides to let its waste be treated and deposited by the community, the community has the duty to manage this waste and use the facilities of its waste management system for this task. The anticipatory planning of the adequate size of the waste management system becomes more difficult.

To sum up, the implications of the recent efforts in Germany to put more emphasis on avoiding and recycling of waste are the following. First, the decision makers had to report a surprising and enormous drop in the amounts of waste that have to be handled by the communities. This was due to the considerable successes of local avoiding and recycling and of the Decree on Packaging Waste. Future developments are highly uncertain, because of the regulation of the new Waste Act, especially with respect to industrial waste.

3.6 The Premises for Decisions about Waste Treatment Facilities

In the preceding sections, I outlined the important conditions for local decisions about waste treatment facilities. First of all, these conditions are provided by the federal legislation on waste management. These legal requirements are, however, supplemented by political, economic and public requirements. This mixture of different, often contradictory, expectations towards the decision process comes into force because of several reasons. First, the legal prescriptions themselves create contradictions or at least demands that are difficult to put together. Second, the decision about waste treatment is not only a legal one. Political and public participation make the decision process susceptible to political opportunism. Together with the institutionalised resistance against waste incineration and the demand to finance all waste management activities by charges to be paid by the citizens, these conditions create a high observational pressure on local decisions about waste treatment. In the following sections, I will try to structure this decision situation, that is characterised by risks, in terms of the three types of decision premises developed in the second chapter.

3.6.1 Programmes

The most important organisational decision premise with respect to risk issues are the programmes. Programmes allocate the attention of decision makers and they allocate responsibility for the consequences of the decision. A goal programme makes the decision making level responsible for the consequences, and not the policy making level.

In the case of German waste management, the programme structure is defined by the local responsibility for *disposal safety*. This is the main requirement for any decision about waste management, and all of the other prescriptions only define what is to be considered a waste management system that provides disposal safety. This goal programme thus allocates responsibility for all consequences of the decisions to the local level. Further prescriptions define how uncertain these consequences are and which type of responsibility has to be taken.

The first important prescription that further defines disposal safety is the Technical Instruction for Household Waste. This technical instruction fixes the technical requirements for a waste management system that can be considered disposal-safe. According to the Technical Instruction for Household Waste, such a waste management system has to contain waste incineration as an element. It is this point that creates much of the risk for local administration.

Public resistance against waste incineration can be considered institutionalised in Germany. All environmental pressure groups try to prevent the further use of this technology, and there are influential pressure groups that create their identity by resistance to it. Furthermore, residents in the locality of the planned waste incineration plants form local protest groups, thus exerting a strong political pressure on local politicians. The political majorities for inconvenient decisions to construct waste treatment facilities are highly contested. It turns out that local politics is highly susceptible to political opportunism. Moreover, affected residents have legal possibilities to avoid or least to delay the decision process.

A further important aspect is the mode of financing. The fact that the construction of a waste incinerator requires long-term financial investment and that waste management measures are to be financed by public charges, leads to a high-degree politicisation of the decision process. Investment in a waste incineration plant binds financial resources for a long time. Due to the high fixed costs of these plants, they have to work to capacity, otherwise the charges for waste rise enormously. The increase of charges as a consequence of planning failures naturally creates political conflicts. The same is true of the other possibility to evade the financial burden of an over-sized waste incinerator, the treatment of waste from other communities. This 'waste import' is normally attacked with political arguments saying that the failure of the decision makers to size the plant correctly makes the respective community a kind of a waste dump for other communities.

The necessity to build appropriately sized waste incinerator leads us to the point that, for the planning of waste incinerators, the decision makers have to make prognoses about the amount of waste that is to be treated. If the plant is oversized, the community can be burdened politically and financially for years. If it is too small, the community cannot guarantee disposal safety. Due to the successes in avoiding and recycling, however, the development of the figures with respect to waste amount has become highly unpredictable. The amounts of waste have decreased dramatically in recent years, and because of the regulations of the new Waste Act of 1996 future developments are highly uncertain.

All of these details of the goal programme 'disposal safety' lead to a situation of high risk for the local decision makers. The consequences of the decisions about waste incinerators are highly uncertain, and the decision makers have to take full responsibility for these consequences.

These are the typical features of goal programmes. In the case of German waste management, a policy field that saw dramatic changes in recent years (SRU 1998: 174), a further important fact can be seen in the lack of organisational routines for the fulfilment of the goal programme. The task of establishing waste management systems that provide disposal safety, including measures of avoidance and recycling, and including waste incineration, is a new one for most of the communities. Uncertainty absorbing routines, that could enable the organisation to handle the problem of uncertainty and responsibility, in most cases do not exist. Thus, the communities have two possibilities. Either they have to develop new routines, or they have to match old routines, developed for different decision situations, to the new task.

The problem is thus to commit oneself to one out of a whole range of alternatives, with the relevant information, and development of further alternatives, being in constant movement. The risk that the chosen course of action will turn out to be wrong and will thus be regretted, is very high. Waste Management in Germany creates a classical situation of decision making under risk.

3.6.2 Channels of Communication

Which actors have to participate in the decisions about waste incineration and which competencies do they have? What does this mean with respect to risk taking in the local decision processes? These are the questions that arise if one asks which channels of communication are relevant in these decision processes. The decisive points in this context are the preferences that have to be considered in the decision process (which can be very heterogeneous and inconsistent in decision processes with multiple actors), the information that influences the decision, and the legitimising effect of the participation of politicians, the public and scientific experts. All these issues refer to the general function of decision premises, which is the absorption of uncertainty.

The preparation of the decisions lies with the professionals in the local administration. From their point of view, especially the fact that the final decision is to be taken by non-professional politicians, whose preferences are very susceptible to political opportunism, creates an element of instability in the decision process. Due to the high political pressure that is exerted on the elected representatives, administratively prepared decisions cannot be sure of political majorities. The acceptability of the decisions can be heightened by the participation of scientific experts, that not only improve the technical quality of the decision, but also provide for more legitimacy.

The legally prescribed, and politically expected, participation of citizens heightens the necessity for the decision makers to make sound and justifiable decisions. The pressure of rationality rises enormously. Moreover, it becomes clear, that the participation of many different actors in the decision process leads to an enormous heterogeneity of preferences to be considered.

3.6.3 Personnel

With respect to personnel, the developments in German waste policy in recent years, have several important implications. I argued above that the establishment of a waste management system has legal, technical, and political aspects. We find these three aspects in the requirements for personnel. What is needed is personnel with multiple qualifications (Cichonski / Heinrichs 1995). However, the traditional staffing of German administration with lawyers retains its important position. The interpretation of the complex legal requirements of German waste policy calls for professional knowledge of legal affairs. Legal expertise, however, is not sufficient for sound decisions in waste management, since there are more aspects about the implementation of a modern waste management system than just legal ones. The most obvious need is, of course, for personnel with technical expertise, since the technical requirements of the decisions about waste management systems have risen enormously. This leads to the importance of technically educated engineers. Since the technical possibilities in waste management develop rapidly, it is necessary to stay in steady contact with recent discussions in journals and on conferences.

Furthermore, the communities need persons with a certain feeling for political processes. The administrators of a politicised administration have to be politicians themselves. They have to consider the possibility that technically sound decisions may not be acceptable politically. They are therefore forced to follow political strategies of consensus building that are a totally different activity from that of finding the optimal technical solution.

Since all these requirements have only arisen in recent years, many communities lack competent personnel to fulfil the tasks of waste management. Moreover, the communities face difficulties when recruiting qualified personnel. The rigid legal prescriptions concerning the civil service in Germany are not very attractive for qualified persons, who normally prefer to choose a career in private enterprises. This will be an important point in both case studies.

The most common reaction of the communities to overcome the problem of lacking personnel is privatisation. This implies either the fulfilment of the tasks of waste management by private, third party firms or the founding of private enterprises run by the communities, who thereby evade the rigid legal requirements concerning civil servants (Schink 1994). Private enterprises are much more able to recruit competent personnel who are able to handle the legal, technical and political requirements of waste management in Germany.

A final point calls for attention in the context of personal decision premises. Since the three types of decision premises can be considered functionally equivalent to a large extent, the inability of programmes and channels of communication to absorb uncertainty leads to a rising importance of personnel in complex decisions. This results in higher demands with respect to qualification, and in more personal stress. But on the other hand, the room for discretion, especially provided by ambiguous and unclear programmes, heightens the importance of personal styles of decision making. This means that different personal styles of making choices make a greater difference if the programmes leave more room for interpretation. Personal initiatives and taking of personal responsibility are more risky for the persons but, in the case of success, are likely to influence the decision process in a significant manner.

3.7 Conclusion

Against the background of the developments as described above, it is not surprising that the present situation in German Waste Management is characterised by the hesitation of the local decision makers to commit themselves to decisions about waste treatment facilities. Many observers state that the necessary decisions are simply not made (e.g. Lemser et al. 1998; Klockow 1995). Within the theoretical framework used in the present analysis, this observation is interpreted in terms of uncertainty absorption: The legal prescriptions that serve as decision premises are not able to absorb enough uncertainty for the decisions about waste treatment plants. The uncertainty that burdens the decision process has to be absorbed by political actions in the community. This is the starting point for the following case studies in which I will try to analyse the efforts of the communities to evade the risk situation caused by the legal prescriptions.

4 Risk and Participation

In the first case study, many of the theoretical points highlighted in the preceding chapters, will play an important role. We find an organisation that is confronted with the new task of constructing a waste management system that includes waste treatment as an element. Furhtermore, the organisation is lacking established organisational routines that would allow much of the uncertainty created by the ambitious and ambiguous legal prescriptions to be absorbed. As a reaction to the problems of unclear responsibilities, of ambiguity and of lacking routines, this organisation initiated a complex procedure of public participation in the decision process. The details of this very interesting case will be developed in the following sections.

The data that provide the basis of the case study were collected within the framework of a research project that was supposed to evaluate the fairness of the participatory procedure. This evaluative project was financed by the Centre for Technology Assessment in Baden-Württemberg and carried out at the Institute for Science and Technology Studies of the University of Bielefeld.

The structure of the case study will be the following. In section 4.1, I will characterise the general organisational context in which the decision making process took place. Section 4.2 is dedicated to the methodological characteristics of the citizens' participation that was carried out as a reaction to the decision problems of the region. This is the basis for the development of four hypothetical functions of such a participatory procedure in a situation of decision making under risk (4.3). Sections 4.4 to 4.7 describe the events during and after the citizens' participation. In section 4.8. I will analyse whether the decision makers of the region succeeded in resolving their decision problems by allowing for informal participation.

4.1 The Organisational Context: A New Organisation

The organisational context of the case is characterised by some peculiarities. The first important point in this context is the fact that the planning of waste treatment facilities is conducted in co-operation by four districts. In order to fulfil this task, the four districts founded a new organisation, the 'Gesellschaft zur Planung der Restabfallbehandlung in der Region Nordschwarzwald', the P.A.N. This new organisation is a private enterprise, however, run exclusively by the four districts. It is therefore a kind of a mixture between a public and a private organisation. The four districts that founded the P.A.N. are the three more rural districts Calw, Freudenstadt, and Enzkreis and the municipality Pforzheim.

The roots of their co-operation can be traced back to 1977 when Enzkreis und Pforzheim made an agreement about the common use of a waste disposal site on the territory of Pforzheim. The agreement stipulated that the follow-up disposal site would have to be built by Enzkreis on its territory. Freudenstadt and Calw show no historical roots of co-operation with other communities (Vorwerk / Timmermeister / Brandt 1997). They were however facing the same problems as Pforzheim und Enzkreis. These problems consisted in difficulties in finding new sites for depositing waste. All communities by the end of the eighties made the experience that any decision about waste disposal sites or about composting plants created strong resistance from the public. Freudenstadt, for example, stopped the planning of a composting plant in the face of public resistance and decided to recycle its biological waste in the composting plant of another community, 120 kilometres away. This is the most striking example in the region of public resistance to waste management decisions, and political hesitation to overcome this resistance. The other communities reacted to the resistance by delaying the decision, for example the Enzkreis when planning a new waste disposal site. (cf. Kämper / Vorwerk 1996).

The interplay of ongoing difficulties in each of the four communities with initial experiences in co-operation between Pforzheim and the Enzkreis lead to the idea of finding a solution to the waste treatment problem at the regional level. In November 1989, Pforzheim decided to take the leadership in the co-operation of the four communities to find a regional waste treatment concept (Vorwerk / Timmermeister / Brandt 1997). The idea to treat the waste through regional co-operation initially arose from the problem of scarce waste disposal sites and from the problem of finding new sites. This idea was reinforced at the beginning of the nineties, when it became clear that the Technical Instruction for

Household Waste in the near future would prescribe waste incineration as an element of any waste management system (cf. above, 3.3.2). In the face of the necessity of building a waste incineration plant, and of the fact that such a plant would not be feasible for one single community, it was decided to found a new organisation with the task of planning the waste treatment concept at the regional level. The communities decided to found a private limited company, that was, however to be run exclusively by the four public bodies; i.e. there is no participation of a private enterprise. Thus, the private limited company in this case is a private enterprise that consists of public partners. The P.A.N. GmbH was then founded by the end of 1992. The task was to plan a waste treatment concept at the regional level, that would be able to fulfil the legal requirements in 2005.

The main conflict with respect to the plans of constructing a waste treatment plant in the region can be expressed in the opposition of 'hot versus cold'. The question is whether the waste is to be treated in an incinerator ('hot') or a biological-mechanical plant ('cold'). During the preparation of the co-operation between the four communities it became obvious that the most suitable location for a waste incineration plant would be Pforzheim. Due to its character as an industrial centre in the region, only in Pforzheim is it possible to use the by-products of waste incineration, heat and energy, in a suitable manner (Interview P.A.N., June 1994). As a reaction, Pforzheim forced its partners to make the so-called 'double resolution', which stated that the P.A.N. would consider 'hot' and 'cold' treatment technologies equally during the planning process. The purpose of this decision is obvious: If this careful consideration of the two technological possibilities would lead to the feasibility of the 'cold' technology, Pforzheim would be relieved of many problems, because the biological-mechanical option does not suffer the serious problems of acceptability like waste incineration. If, on the other hand, waste incineration would turn out to be necessary, the hope was to minimise public resistance by reference to the 'double resolution'. At this point, a general tendency of the decision making process in the region is already obvious. The decision makers try to demonstrate to the public that their decisions are choices out of alternatives and that, against many suspicions, waste incineration is not the automatic result of the decision making process.

Furthermore, at this point the main conflict in the co-operation of the four communities appears. Given that a solution to the waste treatment problem was to be found at the regional level, and given that the decision would lead to the construction of a waste incinerator, Pforzheim would be the only suitable location for the plant. Together with the legal requirements imposed by the Technical Instruction for Household Waste the co-operative planning of the four communities seemed to lead almost automatically to only one possible outcome: the construction of a waste incineration plant in Pforzheim. For the understanding of the decision making process in the region this is one of the most important points to be kept in mind. Throughout the whole decision making process in the Nordschwarzwald, Pforzheim's effort to avoid this automatic result of the decision was observable. The general tendency in this respect was the following: if it would not be possible to avoid a waste incinerator in Pforzheim, the municipal politicians desperately tried to make this conclusion a real choice, i.e. to examine alternatives before making the decision. The intention was thus to escape the automatism that seemed to lead to a waste incinerator in Pforzheim (Interview P.A.N., June 1994).

The newly founded private limited company, the P.A.N., has complicated formal channels of communication and therefore rather opaque decision making procedures. First of all, there is the board of directors, which consists of the heads of the four administrations. The second important part of the structure is the supervisory board. The managing director is the mayor of Pforzheim. Finally, there are two company secretaries, one being responsible for planning, the other one for financial matters. An important point for understanding the political conflicts about waste treatment in the region is the fact that the managing director and the company secretary responsible for planning are representatives of Pforzheim. Pforzheim thus plays a dominant role within the fragile construction of the P.A.N. (Kämper / Vorwerk 1996).

The formal decision procedure is the following. The 'operative core' of the P.A.N., mainly consisting of the company secretary for planning and a civil servant of Pforzheim elaborates a draft that is then passed to the supervisory board and the Gesellschafterversammlung. On this basis a suggestion is made for the four local parliaments. In order to make the decision, the four parliaments have to take identical decisions. Only on the basis of four identical political decisions can the P.A.N. take action with respect to the planning of the waste treatment concept. In the context of the above mentioned conflicts between the four communities, concerning technology and location of a waste treatment facility, the rule of unanimity in making common decisions affects the decision making process seriously. For the operative core of the P.A.N., the task is then to find drafts that are likely to find consent in four independent local parliaments with different party composition and underlying different political dynamics.

To sum up, the decision situation in the region displays some specific characteristics. Firstly, we observe a planning process that takes place through co-operation between four districts. These four political bodies enter into the co-operation with different experiences in waste management planning. Pforzheim and Enzkreis have experiences in mutual co-operation. They were forced to enter into co-operation because of scarce depositing resources and political problems in finding new sites for waste disposal. Calw and Freudenstadt faced the same problems of almost full waste disposal sites and difficulties in overcoming political resistance to new sites. For them, however, the co-operation especially with Pforzheim seemed to be a no-regret strategy since the possibility of constructing a waste incinerator in Calw or in Freudenstadt was extremely low. Pforzheim, on the other hand, is dependent on the co-operation with the Enzkreis, because, as a municipality without large territory, it faces serious problems of depositing waste on its territory (Interview engineering office, July 1996).

The formal decision making procedures of the P.A.N. suggest that this organisation is a rather fragile construction. The precondition for collective action of the four districts are identical decisions of the four local parliaments. In the previous paragraph, the heterogeneous preferences of the four districts have been sketched. It is therefore clear that the institutional precondition of unanimity restricts possible decision outcomes of the P.A.N. The conflicting preferences within the P.A.N., together with the restricting decision making procedure, tighten the possible paths of action of the organisation.

The final characteristic specific to the region has already been mentioned. The P.A.N. is a new organisation facing the new and complex task of planning a waste treatment system at the regional level. Established routines that would allow the problem to be tackled do not exist. There are no experiences with the co-operation at the regional level, because the planning of a waste treatment system is the first time that these four districts work together. The connection between actions and outcomes is not known. The only thing that is known from the past and can be taken for granted is the fact that decisions about waste facilities in the regions face serious problems of acceptability and create intensive political conflicts.

Thus, the decision situation displays certain characteristics that are specific to the region: conflicting preferences, negative experiences with waste management planning in the past, and a lack of organisational routines that would allow to absorb uncertainty. All this must be seen against the background of the general situation described in the third chapter. The decision makers in the region face risks, because they are responsible for the occurrence of uncertain future events. There are serious ambiguities about the interpretation of the central legal prescription, the Technical Instruction for Household Waste. The information most necessary for the construction of a waste treatment facility, the amount of waste that is to be expected, is extremely uncertain because of the dramatic drop of waste in recent years. Finally, everything concerning the waste treatment concept has to be financed by charges that are paid by the citizens. Any failure in the planning that leads to a rise in the charges is likely to create heavy conflicts in the region and might lead to the loss of political majorities.

Ambiguity, uncertainty, and responsibility are therefore the features of the situation in the region. Against the background of this diagnosis of the situation, I will analyse the procedure of citizens' participation that was initiated by the P.A.N. shortly after its foundation.

4.2 Characteristics of the Citizens' Participation

In the Spring of 1993, only a few months after the foundation of the P.A.N., the company secretary responsible for planning got in contact with a representative of the also newly founded Centre for Technology Assessment in Baden-Württemberg (Akademie für Technikfolgenabschätzung in Baden-Württemberg; hereinafter called Academy). Having heard a presentation of the scientist on the theoretical concepts of the Academy concerning informal procedures of public participation, the company secretary contacted the Academy (Interview P.A.N., March 1994). The result was, after a preparatory period starting in March 1993, a contract of co-operation between the P.A.N. and the Academy, signed in October 1993. This contract concerned the carrying out of a procedure of citizens' participation in the framework of the planning process of the P.A.N. Since the theoretical and methodological background of the procedure is rather complex, I will dedicate the following sections to the description of the underlying conception.

4.2.1 Methodology

The citizens' participation was divided into three phases. The first phase was dedicated to a prognosis of the expected amount of waste that will have to be treated. The second phase was supposed to find the treatment technology. Finally, in the third phase the location of the treatment facility was to be found. For these three tasks, different forms of citizens' participation were employed. In the first two phases, the procedure took place in the form of a *mediation*; the third phase was organised with *citizens' forums*. Each phase ended with the formulation of a citizens' report that was supposed to be considered in the decision making procedure of the P.A.N.

Both mediation and citizens' forum are general forms of citizens' participation that were applied in a specific form in the participatory procedure in the region. The characteristics of the general forms and the specific application will be explained in the following two sections.

4.2.2 Mediation

The general idea of mediation is a simple one: two or more conflicting parties try to resolve their conflict with the help of a neutral person or organisation. Although a very old concept, in recent years it has become important in various fields like mediation between victim and perpetrator in criminal law, or in cases of divorce when there are conflicts about children's education. The more general label for these efforts to relieve formal court legal procedures is Alternative Dispute Resolution (ADR). In the United States, since the beginning of the seventies, mediation has also been used to resolve environmental conflicts (Bingham 1986; Holznagel 1990). Around 1989, in Germany a discussion was also initiated whether the idea of conflict resolution by a neutral mediator was suitable for the problem of conflicts about environmental issues, especially for problems of siting potentially hazardous industrial plants (Hoffmann-Riem / Schmidt-Aßmann 1990; Gusy 1990; Zieschank 1991). The extensive discussion about environmental mediation cannot be reconstructed here. It is important to know that by the beginning of the nineties there was a great hope in Germany that this instrument would allow for citizens' participation in contested administrative decisions and would therefore be able to abate the intensive conflicts about risky technologies. This led to the carrying out of several mediation procedures in Germany (Dally et al. 1994; Fietkau / Weidner 1994; Gans 1994; Gaßner et al. 1992).

In the participatory procedure that is in the focus of the present analysis, the concept of mediation undergoes several modifications. The main difference to conventional concepts of mediation lies in the result of the procedure. Whereas in the classical concept of mediation the result is supposed to be a decision, in the Nordschwarzwald the procedure aimed at a citizens' report that was supposed to influence the decision making process of the P.A.N. The political and administrative decision makers were free to consider the citizens' report in their final decision. In the complex formal decision procedure of the P.A.N., the citizens' report was directed to the advisory board, that was supposed to make a draft for the four local parliaments that considered the vote of the consensus conference.

This peculiarity of the mediation in the Nordschwarzwald implies that, as a further difference to conventional mediations, no decision maker participated in the procedure. The consensus conference was mainly composed of regional pressure groups interested in problems of waste management. The task of the mediator was to help these pressure groups to get information and to come to a consented vote in the citizens' report. Decision makers of the P.A.N. and of the administration of the four communities were present in order to give information upon request. The same was true of technical experts. These persons, however, were not formal participants in the mediation. Politicians and administrators of the region were just the addressees of the citizens' reports. This is the main difference to other forms of mediation, that aim more directly at the resolution of conflicts between decision makers and those affected.

The main methodological element of this concept, besides the idea of neutral mediation, was the value-tree-analysis (cf. Keeney et al. 1984). The value-tree-analysis was supposed to allow the interest groups in the consensus conference to establish their own criteria and to evaluate all possible decision alternatives in terms of these criteria. It was supposed to allow a systematic judgement by the interest groups (Interview Academy, January 1995).

This methodological framework of mediation was applied in the first two phases of the procedure. In the first phase, the interest groups in the consensus conference had the task of giving a prognosis of the amount of waste in the year 2005. The information necessary was mainly provided by the technical experts of an engineering office that advised the P.A.N. during the planning procedure.

In the second phase, organised according to the same principles, the consensus conference was supposed to give an evaluation of the alternative technologies to handle the waste. The question in this phase was therefore 'hot' or 'cold'? Or, in other words, the consensus conference was to find out whether the waste of the region should be treated with the biological-mechanical technology, or with a waste incineration plant. This is one of the central issues in German waste management (cf. Gaßner / Siederer 1997; Kremer 1994; SRU 1998).

4.2.3 Citizens' Forums

The Citizens' Forum is a form of citizens' participation with features different from mediation. It is mainly based on the concept of the planning cell, developed by German sociologist Peter Dienel (Dienel 1992). The planning cell aims at the participation of lay people in urban and environmental planning processes. The underlying assumption is that the local and implicit knowledge of lay people who live in the town where the respective measure is planned can contribute important aspects to the decision, that technical experts without local knowledge normally fail to notice. The contribution of the citizens is therefore their local knowledge and their fresh lay perspective on the respective problem.

The planning cell is composed of randomly chosen citizens; by this method theoretically every citizen of a municipality has the same chance of becoming member of the planning cell and thus to influence the planning process. On the other hand, and this is one of the most interesting aspects of the method, the initiators have no control over the composition of the planning cell. The participants can be engineers, professors, workers, housewives, unemployed persons, etc. The planning cell then takes place in 5 to 7 consecutive days, in which the participants are provided with all the relevant information. Because the participants have to take holiday from their usual job for this period, they get an expense allowance. The result of the planning cell is a citizens' report that is directed at the administrative or political decision makers.

The planning cell has mainly been used in processes of urban planning. The success of this form of citizens' participation is amazing (cf. Rehmann-Sutter et al. 1998). Even experts often appreciate the quality of the citizens' reports that the planning cells deliver. In the Nordschwarzwald, the managers of the participatory procedure used a modified version of the planning cell, the so-called citizens' forum (Wienhöfer 1996), in the third phase, the search for the location of the waste treatment plant. The modifications are the following.

The first important difference concerns the composition of the forums. One of the aims of the participatory procedure in the third phase was to overcome the Not-in-my-backyard phenomenon (Nimby). Therefore, the forums were composed according to the principle of parity: On the basis of a preliminary selection of possible locations by the engineering office, the participants were chosen randomly out of the potentially affected municipalities. The participants were then divided in ten citizens' forums. Thus, each forum consisted of inhabitants of each potential locality for the waste treatment plant. As a result, instead of one planning cell, there are ten citizens' forums. The task of transforming the reports of the ten forums into one unitary citizens' report was then to be performed by a conference of delegates from each forum.

The second important deviation from the classical planning cell was the fact that the forums did not take place in five or six consecutive days. Instead, the forums met once a week for six consecutive weeks. The intention behind this measure was to give the participants the possibility of staying in contact with the other citizens of their municipality. The expected disadvantage was that the dynamic processes of group building, one important precondition for the success of the planning cell, might be disturbed by these interruptions. However, as will be shown below, this anticipated disadvantage did not play an important role in the third phase of the procedure.

The third modification of the planning cell concept was the strong reliance on the value-tree-analysis. The value-tree-analysis was the central methodological element of the third phase. The participants of each forum raised their own criteria for evaluating different potential locations for the waste treatment plants. With the help of these criteria, they were able to make a systematic comparison. Due to the methodological basis of the value-tree-analysis, this evaluation was also transparent for outsiders. After the conference of the delegates, the third phase also ended with the delivery of a citizens' report to the supervisory board of the P.A.N.

After this rough sketch of the methodology of the procedure, in the next section I will turn to the question of what contribution a citizens' participation can provide in a situation of decision making under risk and ambiguity.

4.3 Potential Functions of the Procedure

Seen against the background of the special decision situation in the region, one can hypothesise several functions of the participatory procedure. These functions can be related to the central features of the decision to construct a waste treatment plant, to uncertainty, responsibility, and ambiguity. The general promise of the participatory concept suggested by the academy was rationality and participation. The aim was not only to let citizens participate and thus to increase the legitimacy of the decision; nor was it only to consider more values and preferences than it would be possible in a conventional decision making process; moreover, the aim was to ensure a systematic and rational consideration of the citizens' values and preferences in the decision process. This was to be provided by the value-tree-analysis. The intention of the academy was the following. The result was supposed to be a contribution by the citizens to the decision that would be fair, competent, and legitimate: Fair, because every participant had the possibility that his preferences and interests would be considered in the decision; competent, because the citizens' reports were supposed to be of high quality and thus be able to improve the objective quality of the decision; legitimate, because the decision makers could prove that the decision, although made under uncertainty, was made in consideration of all information that was available at the time of the decision, including citizens' preferences (cf. Renn et al. 1995).

According to the managers of the procedure, these are the possible contributions of the citizens' participation to the waste treatment planning in the region. With the concepts developed in chapters one and two, and against the background of the problems of decision making in German waste management sketched in chapter three, I suggest a different evaluation of the potential functions that the citizens' participation can fulfil within the decision making process. The problems for the decision makers when planning a waste treatment plant are responsibility for the consequences, uncertain occurrence of the consequences, lacking routines together with ambiguous preferences, and contested public acceptability of the decision. A procedure that allows for citizens' participation can only be successful when it offers solutions to these fundamental problems of organisational decision making under risk.

Firstly, I stressed the fact that in decisions about waste management systems the decision makers have to take full *responsibility* for the consequences of the decision. The planning of a waste treatment plant means the carrying out of a goal programme. Thus, the responsibility for bad results or for harmful unintended consequences cannot be passed to another political level (Eckhoff / Jacobsen 1960; Hiller 1993). Any failure in the planning is likely to create strong political conflicts in the communities and can lead to the loss of jobs for administrators or to the loss of political majorities.

Secondly, whether the decision will lead to a success or a failure, depends on *uncertain* circumstances. Among the relevant information for the decision about a waste treatment plant are the following: the amount of waste that is to be treated, legal prescriptions that are to be fulfilled, political majorities on the state and federal levels, the state of the art in waste treatment technology, prices for waste treatment technology. All of these circumstances affect the success or failure of the decision, and they are all in constant movement in the field of German waste policy (cf. above, chapter 3). The decision has therefore to be made under high uncertainty. Together with the unavoidable responsibility, this creates a situation of risk (cf. Brunsson 1985).

Thirdly, and now we turn to the specific characteristics of the situation in the Nordschwarzwald, there are conditions of *ambiguity*, as defined by March and Olsen (1976). Since the P.A.N. is a newly founded organisation, it lacks established routines that would allow much of the uncertainty involved in the decision to be absorbed. Moreover, there is an ambiguity about the preferences of the members of the P.A.N. Since the final decisions in the P.A.N. are made by four independent local parliaments underlying different political dynamics, there is ambiguity about the evaluation of past, present, and future events. Decision making, evaluation of success or failure, and learning from experience are very difficult under this condition of unclear, but very likely conflicting, preferences among the four communities.

A further aspect of ambiguity is introduced by the contested legal prescription, mainly the Technical Instruction for Household Waste. The interpretation of this very important decision premise is politically contested at the local, the state, and the federal level. The interpretation of the ambiguous prescription is dependent on political factors. Since there seem to be several ways to fulfil the requirements of the Technical Instruction for Household Waste, it is far from being clear what exactly is to be done.

Finally, there is the problem of *contested acceptability* of decisions to build waste treatment plants. In sections 3.3 and 3.4 I mentioned general problems of legitimising goal-programmed decisions by a preceding procedure. This is of course true as well for the specific decisions in the

Nordschwarzwald. They are amplified by the fact that waste treatment plants are no longer permitted in the planning permission procedure but in the more simple permission procedure under the Nuisance Act. The consequence for the region is the following: Since the formal administrative decision making procedures are likely to fail in providing legitimacy, i.e. in providing the necessary consensus and acceptance of the decision, the P.A.N. has to look for different forms of resolving the problem of acceptability.

In the following sections, I will explain what contributions of the citizens' participation in the Nordschwarzwald one can expect against the background of these fundamental decision problems.

4.3.1 Responsibility

With respect to the problem of high responsibility, Brunsson (1985) suggested two possible solutions. According to Brunsson, in situations of risk, responsibility can be shared, or it can be reduced. Shared responsibility requires the participation of many persons in the decision, the reduction of responsibility can be achieved by a rationalisation of the decision making process.

First of all, a successful participation of citizens and regional interest groups may help to *distribute* responsibility. The more participants there are in a decision, the more difficult it is to identify responsible persons. This possible effect of letting a large number of people participate in decisions is widely acknowledged in the literature on organisational decision making (Luhmann 1964; Brunsson 1985; Hiller 1994). The precondition for this effect is that the citizens' reports provided by the citizens and interest groups in the three phases of the procedure exert a real influence on the final decisions. Within the complicated constructions of the P.A.N. and the participatory procedure, it is however a significant problem to make clear that the citizens' reports are considered in the decisions of the P.A.N. I will turn to this point later in the case study.

The *reduction* of the responsibility the decision makers have to take can be achieved by the demonstration of rationality in the decision making process (Brunsson 1985). The argument is that in a rational decision making process, all participants see the uncertainty under which the decision has to be made. It becomes clear that under conditions of uncertainty, there is no single best solution. This might lower the responsibility the decision makers have to take when something goes wrong. To achieve this effect, it is important to demonstrate that the decision considers all relevant information that is available at the moment of the decision. This can show that uncertainty is unavoidable and therefore reduce later conflicts about alternative ways of action.

In the concept of the procedure, especially the use of the value-tree-analysis carries the promise of rationality. By this means, the contribution of the citizens was supposed to be systematic and free of emotional influences. With respect to the P.A.N. the rationalisation effect was supposed to be the consideration of more preferences and the collection of more information before the decision. In this perspective, the citizens' participation is a demonstration of decision rationality.

In a later book by Brunsson (1989), we find, however, a further interesting point. Brunsson states that organisations that have to handle conflicting institutional demands tend to decouple 'talk' and 'action'. Talk is exactly the demonstration of decision rationality, the consideration of values and information in the decision as described. Action is the segment of the organisation that really makes the decision and normally will lack the traits of formal rationality. There is thus an internal differentiation between the more symbolic consideration of values, preferences, and information, and the more instrumental part of the decision process, that normally is not able to consider all these additional aspects (cf. Feldman / March 1981). In this perspective, such an explicit demonstration of rationality is, in the first place, a purely symbolic act. Whether these symbolic efforts have influence on the action segment of the organisation seems to be an empirical question. While Brunsson (1989) stresses the argument that talk and action are always very loosely coupled, other scholars point to the possibility that symbolic efforts of organisations to demonstrate rationality sooner or later will develop a certain momentum, and will in a self-dynamic process exert influence on the action segment of the organisation (Feldman / March 1981; Japp 1996; Hasse / Japp 1997). For the P.A.N. these arguments imply that the reduction of responsibility will succeed if it is possible to demonstrate that the efforts towards more rationality in the decision making process have a significant effect on the final decision about the waste treatment concept of the region.

There is however a second possible positive effect of the participation, even when real participation does not take place. If the organisation succeeds in demonstrating its difficulties and the obligations it has to fulfil with the decision, this can also lower the burden of responsibility. If the P.A.N. can show that the Technical Instruction for Household Waste forces the communities to build a waste incinerator, and if it can show that all conflicts about the interpretation of this legal prescription will not change this obligation, then a final decision to construct a waste incineration plant in the region will not be loaded with high loads of responsibility. This is because it becomes clear that there is no choice; if there is no choice there is no responsibility. The case study will discuss the question whether this effect could really take place in the region.

4.3.2 Uncertainty

The second fundamental problem of the decision in the region is the enormous uncertainty that has to be absorbed by the decision. The uncertainty refers to several aspects of the decision. First of all, the most important information for the planning of a waste treatment plant, the expected amount of waste, underlies massive uncertainties. The reasons for this development have been discussed in the third chapter. The effect for the communities in general and for the region Nordschwarzwald in particular is that it is not known what size of the treatment plant would be suitable. It has to be big enough to ensure the disposal safety, but it must not be too big, because otherwise the waste charges to be paid by the citizens have to be raised. Second, the decision makers face the uncertainty of acceptance. Whether the decision about a waste treatment facility will be acceptable politically, cannot be known in advance. A final aspect of uncertainty relates to the legal, technical and economic circumstances of the decision. The fact that the legal prescriptions are ambiguous has already been stressed. This creates of course uncertainty for the decision making process. Of equal importance are the technical and economic aspects of the planning of a waste treatment concept. The technology of waste treatment is in constant dynamic development, and so are the prices for the plants. Moreover, due to the paradoxical effects of German waste policy since the beginning of the nineties, the prices for external treatment in different communities are very unstable. When the P.A.N. made its final decision, in spring 1998, they were very low. It is however very likely that they will rise enormously in the years up to 2005, when the effect of the temporary regulation for the implementation of the Technical Instruction for Household Waste is due to end.

The potential contribution of the citizens' participation to the reduction of these uncertainties is the following. If the citizens can agree about the expected amount of waste, about the suitable technology to treat the waste, and about a location for the plant, and if this vote would be quite close to the report of the engineering office, much of the uncertainty described above would be absorbed. The achievement of a consensus of the citizens that is more or less in accordance with the results of the experts' examinations was the main goal of the managers of the procedure. This would have been the optimal result, because it would have contributed to the reduction of uncertainty. Of course, a consenting citizens' report in the Nordschwarzwald does not mean that the technological, legal and economic dynamics that create the uncertainty for the decision would go away. It would however be possible to neglect a certain amount of the given uncertainty. In other words much of the uncertainty would be absorbed.

However, as should be clear from the sketch of the many factors that introduce fundamental uncertainty into the decision making process, the possibility that a citizens' participation can contribute a solution to this problem is modest. As I will argue in more detail below, the hope that a citizens' participation could help to find the best decision misses the complexity of the problems in complex planning situations. The expectation that people in a discourse are able to find the single best solution if they have time to find a consensus on the basis of objective argumentation, is unrealistic in a complex situation of organisational decision making. This conception, which has clearly its roots in Habermas' theory of communicative action (Habermas 1981) seems to be inappropriate for the complex problems of risky decisions in modern society. This argument will be elaborated in section 4.8.2.

4.3.3 Ambiguity

In the literature on organisational decision making, the term ambiguity refers to many factors. The most important of these are the lack of clear and controllable routines (the so-called organisational technology), and ambiguity about preferences (March / Olsen 1976; Weick 1979). I argue that in the case of the P.A.N. the conditions of ambiguity are reinforced by the fact that it is a newly founded organisation.

In the first place, the lack of routines means that the organisation has no established knowledge about which possible actions lead to which outcomes. Routines allow the organisation to absorb uncertainty in situations of risk and thus to remain able to act. If there are no uncertainty absorbing routines, the organisation has to develop measures to absorb uncertainty (Weick 1979). The lack of knowledge of how to bring about certain outcomes is of crucial importance in our case because in German waste management, the communities are *responsible* for the occurrence of the outcomes.

The planning of a waste management system under the given conditions is a new task that creates difficulties even for one single community (cf. chapter 5). In the Nordschwarzwald, the situation becomes more complicated by the co-operation of four communities with probably conflicting preferences. Although the problem of conflicting preferences plays a crucial role in the Nordschwarzwald, I argue that the situation of four co-operating political and administrative organisations implies more aspects than only conflict of interests. The problem is a more fundamental one in the lack of causal knowledge about which decision leads to which outcomes with respect to the political and public acceptability of decisions and thus to the continuation of the co-operation.

Against the background of this problem, the carrying out of the citizens' participation can be seen as an enactment in the sense suggested by Karl Weick (1979). The participation of citizens can help to experiment with possible action alternatives, it can create an impression about the acceptability of certain decisions in the public and in the four communities. The organisation tries to develop knowledge about itself and about its environment, and it tries to reduce conflicts and ambiguities about preferences. At the end of a successful enactment, the organisation has certain causal assumptions, such as: a waste incinerator in Freudenstadt is unacceptable, the conservationist pressure groups in the region are no serious partner and can therefore be neglected, the necessity of building a waste incinerator can be made comprehensible to the public etc. These assumptions can absorb uncertainty and thus enable the organisation to make decisions.

4.3.4 Legitimacy and Trust

A final argument can be made with respect to the problem of public acceptability of the decision about a waste treatment plant in the region. The problematic acceptance of such decisions in Germany has mainly been ascribed to weaknesses in the formal administrative decision making procedures, like the planning permission procedure (cf. e.g. Gusy 1990). This critique has been one reason for the efforts to establish more informal possibilities for citizens' participation, including mediation and planning cells. The expectation is that these forms of participation allow for a fair consideration of the preferences and interests of citizens affected by the respective decision.

However, in chapter three (cf. 3.3.1), I argued that for example the problems of the planning permission procedure can be explained more fundamentally by the time-orientation of complex planning decisions. These decisions are goal-programmed decisions, i.e., the knowledge whether they are correct, whether they reach the prescribed goal, will only be known in the future. This is a fundamental difference to decisions programmed on a conditional basis. Whether the rule if - then has been correctly performed can be observed when the decision takes place. A formalised procedure can report this correct fulfilment of the norm because the criteria for the correctness of the decision are already known. This allows a legitimisation by procedure (Luhmann 1983). These conditions are not given with decisions programmed towards the reaching of a goal. This is the reason why formalised administrative procedures normally fail to ensure the legitimacy of complex planning decisions: whether the decision is correct, can only be known in the future and not during a preceding procedure.

With respect to the citizens' participation in the Nordschwarzwald, this is an important argument, because the aim was to legitimise a risky decision by a procedure (Renn / Webler 1994). The goal was to improve the perceived shortcomings of formal procedures. Mainly, the participation should take place earlier in order to exert influence in the moment of the real decision, and the participation takes place with the help of a neutral mediating institution that ensures the fair participation of the citizens. However, such a conception of a preceding participation runs into the same problems of time-orientation as formal administrative procedures.

The literature on organisational decision making suggests another possibility for organisations to ensure the acceptability of their decisions. If it is not possible to create legitimacy for each single decision, the organisation has to establish a general trust of its environment in the rationality of its decisions (Luhmann 1964: 111). This trust can be established by the formal structure of the organisation, demonstrating rationality (Luhmann 1964: 112; Meyer / Rowan 1977). With special reference to conflicts about risky technologies, Brian Wynne (1987) has pointed to other possibilities to establish a background of trust in contested decisions. According to Wynnes suggestions, trust in an organisation's decisions can be created by fair decision making procedures, by open access to relevant information for the public, and by high performance in risk issues in the past.

With the help of these hints we see the potential contribution of the citizens' participation in the Nordschwarzwald to the improvement of the acceptability of the P.A.N.'s decisions. The intention to reach more fairness in citizens' participation than is possible in formal administrative procedures cannot overcome the time limitations of any preceding procedure, but it can help to establish general trust in the decisions of the P.A.N. The same is true of the access to information that is necessary for the carrying out of such a citizens' participation. As will be described below, the representatives of the P.A.N. that were involved in the procedure definitely tried to give access to all relevant information to the participating citizens and interest groups. The aim to create an open information policy with respect to the citizens' participation was obvious. Whether these attempts were sufficient to create public trust in the P.A.N. will be examined in more detail in the sections below. Possible factors that could hinder the creation of trust have already been mentioned: the problem of different time orientation in the citizens' participation and the decision itself, and the possible failure of the formal decision making structures of the P.A.N. to create trust.

Summing up the arguments of this section, one can identify the following potential contributions of the citizens' participation to the decision making process in the region. Firstly, the participation can help to distribute and to reduce *responsibility*, if it is possible to demonstrate that the citizens and interest groups came to their votes in a rational and systematic manner, and if it is possible to demonstrate that these contributions are considered systematically in the decision of the P.A.N. Secondly, *uncertainty* can be reduced, if in the course of the procedure one decision alternative turns out to be the single best one, and if this alternative is supported by the citizens and by the technical experts. Thirdly, the procedure can reduce the *ambiguity* of the situation if it helps to develop a routine that allows the heterogeneity of preferences within, and ignorance about the environment of, the P.A.N. to be overcome. Finally, by giving access to relevant information and allowing fair participation, the P.A.N. can create *trust* in its decisions and thus overcome the structural problem of contested legitimacy of goal-programmed decisions.

The following analysis of the procedure will be guided by these possible solutions of the four fundamental decision problems in the situation in the Nordschwarzwald. The analysis however has to be prepared by a description of the events during the procedure. This will be done in sections 4.4 to 4.6. Section 4.7 will sketch the impacts of the results on the process of decision making in the Nordschwarzwald. Section

4.8 is dedicated to the analysis of the events in perspective of the four potential functions of the participation.

4.4 First Phase: Mediation and Waste Prognosis

4.4.1 The Task of the First Phase: Waste Prognosis

The first phase of the citizens' participation began in March 1994 and ended in August 1994. The task for the citizens' and interest groups was to give a prognosis of the expected amount of waste that is to be treated in the year 2002. With this task, the desired contribution was either to reduce uncertainty about the development of the waste amounts, or to create consensus about the uncertainty, thus to demonstrate that the decision about the size of the planned waste treatment plant has to be made under fundamental uncertainty with respect to this absolutely central information. The question of the expected amount of waste is a central one, because almost all waste treatment plants in Germany that are already in function, are inappropriately sized, i.e. they are too big and therefore create enormous costs for the respective communities. A consensus with the citizens about the waste amount that is to be expected in a few years can therefore be a very important contribution to reduce conflicts after the final decision. The issue of waste amount is crucial for the decision about a waste treatment plant, firstly because waste incinerators, if they are too big, are suspected to have the effect of discouraging efforts to avoid and recycle waste. Secondly, the waste prognosis touches the choice between 'hot' or 'cold' treatment technology, because a waste incinerator can only be run with a certain minimum amount of waste.

4.4.2 The Consensus Conference

The first phase was organised as a mediation. That is, the academy served as a neutral, mediating institution. The task of the academy was to contact the relevant groups, to organise the consensus conference, and to give help with the formulation of the citizens' report on the waste prognosis. The mediation itself took place in the so-called consensus conference.

In the initial phase of this first part of the procedure, the academy contacted all groups in the region possibly relevant to and interested in the topic. Among these were economic and agricultural interest groups, environmental pressure groups, citizens' action groups, and many more.

Due to the complexity of the topic and the rather early stage of the participation with respect to the whole decision making process, the academy faced problems in convincing the relevant groups to participate in the consensus conference. This was a consequence of the general concept of the procedure to initiate a participation long before the actual conflict arises, in order to have room for real participation. However, the conflict was so far away, that many of the relevant groups did not see the necessity to invest time and personal resources into the participation in the consensus conference.

The eventual composition of the consensus conference was the following. In the first place there were conservationist pressure groups, like the BUND (Bund für Umwelt- und Naturschutz in Deutschland; German Association for the Protection of Environment and Nature) and the Besseres Müllkonzept, a pressure group which specialises on waste issues, with a strong identification with the goal of avoiding waste incineration. The second important cluster were agricultural pressure groups, some of them had economic interests in composting biological waste. Thirdly, economic interest groups of the region were participating, namely the Industrie- und Handelskammer (Association for Industry and Trade), and the Einzelhandelsverband (Association for Retail Trade). The fourth group were several citizens' action groups. Among these were groups which were founded in order to prevent some of the several projects to build waste disposal sites in the region, and others without any specialisation in waste issues, which only have the task of representing citizens' interests in municipal decision processes.

4.4.3 Proceeding in the First Phase

The first phase began in March 1994, with the first consensus conference, that took place in Calw. The phase ended in August 1994 with the fifth consensus conference. The method in the first phase was mainly characterised by the reliance on the expertise of the engineering office that was engaged by the P.A.N. to carry out the technical aspects of the planning process. This was necessary because the issue of waste prognosis is too complex to be tackled only by the everyday knowledge of citizens' groups. The consensus conference relied therefore on the methodology and the data provided by the report of the engineering office. The specific contribution of the citizens' groups were values. One example can illustrate this combination of experts' knowledge and citizens' values. In the report of the engineers, the assumption was made that a rise of living standards would lead to more waste production, because consumers would buy more products. The consensus conference concluded from the possible rise of living standards in the future that consumers with more money would tend to buy ecologically friendly products, that are more expensive but lead to less production of waste. From the same assumption, that living standard will rise in the future, experts and citizens came to a opposing prognosis of the development of waste production.

On the basis of this method, in August 1994 the consensus conference delivered a citizens' report on the future development of the waste amount in the region. The prognosis assumed an amount between 137,000 and 153,000 tons for the year 2002. The report of the engineering office assumed between 132,000 and 179,000 tons by the year 2002. The prognoses of the citizens and of the engineers were thus quite close. Compared to other prognoses in different regions and communities, both the citizens' and the experts' report were very optimistic with respect to the future development of waste production in the region (Interview engineering office, January 1995). The citizens' report was officially delivered on the 19th of September 1994 at a press conference.

After this, the supervisory board of the P.A.N. presented its draft for the conference of the partners of the P.A.N. In this draft, the supervisory board assumed a waste amount of 155,000 tons for 2002. Thus, the supervisory board of the P.A.N. obviously tended to accept the more optimistic prognosis of the consensus conference.

With this result, the first phase of the citizens' participation could be considered a success. This was not just true of the obvious effect of the citizens' report on the draft of the supervisory board. Moreover, due to the high motivation of the citizens' and interest groups and the effective and neutral management of the procedure by the academy, the consensus conference developed a highly co-operative and argumentative style of working. Although from the point of view of the participating experts, some of the optimistic assumptions of the citizens were not justifiable scientifically (Interview engineering office, June 1994), the final report of the citizens proved to be of considerable quality.

As will become clear in the following sections, an overly optimistic evaluation of the first phase had to be corrected afterwards. It turned out that the issue of waste prognosis did not entail as many conflicts such as the choice of the treatment technology. In the second phase, therefore, the consensus conference had to handle more conflicts between the groups. Moreover, it turned out that the draft of the supervisory board was far from being the final decision. Since in the following years the waste amount declined dramatically, both the experts' and the citizens' prognoses were far too pessimistic. In 1997, the P.A.N. had to assume about 83,000 tons for the year 2002. Thus, no influence of the citizens was observable, because they had no possibility to make a new prognosis. The apparent success of the first phase, seen immediately after its end, disappeared as things developed in the planning process.

4.5 Second Phase: Mediation and the Choice of Technology

The second phase of the citizens' participation began in August 1994 with the fifth consensus conference and ended in December of the same year with the tenth consensus conference. The task was to vote on the very contested issue of treatment technology.

4.5.1 Changes in Method

The second phase was characterised by some differences with respect to the initial phase of the procedure. First of all, the importance of the engineering office declined. This was for two main reasons. The constant presence of the technical experts in the consensus conference had proved to be very cost-intensive (Interview Academy, December 1994). Furthermore, the participating citizens' groups suspected the neutrality of the office with respect to the contested issue of choice of technology (Interview BUND, June 1994). As a result, the necessary information was provided by external technical reports and by presentations of external experts on waste treatment technology. In order to enable the citizens' groups to evaluate the importance of the incoming information, the value trees for each group were completed and thus served as a guideline for the citizens to collect and filter the necessary information (Interview Academy, January 1995).

With respect to the composition of the consensus conference, it is important to state that the organisational basis of the conference diminished step by step. The industrial interest groups no longer participated. The effect was a certain dominance of green groups in the conference. After the second phase, it turned out that the suspicion of environmentalist dominance affected the political weight of the second citizens' report (Interview P.A.N., July 1996). Furthermore, due to the extremely complex topic of waste treatment technology, the citizens' groups, most of them poorly organised, faced organisational problems. The most important of these was the problem of representation. The representatives in the consensus conference were no longer able to feed back the developments in the conference to their groups. Many of the people participating in the consensus conference could therefore no longer be considered representatives of their groups. Moreover, the problems in representation led to conflicts when, by the end of the second phase, influential participants of the consensus conference seemed to be willing to agree on a compromise. However, this change in position was not possible because the organisation they represented did not support the compromise (cf. Kämper / Vorwerk 1996).

4.5.2 Conflicts by the End of the Second Phase

By the end of the second phase, it turned out that the issue of waste treatment technology was a more contested one than the question of waste prognosis. The positions of the groups can be summarised as follows. In the first place, there were well organised environmental pressure groups with a very clear position on the question of waste treatment: a strong resistance to waste incineration was their main interest, in some cases this resistance even defined the identity of the groups (Interview BMK, August 1995). The position of these groups against waste incineration was based on a considerable amount of technical knowledge concerning all aspects of modern waste management. These groups were by far the best informed ones in the conference and were therefore able to influence some other groups to a certain degree. Furthermore, there were groups without specialisation on issues of waste management or on general environmental matters. These groups initially were more or less undecided on the question which technology should be used to treat the waste of the region. Finally, there were two groups in the consensus conference that were citizens' action groups with the goal of blocking planning procedures in the region to build waste disposal sites. The members of these groups lived right next to the proposed waste disposal sites and were thus immediately affected. With respect to waste treatment, their position was very clear: They supported waste incineration, because this technology promised to reduce the volume of the waste significantly. The hope was therefore that waste incineration in the region would stop the projects of waste disposal sites that were then no longer necessary (Interview citizens' action group, March 1994).

Against this background the result of the second phase is not surprising. The specialised and well organised environmentalists were able to convince the undecided groups to vote for the biological-mechanical option (Interview BUND, December 1994). The groups that tried to avoid waste disposal sites voted for waste incineration. Since the mediation in the second phase was not able to resolve this conflict, the result was a citizens' report with two votes. A majority of nine groups was in favour of biological-mechanical waste treatment, while a minority of three groups preferred the option of waste incineration.

4.5.3 The Second Citizens' Report and its Public and Political Reception

The consensus conference was not really able to resolve the conflict between the 'hot' and the 'cold' option. The result was a citizens' report with two votes. The crucial point with respect to the majority vote was the fact that it was in conflict with the legal requirements of the Technical Instruction for Household Waste that prescribes waste incineration in the long run. The risk was that a citizens' report neglecting the legal situation would have no influence at all in the political process. The academy, responsible for the management of the mediation, therefore suggested to insert a sentence into the majority vote, saying that the consensus conference would agree with the search for a location for a waste incinerator, unless the legal requirements changed. For the academy, this was the only possibility to produce a result of the second phase that could be used politically. It is important to state that this sentence did not contain a vote for waste incineration; it was merely the concession that the search for a location for a waste incinerator would be inevitable, if the decision makers would be forced to by the Technical Instruction Household Waste. It was therefore supposed to maintain a certain political influence of the consensus conference by not imposing unrealistic demands on the decision makers of the region.

The effect of this short sentence was, however, devastating. In the media and in the political discussion of the region, the citizens' report was received as a vote for the combination of biological-mechanical treatment and incineration. For the citizens' groups, especially for the environmentalist pressure groups, the public impression that they would have voted in favour of waste incineration, was unbearable. The citizens' vote was too differentiated for the public discussion in the region. The reaction of the groups was to quit the procedure. Although they were supposed to participate as well in the third phase, they declared publicly, i.e. in the regional press that the procedure had failed and that they would quit. The public impression was therefore that the second phase of the citizens' participation had failed.

The political influence of the citizens' report on waste treatment technology was as ambiguous as the report itself. A few days after the delivery of the report, the advisory board of the P.A.N. presented its draft for the four local parliaments. This draft recommended to not decide the issues of waste technology but to assume for the period of search for the location a combination of biological-mechanical treatment and waste incineration. This draft was accepted by the four parliaments. This non-decision was ambiguous with respect to the crucial question of a possible influence of the citizens' report on the process of decision making of the P.A.N. In the first place, the participants of the consensus conference also admitted that the formal consideration of the P.A.N. to integrate an element of biological-mechanical technology into the waste treatment concept was a success (Interview BUND, December 1994). The general impression was that, without the citizens' participation, the P.A.N. would have considered only the option of waste incineration. The influence of the citizens' report at this stage of the decision making process was, however, only speculation. Of course it would have been possible that the P.A.N. would have considered the biological-mechanical option even without the citizens' report (Interview P.A.N., December 1994). And in the end it was far from clear, whether the pre-decision (to assume a mix of technologies for the search of locations) contained the final decision on treatment technology: still it was possible that in the end the region would rely only on waste incineration, and would therefore ignore the citizens' report completely.

The end of the second phase was therefore characterised by ambiguities. The citizens' report did not offer a simple answer to the question 'What do the citizens prefer?', the decisions of the P.A.N. and of the four communities hesitated to make a decision on the contested issue of waste treatment technology, but tried to keep open as many alternatives as possible. It was very difficult to identify the influence of an ambiguous citizens' vote on a political non-decision.

The ambiguous result of the second phase of course had grave negative effects on the third phase, in which randomly chosen citizens were supposed to assist in the search for locations for the waste treatment plants in the region.

4.6 Third Phase: Citizens' Forums and Siting

In January 1996, the third phase of the citizens' participation began. The task of finding suitable locations for two bio-mechanical treatment plants and one waste incinerator was carried out by 200 randomly chosen citizens of the region, with the help in management and information by the academy.

4.6.1 The Citizens' Forums

The main problem for the third phase was the ambiguous output of the second phase. Since the decision about the technology of waste treatment was not yet made, it was difficult to organise the participation of citizens in the search for a location. The ambiguous point of departure for the third phase was the following. The four districts had decided to not decide on technology, but to assume a combination of two bio-mechanical treatment plants and one central incineration plant for the period of search of locations. The task for the citizens was then to search for three locations, with the uncertainty that maybe they would search for locations for plants that would never be constructed.

The basis for the third phase was a preliminary study of the engineering office that pre-selected possible locations for the waste treatment plants. The academy then chose randomly citizens from the respective municipalities. The citizens who were willing to participate then formed ten citizens' forums that were composed of inhabitants of each possible location for a waste treatment plant. The result were six citizens' forums for the bio-mechanical plants, and four that were supposed to search for a location for a waste incinerator. All citizens' forums were managed by two employees of the academy. The forums met on six evenings in six consecutive weeks. The method was to erect value trees that would allow the citizens to generate their own criteria to compare the locations and to process all the necessary information that was provided in several ways. After the fifth meeting, each citizens' forum elected two delegates that participated in the delegates conference. The task of this conference was to put together the ten reports into one single citizens' report on possible locations.

4.6.2 The Third Citizens' Report and its Political Reception

The result of the third phase was a citizens' report with an unanimous vote. However, this unanimous vote contained two scenarios. Dependent on the possibility of transporting the waste by railway, the citizens' forums proposed two possible combinations of locations. In both scenarios, the location for the waste incinerator was Pforzheim, one bio-mechanical plant was suggested to be in the north of the region (Pforzheim, Enzkreis), and the second one was supposed to be located in Freudenstadt, in the south of the region.

After the end of the third phase of the citizens' participation in July 1996, the advisory board communicated its draft for the four local parliaments. This draft contained a surprise. Within a concept of a technical combination of waste incineration and bio-mechanical treatment it proposed a decision for a bio-mechanical technology, the so-called Trockenstabilat. This technology allows to transform waste into a form in which it can be stored for a long period (Wiemer et al. 1995a; 1995b). This technical possibility promises a flexibility, since it becomes possible to react to fluctuations in the amount of waste. With respect to the decision about the location for such a plant, the important point is that for the storage of the treated waste, one needs storing capacities that are only available on waste disposal sites. This means that the choice of technology predetermines the choice of location: the plants have to be constructed on waste disposal sites.

Although this appeared to be a technically sound suggestion, the political effect was difficult to manage. Whereas the engineering office and the citizens' forums had considered lots of criteria in order to choose the optimal location for the plants, the draft of the P.A.N. considered only one: proximity to a waste disposal site. The result was the suggestion of two bio-mechanical locations that deviated from the vote of the citizens and of the engineering office. With respect to the location for the waste incinerator in Pforzheim, there was no dissent. Since Pforzheim as a location for the waste incinerator was no surprise, the impression arose that the time consuming work of the citizens' forums was completely ignored.

4.6.3 Political Developments after the Third Phase

The draft of the P.A.N. from June 1996 was only a suggestion for the four local parliaments of the region. After the communication of this draft, the interesting question was whether it would be possible that the four communities would come to identical decisions on the basis of the P.A.N. draft. This demand of identity referred to all parts of the decision: the assumed amount of waste of 83,000 tons per year, the choice of technology for two plants of the Trockenstabilat technology and one central waste incinerator, and for the locations of the plants on the waste disposal sites in Freudenstadt and in Enzkreis, and of the waste incinerator in Pforzheim. In the end, it took the four parliaments one year to come to the decisions. It turned out, however, that it was not possible to organise the necessary political majorities for the draft of the P.A.N. Not surprisingly, it was the communities of Freudenstadt and Pforzheim, most heavily affected by the concept of the P.A.N., who were not willing to accept waste treatment plants on their territories.

The first political decision after the communication of the P.A.N. draft was made by Calw. In November 1996, the Kreistag of Calw accepted the concept, including all parts of the decision (Pforzheimer Zeitung, 5.11. 1996). Of course, this was no surprise, because Calw did not have to accept any burden of a plant on its territory. Calw was the only clear winner of the concept, because it offered a solution to the problem of waste treatment without political burdens.

January 1997 saw the second positive vote, the 'yes' of the Kreistag of Enzkreis. This meant that Enzkreis was the only one of the four communities willing to accept a waste treatment plant on its territory, thus paying a certain contribution to the solution to the waste treatment problem of the region. The interesting point with the decision of Enzkreis was that, anticipating the decision problems in Pforzheim and Freudenstadt, the Kreistag stressed the necessity of making the final decision quickly. Furthermore, the Kreistag stated that it would be unacceptable to spend money on further investigations. However, Enzkreis made the agreement with the P.A.N. concept contingent on the economic superiority of the concept to the possibility of external treatment of the waste. This comparison was still to be carried out (Pforzheimer Zeitung, 21.1. 1997).

The decision of Enzkreis put Pforzheim under pressure to decide in favour of the P.A.N. draft, i.e. to agree with the construction of a waste incinerator in Pforzheim. This pressure generated strong public resistance in Pforzheim. In a public hearing in Pforzheim, the organised resistance against waste incineration resulted in heavy conflicts including personal insults of the political decision makers (Pforzheimer Zeitung, 16.1. 1997). Here for the first time it became clear that to a certain extent the efforts of the P.A.N. had failed to make a decision for waste incineration comprehensible. The public resistance against the suggestion of the P.A.N.

succeeded in influencing the decision in Pforzheim. Since the decision of the Enzkreis was already known, the decision in Pforzheim, communicated in February 1997, was the first negative signal on the P.A.N. draft. The Stadtrat of Pforzheim in principle agreed on the draft, but made this agreement contingent on the carrying out of further examinations. Especially it was demanded to examine the possibility of treating the waste outside the region (Pforzheimer Zeitung, 19.2. 1997). As a matter of fact, this meant a disagreement because after the long period of preparation of the decision, it was extremely unlikely that the other partners of the P.A.N. would agree on the search for additional information, implying the further loss of time and money. Furthermore, the Enzkreis had already stated clearly that this would be unacceptable. The hesitation of Pforzheim to make a decision in favour of the P.A.N. draft seems to be comprehensible: the construction of a waste incinerator on its territory was exactly the decision Pforzheim desperately tried to avoid since the regional co-operation had begun.

Before the decision was made in Freudenstadt, several important developments with respect to the acceptability of the P.A.N. draft and with respect to possible decision alternatives took place. First of all, step by step it became clear that the partners of Pforzheim in the P.A.N. were not willing to pay for the further investigations Pforzheim had asked for. Furthermore, some actors in the Nordschwarzwald intensified the efforts to find solutions without the necessity of building a waste incerating plant. Enzkreis, for example. had initiated a formal question to the Ministry for the Environment of the state Baden-Württemberg about the possibilities to permit waste treatment concepts according to clause 2.4 of the Technical Instruction for Household Waste (i.e. a waste treatment concept without waste incineration, c.f. above 3.3.2). The answer of the ministry was clear and left no doubts: the clause 2.4 would not be applied in the state Baden-Württemberg (Pforzheimer Zeitung, 29.4. 1997). Simultaneously, Calw initiated the search for solutions alternative to the co-operation within the P.A.N. In case the co-operation failed, the community initiated negotiations with other possible partners, that would offer the external treatment of the waste of Calw (Pforzheimer Zeitung, 22.4. 1997). An effort in the direction to avoid the fulfilment of the legal requirements imposed by the Technical Instruction for Household Waste was the suggestion of environmentalists in Pforzheim to institute proceedings against the Technical Instruction (Pforzheimer Zeitung, 22.3. 1997).

A final development was the activities of some politicians in Pforzheim, who got in contact with the community of Münster in northern

Germany. Münster was at that time developing a technology for waste treatment that promised to fulfil the criteria if the Technical Instruction for Household Waste without incineration. This new technology (Naßoxidation) is not yet fully developed. However, it seemed to create new possibilities to escape the obligation to construct waste incineration plants (Pforzheimer Zeitung, 31.5. 1997). For the decision situation in the Nordschwarzwald the implication is the following: the emergence of this new technical possibility heightens the fear that a commitment to the technology of waste incineration in the future could turn out to be a mistake.

All of these events, which accompanied the efforts of the P.A.N. to find political support for its draft, had important impacts on the decision situation in the Nordschwarzwald: the solution suggested in the draft was questioned, because alternative courses of action seemed to be promising. The risk of a commitment to a technical solution that in the future would turn out to be wrong seemed to rise. Or, in other words, the contingency and the selectivity of the P.A.N. draft were stressed; the proposed decision was seen against the background of different possibilities. The probability of its acceptance became lower.

In June 1997, the Kreistag of Freudenstadt communicated a clear 'no' to the P.A.N. draft. This decision was made unanimously. The suggestion to construct a bio-mechanical plant in Freudenstadt obviously was unacceptable for the local politicians. The official reason for the disagreement was the economic aspect of the concept. A bio-mechanical treatment before the incineration was seen as a source of additional costs without any ecological benefit. Furthermore, it was clearly stated that the demand of Pforzheim to initiate further investigations before constructing a waste incinerator would be unacceptable (Pforzheimer Zeitung, 11.6. 1997).

Thus, in June 1997, almost one year after the delivery of the P.A.N. draft on a waste treatment concept, it was clear that this draft was not acceptable politically. The result of these disappointing developments after the third phase of the citizens' participation made further common action of the four communities almost impossible. The following autumn saw efforts of the four partners to look for alternative solutions to the waste treatment problem. The final point of this development was the end of the P.A.N. in March 1998. It had not been possible to find a common solution to the waste problem at the regional level. Therefore, the P.A.N. was dissolved. In the future, the four partners will try independently to make contracts with existing waste incinerators in order to treat their waste externally (Pforzheimer Zeitung, 31.3. 1998).

4.7 The Impacts on the Political Decision Making Process

It is very difficult to speculate about the impacts of the citizens' participation on the actual decisions made in the region. Throughout the decision making process, preliminary decisions were taken which, due to their ambiguous character, gave leeway to all kinds of interpretation concerning the central question with respect to the citizens' participation: has the citizens' participation had any impact on the decisions of the four communities? After the end of the regional co-operation in March 1998, of course these considerations have become less important: since the addressee of the citizens' participation has been the P.A.N. and since the P.A.N. does not exist any more, the suggestions of the citizens did not influence the decisions of the organisation.

4.7.1 First Phase: Correction of the Waste Prognosis

By the end of the first phase, the evaluation of the citizens' participation was positive. The citizens' report had assumed a more optimistic development of the waste amounts than the engineering office. The P.A.N., being confronted with two prognoses, decided to accept the figures of the consensus conference.

In the aftermath, however, this considerable success underwent a re-evaluation. The corrected waste prognosis of the P.A.N. in 1994 assumed 155,000 tons as a basis for the decision about the waste treatment concept. Since in the following years the waste amount declined dramatically, both the experts' and the citizens' prognosis were far too pessimistic. In 1997, the P.A.N. had to assume 83,000 tons per year. Thus the contribution of the citizens, the result of five months of work, was without any value for the planning process.

Of course, the consensus conference cannot be blamed for misjudging the dynamic unforeseeable development of waste production, nor can the P.A.N. be accused for ignoring the citizens' vote. The problem of the first phase is more related to the general characteristics of the decision situation that have been developed in the third chapter (cf. especially 3.5). The central information for the construction of a waste treatment facility is the question how much waste is to be treated. The developments that influence this information are in constant movement. The amount of waste to be treated is influenced by economic, technological, legal and political developments. The result is a high uncertainty for the decision makers. However, in order to plan a waste treatment facility, at a certain point in time the decision makers have to absorb this uncertainty, they have to assume a figure, although knowing that the development does not stop.

In this situation, the decision makers of the P.A.N. tried to combine anticipation with consensus. The aim was to fix the prognosis in advance and to do this in consensus with interested citizens' groups. The developments after the first phase suggest that this approach is not appropriate to situations of risk, that are characterised by the problem of regretting a decision in the future that seem to be right in the present. The problem of judging a decision differently in the present and in the future can obviously not be resolved by attempts to improve anticipation.

4.7.2 Second Phase: The Non-Decision About Technology

As has been argued above, the influence of the second citizens' report on the choice of treatment technology, is highly ambiguous. The result of the second phase was a citizens' report with a majority vote in favour of the bio-mechanical technology and a minority vote arguing for waste incineration. On the basis of this citizens' report and the report of the engineering office that suggested a combination of 'cold' and 'hot' technologies, the draft communicated by the advisory board of the P.A.N. contained no real decision. The choice between bio-mechanical technology and waste incineration was not made; instead, the P.A.N. assumed a combination of the two technologies for the period of location search. This non-decision was supposed to keep open all possible alternatives with respect to the contested question which technology should be used for the waste treatment of the region.

It is difficult to assess whether the citizens' report with its clear majority for the bio-mechanical option exerted any influence on the decision of the P.A.N. not to commit itself to the incineration technology. In the interviews conducted for this case study, many representatives of the P.A.N. expressed the belief that the non-decision of December 1994 was the only possibility to keep together the four partners of the P.A.N. (Interview P.A.N., July 1996). A choice of any of the options - bio-mechanical treatment vs. incineration - would have made impossible the co-operation of the four communities. It is however very likely that the citizens' report facilitated this political move (Interview P.A.N., December 1994).

4.7.3 Third Phase: The Ignoring of the Citizens' Report

With respect to the third phase, the assessment of the impact of the citizens' participation faces the same ambiguities as after the second phase. The citizens' report and the report of the engineering office unanimously suggested Pforzheim as a location for a possible waste incineration plant. These suggestions were considered in the draft of the P.A.N. communicated in July 1996: For the planned waste incinerator it left the choice between two alternative locations in Pforzheim. With the locations for the bio-mechanical plants, the situation was more complicated. The citizens' report and the study of the engineering office dissented in this issue. The draft of the P.A.N. ignored both. The advisory board of the P.A.N. had committed itself to the Technology of Trockenstabilat. This technology promises to solve one of the most difficult problems in waste management, the risk of unpredictable amounts of waste. Trockenstabilat, as a treatment before waste incineration, produces a storable substance, thus buffering the incinerator against fluctuations in waste amounts. However, since the use of this technology requires large storage facilities, it restricts the choice of location to one criterion: the plant has to be located on a waste disposal site. Thus, with the decision for this technology the P.A.N. ignored all the complicated and time-consuming considerations of the technical experts and the citizens' forums. Although being sound from the technical point of view, the decision created the impression of completely ignoring the citizens' vote.

With respect to the pre-decisions that were made by the P.A.N. after each phase of the P.A.N., the assessment of possible impacts of the participation on the decision making process cannot present clear results. After the first phase, a clear impact was observable, which, however, was minimised due to the developments of the waste amounts later on. The possible contributions of the second and the third phase are difficult to evaluate since the report delivered by the technical experts made similar suggestions. For the third phase, one can even identify a clear disregard of the citizens' report, since the locations for the bio-mechanical plants were chosen without any reference to the vote of the citizens' forums.

The influence of the participation being modest on the pre-decisions, there is no influence at all on the final decision of the P.A.N. concerning the waste treatment concept of the region. This is because in spring 1998, the four communities decided to stop their co-operation. Now, each of the former partners is trying to find a solution of their own. This can only mean that they try to find external possibilities to treat the waste. Since a waste treatment plant for only one of these communities is not suitable, the most likely solution will be that the communities of the region will try to make contracts with existing waste incinerating plants. The decision to solve the treatment problem without regional co-operation and by treating the waste externally does not make any use at all of the information made available by the extensive citizens' participation.

Since the participation was supposed to contribute to the co-operative planning of the region and to solve problems of this common decision about a waste treatment concept, one has to state that the procedure could not make this contribution. In the following section, I will try to analyse this failure. The general argument will be that this form of participation was not appropriate to the specific situation in the Nordschwarzwald. The participation was not able to tackle the central decision problems in the region I outlined above: high responsibility, uncertainty, ambiguity, and contested trust and legitimacy.

4.8 Risk and Participation: Results

By the beginning of 1998, it became clear that the P.A.N. was not willing to take the risk of constructing a waste treatment plant under the given circumstances. It is however very important to underline that this course of action does not imply the avoidance of risks. With their strategy to treat the waste in external, already existing treatment plants, the four communities of the region Nordschwarzwald of course run the risk of being dependent on the decisions of the owners of these external treatment plants. Although the prices for waste incineration were quite low in 1998, it is very likely that these prices rise enormously by 2005, when incineration will be obligatory (cf. section 3.3.2). Therefore, it is very difficult to get contracts that last beyond 2005. The attractive conditions for external treatment are very likely to turn into a financial burden for those communities who rely exclusively on this option. Although this risk has been seen in the P.A.N., the decision makers obviously preferred to run this risk instead of the risk of constructing a waste treatment plant against the strong political resistance in the region.

In order to discuss the role of the citizens' participation in this process of avoiding one risk and running into another one, in the following sections I will analyse the contributions of the participation in terms of its four potential functions identified above in section 4.3.

4.8.1 Responsibility

The result of the decision making process in the Nordschwarzwald is obvious: The P.A.N. tried to make a decision about a common regional waste treatment concept but in the end failed to make this decision. With the theoretical framework developed in the first two chapters of this study, the explanation for this failure is that it was not possible to create structures that would have allowed to re-allocate or reduce responsibility. This is one reason why the four partners in the P.A.N. were not able to come to a decision.

In section 4.3.1 I argued that the amount of responsibility, that is characteristic of the decision about the waste treatment concept in the Nordschwarzwald, could be lowered by two mechanisms. The responsibility can be *shared* by allowing for citizens' participation, and it can be *reduced* by trying to rationalise the process of decision making.

Borrowing an argument from Brunsson (1985), one can say that the sharing of responsibility can take place by allowing for more participation in the decision. If many persons make an unanimous decision, the responsibility, especially for negative outcomes, is shared. In the Nordschwarzwald, for several reasons this sharing of responsibility did not work. Roughly speaking, one can identify obstacles on the side of the groups participating, and on the side of the political and administrative decision makers.

First of all, during the conflicts in the Nordschwarzwald it became obvious that environmentalist pressure groups have major difficulties in sharing responsibility for political and administrative decisions in risk issues. Such pressure groups do not have the organisational capacities to participate in political compromises. In the case of the Nordschwarzwald, the more influential groups that participated in the second phase, the choice of treatment technology, had a clear position in the respective issue: they reject the technological option of waste incineration and argue for bio-mechanical treatment of the waste. This position even defined the identity of these groups. Thus, when after the delivery of the second citizens' report in the public discussion the impression emerged that the environmentalists had voted in favour of a combination of bio-mechanical treatment and waste incineration, the groups had to pull the emergency brake. They had to quit the participation, and they did this by stating their disappointment in the regional newspapers. The public impression, that they had compromised in this extremely important issue was not bearable for these groups. Since the main channel of influence for environmentalist pressure groups is the public sphere, i.e. the exertion of pressure through newspapers and all forms of public protest, for them it is very important to have clear positions in the contested issues. Furthermore, the members of these groups very often are not willing to follow political compromises, since these compromises can endanger the identity of an environmentalist pressure group.

On the side of the decision makers one can see that it seems to be quite difficult to consider explicitly a citizens' report in a formal decision. In many interviews with participants and observers of the citizens' participation, the demand was formulated that the decision makers must not escape their responsibility for the risky decisions to be made (e.g. Interview Association for Retail Trade, December 1994). The explicit reference to the contribution of the consensus conference and citizens' forums would have been interpreted as an escape from the formal responsibility. It seems that in German political culture informal procedures of citizens' participation are not able to re-allocate responsibility, because the reference of decision makers to an informal participation is interpreted as a shifting of responsibility to the citizens. By many interviewees, this option was seen as an escape from the structures of representative democracy.

Finally, even a rough analysis of the citizens' reports makes clear that these reports were too ambiguous to help find a clear political decision. The citizens' reports contained many compromises, especially in the contested issues. Thus, they also contained all the possible interests that can be found in the political conflicts about waste treatment. As a result, almost all political actors in the region could interpret the citizens' reports as a support for their own position (Interviews P.A.N., July 1996). Such ambiguous reports are not able to support a certain political decision and thus to distribute responsibility for such a decision.

With respect to the mechanism of reduction of responsibility by rationalisation, one can clearly identify an important contribution of the sophisticated methodology of the citizens' participation. In each of the three phases of the procedure, the citizens came to their reports in a very systematic manner. This careful method was provided by the use of the value tree analysis and by the effective management by the academy. The citizens' reports were free of any emotional judgement and were in general accordance with the reports provided by the technical experts. The additional information that was provided by the citizens' reports had, however, no impact on the decisions about the waste treatment concept of the region. Therefore one cannot speak of a successful rationalisation of the decision by the citizens' participation. The aim of reduction of responsibility by more decision rationality would have been reached if the additional information would have demonstrated the necessities and obligations implied in the decision to be made.

To sum up, it becomes clear that the citizens' participation did not generate structures that allowed the re-allocation and reduction of responsibility. In the theoretical perspective of this study, the failure of the P.A.N. to reduce or distribute the responsibility connected with the decision about the regional waste treatment concept is one of the crucial factors to explain the failure of the regional co-operation in the Nordschwarzwald.

4.8.2 Uncertainty

The possible contribution of the citizens' participation to the uncertainty problem has been discussed in section 4.3.2. The uncertainty to be absorbed by the decision of the P.A.N. would have been reduced if during the citizens' participation one decison alternative would have turned out to be the best one and if this alternative had been chosen unanimously. The result of the process shows, however, that the amount of additional information that was produced during the citizens' participation could not reduce the uncertainty. Probably the uncertainty about the alternative to choose was even increased. Several theoretical conclusions can be drawn from this observation.

First of all, and most importantly with respect to problems of decision making under risk, in the case of the Nordschwarzwald one can see that it is difficult to find the point at which the available information can be considered as certain. The problem is a) that the information necessary to make the decision changes constantly and b) that the three main aspects of the decision - waste amount, technology, and location - are highly interrelated. The citizens' participation with its three phases, each of them dedicated to one part of the whole decision about a waste treatment plant, demonstrates this point very clearly.

After the first phase in summer 1994 and on the basis of the experts and the consensus conference, the P.A.N. communicated a draft that assumed an amount of waste of 155,000 tons for the year 2002. Already the figures of the year 1995 fell below this prognosis. In 1997, one year after the end of the citizens' participation, the P.A.N. had to assume an amount of waste for the whole region of 83,000 tons. This dramatic decrease of the waste heightened significantly the risk of building an ill-sized waste treatment facility. On the basis of this information, the choice of technology became an important issue and especially the aim of technical flexibility. The big surprise of summer 1996, the technology of Trockenstabilat promised a solution to exactly this problem: it seemed to be possible to react to fluctuations in the waste amount in a flexible manner. This would have been possible by a combination of the Trockenstabilat technology with a conventional waste incinerator. A further important point was that with the choice of technology also the choice of location for the respective plants was implied. Since sufficient storage capacity was needed, the plants had to be located on existing waste disposal sites.

However, these developments - from the dramatically decreasing waste amounts to the goal of technical flexibility to the choice of waste disposal sites as locations - could not be considered in the citizens' participation. There was no possibility to re-examine the waste prognosis of summer 1994, thus the possibility that the citizens could influence the decision about the assumed waste amount did not exist. The citizens' vote about the choice of technology - delivered in December 1994 - was also obsolete when the P.A.N. tried to make the final decision about this issue in summer 1996. Finally, the citizens' suggestion for the locations of the waste treatment plants could not consider the fact that the P.A.N. had pre-chosen the technology of Trockenstabilat. Therefore the citizens' vote could not be considered by the draft of the P.A.N. communicated in July 1996.

Since the developments of the technical information necessary to make the decision constantly overtook the citizens' participation, it was not possible to consider the citizens' votes in the drafts of the P.A.N. as they were no longer appropriate to the situation. A citizens' participation, however, can only fulfil its function in a decision making process if it is possible to demonstrate that the citizens execute a real influence on the decision.

With the example of these difficulties of the citizens' participation in the Nordschwarzwald, one can demonstrate the principal problem of decision making under risk. The problem is one of time binding, i.e., the problem is that the decision makers have to commit themselves to a decision even if the surrounding world and with it the relevant information is in constant movement. With this decision the uncertainty of the information has to be absorbed, the decision makers have to assume certainty of the information because otherwise they are not able to decide. This obligation to assume certainty in an uncertain world is the very problem of decisions under risk.

A final consideration can be made with respect to the role of information in this context. If the decision problem consists in the assumption of certainty in the face of uncertainty, then too much information can block the process of decision making. The discussion in the Nordschwarzwald has shown that during the search for additional information more suitable alternatives came into consideration, all burdened with uncertainty, but all offering potential courses of action. The burden for the decision is to choose one of these uncertain but potentially promising alternatives. In fact, the final draft of the P.A.N. ignored much of the information that was provided by the technical experts and by the citizens: the suggested choice of technology confined the criteria for a possible location for the bio-mechanical plants to one single consideration. Of course, this ignoring of available information can be judged as irrationality. I argue that in the face of the amount of available information in the Nordschwarzwald, ignorance was the only way for the P.A.N. to come to a decision. Ignorance was the only way to absorb the uncertainty that was generated by the information.

However, this way of decision making had negative political effects. Since the carrying out of the citizens' participation had generated hopes and expectations that the citizens could really participate in the decision, the ignoring of the citizens' contribution to the decision making process led to great disappointment. The political damage is likely to be great in the long run.

4.8.3 Ambiguity

With respect to the decision problem of ambiguity, I argued that in the special situation in the Nordschwarzwald ambiguity arises out of two facts: Firstly, the P.A.N. is a newly founded organisation without established routines that could be applied to the decision situation; secondly, the P.A.N. is characterised by unclear, but probably conflicting preferences. In other words, the P.A.N. has poor knowledge about itself, about its environment and thus about how to carry out its task of planning a waste treatment system for the region.

The way in which the citizens' participation contributed to a possible solution to this problem can be highlighted by the events after the third phase, from July 1996 until the 'No' of Freudenstadt to the P.A.N. draft in summer 1997. After the third phase, the supervisory board of the P.A.N. communicated the decision draft containing the relevant choices for the waste treatment concept of the region: it fixed the assumption about a certain waste amount, suggested the technological combination of Trockenstabilat and waste incineration, and proposed the locations for the three waste treatment plants necessary within this concept. With this draft for the first time the P.A.N. dared to propose choices in all the contested issues of the decision about the regional waste treatment.

It is possible to speak of daring because the draft contained the suggestion to build bio-mechanical treatment plants in Enzkreis and in Freudenstadt. The option to build waste treatment plants outside Pforzheim had never before been considered explicitly in the decision making process in the region. The P.A.N. was encouraged by the positive results especially of the third phase, when it was possible to generate comprehension in the citizens' forums of the legal obligations and of the necessities to take burdens in finding a solution to the waste problem of the region. It was even possible to come to a unanimous citizens' vote about the location of a waste incinerator, and this vote was done with the participation of citizens that lived right next to the proposed location. Therefore, the supervisory board of the P.A.N. took the risk of proposing the concept of a combination of bio-mechanical treatment and waste incineration.

However, during the events after the third phase, the belief that the combination was a suitable solution for the region turned out to be wrong. The impression created by the successful third phase of the citizens' participation, that even uncommon solutions could be acceptable, was not true of the political reality in the region. The local parliaments of Pforzheim and Freudenstadt stated their 'no' to the P.A.N. draft, thus reducing significantly the ambiguity within the P.A.N. about the appropriateness of certain courses of action, however in a different manner than was expected.

The citizens' participation did not succeed in resolving the problem of ambiguity within the P.A.N. The ambiguity diminished only when it became clear that the four regional partners were not able to find a co-operative solution. The impression created especially by the third phase, that the concept of combination would be acceptable and comprehensible, turned out to be an illusion.

4.8.4 Legitimacy and Trust

The last problem I identified in the decision making process in the Nordschwarzwald, and to which the citizens' participation could contribute a potential solution, is the problem of contested acceptance of such a risky decision. I argued above that the public acceptance of risky decisions can be ensured by measures of trust building. Especially if an organisation has difficulties in legitimising every single decision, it has to try to establish a general climate of trust. If the public has a general confidence in the structures and procedures of the organisation, than it might be willing to accept decisions, even if they create burdens and if they can be questioned.

The generation of this general trust can be provided by the formal decision making structures of the organisation or by special measures directed to the creation of trust, like giving access to relevant information, organising fair decision making procedures and additionally by high performance in risk issues in the past.

Before the citizens' participation was initiated, the mistrust in the decision making capacity of the P.A.N was manifest in a suspicion that was stated by many of our interviewees by the beginning of the procedure. The well-informed environmentalist pressure groups in particular thought that the majority of the decision makers in the P.A.N. definitely preferred the technology of waste incineration (Interviews BUND, March 1994). It was therefore suspected that the decision was already fixed and that there was no real choice at all.

The first effort within the context of the P.A.N. to do something against this general mistrust was the double resolution of the Stadtrat in Pforzheim, saying that during the planning process in the region, waste incineration and bio-mechanical technologies would be considered equally. However, as our first interviews showed, this measure was not yet able to create a certain degree of trust, since by the beginning of the participation many environmentalists were of the opinion that waste incineration was the pre-selected option for the waste treatment problem of the region.

During the participation, however, it turned out that the group representatives that participated actively in the procedure, were willing to change their opinion. It became clear that many officials of the P.A.N. also tried desperately to avoid the necessity of constructing an incinerating plant (Interview BUND, December 1994). This modest success in creating trust at least among the participants of the procedure was due to the fact that the P.A.N. tried to give access to all relevant information during the participation. The representatives of the P.A.N. that were present in the participation gave the impression of co-operation and collegiality. As a result, in the citizens' participation it was possible to create trust in the sense that the suspicion of a fixation on waste incineration could be put aside (Interview BMK, July 1996).

However, the events after the citizens' participation showed that it was difficult to transport this trust into the wider public. During the conflicts about the P.A.N. draft of June 1996, many arguments in the public discussion made the accusation that the choice for waste incineration had been pre-fixed throughout the planning process and that the decision makers had not considered alternative courses of action carefully (e.g. Pforzheimer Zeintung, 16.1. 1997). The arguments sounded like the citizens' participation with its co-operative atmosphere and style of working had never taken place.

Several explanations are possible for this failure to create general trust in the organisations' decision. First of all, although the P.A.N. was a newly founded organisation, many of the waste management decisions the four communities made in the past, were implicitly attributed to the P.A.N. Especially failures in planning for waste disposal sites (Enzkreis) and explicit pre-commitments to the technology of waste incineration (Calw) burdened the struggle for trust of the P.A.N. (Interview BUND March 1994; Interview Citizens' Action Group March 1994).

A further important point in this context is the above mentioned fact that the formal decision making procedures of the P.A.N. between supervisory board, Gesellschafterversammlung and the four local parliaments were rather opaque. The lack of transparency in the processes of decision making of the P.A.N. undermined the successes in creating transparency during the citizens' participation. Furthermore, the opaqueness of the structures led to the above mentioned problems of identifying the concrete contributions of the citizens' reports on the decisions of the P.A.N.

Opaqueness, however, was also a characteristic of the citizens' participation itself. Although the participants gained insight into the problem of decision making in waste management, the participation itself was too complicated to transport these progresses into the wider political discussion of the region. This gap between developments within the citizens' participation in the direction of co-operation and transparency and the political reality of the region was one of the main obstacles to a real success of the participation in resolving the decision problems in the region.

4.9 Conclusion

In terms of a theoretical perspective that accounts for decisions as a reaction to expectations, and that conceives of risk as a problem of time binding, one can make the following conclusions with respect to the case of the Nordschwarzwald. Due to the general conditions of German waste management and due to the special characteristics of the situation in the Nordschwarzwald, the P.A.N. was under high decision pressure. In this situation, created by behavioural expectations from the environment of the P.A.N., the problems were the high responsibility for the consequences of the decision, the uncertainty about the relevant information including technical and legal uncertainty, and poor knowledge about the organisation itself. Finally, Pforzheim found itself in the difficult situation that the necessary solution to the waste treatment problem of the region, waste incineration, seemed to lead automatically to an incinerating plant in Pforzheim.

The events during the decision making process in the Nordschwarzwald suggest the interpretation that Pforzheim did not really try to avoid this result of the planning process. Instead, some influential persons tried to make this foreseeable outcome the result of a real choice. The double resolution about the equal consideration of both technological options points in this direction, as does the whole citizens' participation. The optimal result of such a struggle for the representation of one's own actions as a decision, as a choice out of alternatives, would have been the following. It would have been necessary to demonstrate that the P.A.N. was really considering all available alternatives, but that the decision makers are obliged to commit themselves to waste incineration, and that, in the comparison with all alternative solutions, Pforzheim was the only suitable location for a waste incinerating plant.

The effect of the decision making process, however, was only half of the optimum. During the planning process, many suitable alternatives for the solution to the waste treatment problem appeared. The decision makers, especially of Pforzheim, demonstrated their search for the optimal decision. They failed, however, to demonstrate the necessity of the only decision alternative that was politically acceptable within the context of the regional co-operation. This was because the construction of a waste incinerating plant in Pforzheim was not convincing in the face of the alternatives that had appeared during the decision making process. Among these alternative solutions were: external treatment, relying on new biomechanical technologies that promise to fulfil the legal requirements, trying to achieve an exceptional permission according to paragraph 2.4 of the Technical Instruction for Household Waste (c.f. 3.3.2), and to ignore the Technical Instruction.

The result of the generation of this range of alternatives without demonstrating the necessity of choosing one of them, was a rise in uncertainty and responsibility, a rise of the risk to be taken with the decision. The discussion about alternative technical solutions and of possibilities to escape the legal requirements of the Technical Instruction for Household Waste created the impression that a commitment to the solution of waste incineration would run the risk of being overtaken by legal and technical developments. The result would have been a burden for the citizens of the region - especially the burden of high waste charges - while it would have been possible to resolve the treatment problem with other solutions. This is classical problem of risk: the risk was to commit oneself to a decision alternative that after the decision would turn out to be the wrong one and would lead to burdens for others. This is the tension between the time dimension - the future shows that the decision was wrong - and the social dimension - people not participating in the decision are affected by its results.

If this analysis of the decision problem is correct, then the failure of the citizens' participation to offer solutions in this situation is no surprise. The methodology and the concept of the participation relied very much on a logic of anticipatory rationality. The intention of the participation model was to fix a consensus, between decision makers and those likely to be affected, about the decisive issues of the decision - amount of waste, technology, location - *before* the decision. The goal was to provide for a better basis of information and for a broader consensus for the decision. The absorption of uncertainty about the three parts of the whole decision was supposed to take place step by step in three phases. However, neither the participants of the procedure nor the decision makers were willing to commit themselves to clear, and unambiguous decisions during the planning process. Before the summer of 1996, the P.A.N. had not even fixed one of the three main parts of the decision. No uncertainty was absorbed until then.

This result suggests that the concept of the participation was not appropriate to the situation in the region. The time problem of committing oneself to a decision under uncertain circumstances can obviously not be resolved by a preceding citizens' participation. This general inappropriateness of the participation concept to the decision situation is reinforced by the special condition of the case, that the co-operation between the four partners was characterised by deep interest conflicts. The political complexity of the co-operation was too great to be resolved by a citizens' participation.

Since the efforts of the P.A.N. in taking the risk of planning a regional waste treatment concept did not succeed, the four communities have turned to another risk: they treat their waste independently and in co-operation with already existing waste incinerating plants. In looking for relevant information for the regional solution, the P.A.N. generated too much uncertainty. This uncertainty mainly existed in the presence of new and promising alternatives, that stressed the selectivity of the regional solution. It became clear that there were lots of other possibilities and it seemed that they were politically more convenient. The risk of a common decision became too high for the communities. As a result of this generation of uncertainty by information, the decision makers hesitated to take the risk of a regional solution and preferred to take the risk of an external solution. The risk of this decision is of course the possible dependency on economic and political developments outside the sphere of influence.

It is difficult to judge whether the final choice of the decision makers in the Nordschwarzwald is right or wrong. Although the general impression of a paralysis, of an incapacity to take a decision, remains, there were good reasons not take the risk of constructing a regional waste treatment structure. The consequences of the decision to sign contracts with external partners can be judged only in the future, more or less by the year 2005. And even then a judgement will be speculative because it is impossible to reconstruct the potential consequences of the decision that was not made in 1998.

For a sociological analysis of organisational decision making under risk the important conclusion is the following. In the Nordschwarzwald we can see the process of how an organisation avoided one risk and preferred to take another. In this case, this took place during the efforts to collect information for the decision that in the end was not made. The uncertainty that was generated during the attempt to improve the informational and political basis of the decision led to an undermining of the capacity of the organisation to make the respective choice. The new and informal structures that were established during the citizens' participation failed to fulfil their function with respect to the problem of making a decision as they did not absorb uncertainty. We therefore see that efforts in the direction of rationality and participation can destroy the prerequisite of a decision. This prerequisite seems to be the ability to assume certainty in an uncertain world. This ability is not achieved by information, but by ignorance. Only by ignorance can the organisation reach the state of assuming certainty in an environment and in the face of a future that are inherently uncertain.

5 Risk and Routines

The second case study presents a different situation with a different decision outcome. Although the legal situation in this case is the same as in the first one, especially the differing organisational conditions led to courses of action and decision outcomes completely different from those observed in the first case. Düren, which is in the centre of the second case study, was one of the first communities in Germany to construct a bio-mechanical waste treatment plant. The main goal of the present chapter is to explain why this most striking and innovative decision was taken in Düren. The making of this decision implied the taking of considerable risks. I will argue that the institutional conditions in Düren absorbed uncertainty and re-allocated responsibility and thus allowed the organisation to take the risks connected with the decision. Thus, the surprising decision outcome, which is in conflict with the legal prescriptions as they appeared in 1998, was achieved due to organisational peculiarities in the community.

The most striking organisational difference is the fact that the community of Düren made all the relevant decisions on its own, i.e. without any formal or informal co-operation with other communities. However, Düren relied on the co-operation with a private enterprise, Trieneckens, which specialises in the construction of landfill sites and in waste treatment technology. In the following sections I will argue that it was this close and long-lasting co-operation in particular that enabled the political and administrative decision makers to absorb many of the uncertainties connected with waste management decisions. The result is a very active and adversarial strategy of handling the decision problems.

The second important characteristic of the situation in the community of Düren is the active role of the higher political levels, the state government (Landesregierung) and the district administration (Bezirksregierung). At these political levels, the strategy to implement the federal waste legislation was active planning and enforcement. This active strategy created political resistance in the community of Düren, which, in combination with the uncertainty absorbing climate of co-operation in the community, led to decision outcomes that were in conflict with the demands of the higher political levels.

The case study shows how a political organisation can be put under pressure from two different directions. On the one hand, the co-operative relationship between the community and the private enterprise suggested the construction of a bio-mechanical waste treatment plant as a sensible and necessary course of action; on the other hand, the district administration tried to force the community to construct a waste incinerator. At a certain point in time, the community was facing two contradictory expectations to take action. In this situation, obviously without any clear preferences, the local decision makers in Düren relied on the uncertainty absorbing co-operation with the private enterprise and thus set themselves against the legal and political pressure to participate in the planning for a waste incinerator.

The interesting point is that the co-operation with the private enterprise was rooted in the planning and running of the community's landfill site. Facing the task of planning a waste treatment plant, the community relied on this organisational routine, the co-operation with Trieneckens. I will argue that this is a classical case of matching an existing organisational routine with a new decision situation, as it is described by March and Olsen (1995). For the analysis of organisational decision making under risk, it will be important to stress the uncertainty absorbing function of organisational routines. The trust in the successful co-operation with Trieneckens allowed much of the information relevant the decision to be neglected.

The preliminary result of this course of action is, of course, not an optimal one. The uncertainty, that was absorbed by the institutional features of the local network, returned after the decision in the form of negative consequences. These negative outcomes put the community under further pressure to make decisions and to adjust its course of action. Düren is forced to learn from its partly negative experience. I will however argue that Düren has also better possibilities to learn from experience, since the situation in Düren, as it could be observed in 1998, is characterised by less uncertainties and ambiguities than at the beginning of the decision process. Uncertainty has been absorbed and ambiguity has been reduced by making decisions. The situation after these decisions is thus characterised by new structural pressure but as well by low uncertainty and low ambiguity.

This interesting development will be described and analysed in detail in this chapter. I will begin by sketching the important organisational conditions of the case (5.1). Section 5.2 will be dedicated to the pressures that were exerted by the higher political levels. This structural development seemed to lead inevitably to the construction of a waste incinerating plant on the territory of Düren. In section 5.3, I will concentrate on the development of the tight co-operation between the community of Düren and Trieneckens. This institutional arrangement suggested the construction of a bio-mechanical waste treatment plant. Only if one keeps in mind the parallel development of both structures, the internal and the external one, is it possible to explain the idiosyncratic decision outcome in Düren. In section 5.4, I will outline how the consequences of the risky decision put the community under pressure to take further action. This will lead to a discussion of the possibilities and obstacles to organisational learning from experience. Section 5.5 presents the conclusions of the case study.

5.1 The Organisational Context

The community of Düren is a small district in the south of the German state of Nordrhein-Westfalen. It is characterised by a more rural structure and by its proximity to the bigger municipalities of Cologne and Aachen (Herbold / Timmermeister / Vorwerk 1998). The waste management system of Düren until recently was mainly based on its large landfill site, located in Horm, close to the City of Düren.

5.1.1 Close Co-operation with a Private Partner

The most important organisational precondition of the decision making process in Düren is the long-lasting and close co-operation of the community with a private enterprise specialising in all kinds of waste management technologies. This firm, Trieneckens, is part of a larger enterprise, the RWE, which is one of the biggest energy and disposal enterprises in Germany. Trieneckens runs the landfill site of Düren. For this task, the Dürener Deponiegesellschaft (DDG) was founded. For many years, the DDG was a 100% subsidiary company of Trieneckens.

The co-operation between Düren and Trieneckens has the traits of a monopoly. Since the beginning of the co-operation with the foundation of the DDG, all new waste management projects of Düren lead the community into a further contract with Trieneckens. The community of Düren follows the strategy of privatising all tasks and services in waste management (Interview administration, November 1995). Thus, the case of a new project - be it a composting plant, a rebuilding project for the landfill site, or the task of planning a waste treatment concept for the community - there is no real competition, but the task is almost automatically passed to Trieneckens. Due to its membership of a larger enterprise, Trieneckens can offer all kinds of services. Thus, no external technical expertise is necessary when a new project is started.

In the political discussions in the community, this close co-operation is often criticised (e.g. Jülicher Nachrichten, 26.5. 1994; Dürener Nachrichten, 28.10. 1995). This is comprehensible since the legitimising function of external expertise cannot be observed in this approach. The suspicion of many critics is that the community of Düren sells its interests to the large RWE company, a company which in the German discussion in general is heavily criticised because of its opaque decision making structures and its strong position in the market for energy and for disposal services and technologies.

The administrative decision makers of Düren concede that the close co-operation with Trieneckens can lead to problems. They claim, however, that the relationship is characterised by strong mutual trust (Interview administration, October 1995). Moreover, the usual contracts with Trieneckens allow a stable sharing of risks, especially of the risk that a waste disposal plant - be it a landfill site, a composting plant or a waste treatment plant - cannot be run to capacity due to fluctuations in the amount of waste. The contracts usually guarantee a fixed price per ton for the community of Düren. Thus, the risk that due to unforeseen fluctuations in the amount of waste the waste charges have to be increased, is reduced to a certain extent.

However, in the interviews with the administration of Düren it became clear that there are also problems with the co-operation. The officials complained about a lack of control of the decision making structures of Trieneckens and of the DDG. This lack of control is mainly ascribed to the membership of Trieneckens and the DDG in a larger company. This company is suspected to have strong commercial interests that may be conflicting with the political interests of the community of Düren. Another example is that the employment of the personnel of the DDG is opaque. The administration of Düren suspects that in some cases employees of the DDG, that formally have the exclusive task to work in the landfill site of Düren, work in other parts of the company as well (Interview administration, October 1995). This is only one example of problematic aspects of the co-operation between the community of Düren and Trieneckens. In the end, however, the officials of Düren see the relationship with Trieneckens as characterised by mutual trust and consider the co-operation a success.

5.1.2 Position within Larger Decision Making Structures

The second important feature of the organisational context in this case is provided by the higher administrative and political levels, that set premises for the waste management decisions in Düren.

First of all, until 1995 one very important characteristic was the waste management policy of the state government in Nordrhein-Westfalen, controlled by the social democrats (SPD). The minister of the environment pursued an explicit strategy of support for the implementation of the waste incinerating technology in Nordrhein-Westfalen. The goal was to be first state in Germany to have the Technical Instruction for Household Waste implemented. To achieve this requirement, the government of Nordrhein-Westfalen prescribed a shorter phase of transition than is contained in the Technical Instruction. The Technical Instruction for Household Waste permits that its prescriptions, especially with respect to the incineration of waste, are implemented only by the year 2005 (cf. above, 3.3.2). Nordrhein-Westfalen tried to shorten this transition period. This policy was connected personally with the SPD state minister of the environment, Klaus Matthiesen. Thus, the ministry of the environment demanded that by 1999 all communities should incinerate their waste before depositing it. This policy was supposed to be implemented by the respective district administration.

In the case of Düren, the district administration responsible is that of Cologne, chaired by the Administrative District Officer (Regierungspräsident) Antwerpes. For the developments in the community of Düren it is important to note that the Administrative District Officer of Cologne has a very peculiar style of decision making. Although an Administrative District Officer is supposed to be only an official, implementing policies of the state, in the case of Cologne he is a person with a very high media profile. The Administrative District Officer of Cologne is one of the few officials in this function known to the wider public. With a certain instinct for media intensive topics, he tends to present decisions as decisions made personally by him. Thus, many policies and requirements that are made by the district administration of Cologne are attributed personally to the Administrative District Officer Antwerpes. This is also true for the Waste Management Plans (cf. above, 3.3.1), communicated by the district administration of Cologne. The waste management plans of the district administration were supposed to implement the waste policy of the state. These plans were attributed personally to the Administrative District Officer and his peculiar style of decision making. This strong personal commitment of the Administrative District Officer and the attribution of the decisions of the district administration to one person heightened the conflicts in Düren significantly. This will be an important point for understanding the developments in the waste management planning in Düren.

Until 1995, the state policy in favour of a speedy implementation of the Technical Instruction for Household Waste, combined with a very active support by the person of the Administrative District Officer, lead to an intense pressure on the community of Düren to participate in plans to build a waste incineration plant. In 1995, the state government of Nordrhein-Westfalen changed, and the new minister of the environment became Bärbel Höhn, a member of the green party. The implications of this political change at the state level for the planning process in Düren will be described in detail in the final sections of this chapter.

The institutional preconditions sketched so far - the close public-private co-operation at the community level and the pressures exerted from the state and district level - led to two separate developments. From both directions one can observe structural developments that suggested certain decisions with respect to the problem of waste treatment in the community of Düren. The *external* development created decision pressure in the direction of a speedy implementation of the Technical Instruction for Household Waste. The demand put forward by the state government and by the district administration was to construct a waste incineration plant on the territory of Düren (5.2). The *internal* structural development was rooted in the co-operation with Trieneckens and led to plans to build a bio-mechanical treatment plant on the landfill site of Düren. This technical measure was initiated in order to improve the quality of the waste. Only against the background of the emerging Technical Instruction for Household Waste and its active implementation by the state level did this possible course of action take the form of a potential alternative to the technology of waste incineration (5.3).

The development from the two opposed directions - the community and the state level - will be described in the following sections. I will argue that the community of Düren chose to follow the course of action suggested by the internal structural development because of two reasons. *Firstly*, the uncertainty absorbing capacity of the routine co-operation with

Trieneckens was higher than that of political prescriptions from the higher political levels. The trust in the co-operation with Trieneckens allowed a known routine - passing over a task to a private company - to be applied to a new decision situation - the planning of a waste treatment plant. This matching of an old rule to a new situation absorbed uncertainty - although its appropriateness to the task of planning a waste treatment facility could be questioned. On the contrary, the pressure from the higher political levels could not absorb uncertainty since during the conflict the lacking information basis of the district administration's strategy became obvious. *Secondly*, the internal structural development promised the re-allocation of responsibilities. During the planning of the plant, Trieneckens was willing to take much of the financial burdens connected with the construction of the waste treatment plant. Furthermore, the contracts between the community and its private partner allocated the financial liability for an ill-sized plant with Trieneckens. On the other hand, the institutional pressure from the higher political levels could not relieve the community of responsibility: the political responsibility for higher waste charges as a consequence of an ill-sized waste incinerating plant cannot be passed to higher political levels.

Thus, the routine of relying on the organisational and technical expertise of a private partner absorbed uncertainty and reduced responsibility. This institutional relief allowed Düren to make a decision that was connected with the taking of considerable risks. The risk taking approach of Düren was thus possible due to institutional conditions.

The effects of this active approach are legal, technical, and economic consequences that lead to new action pressure. On the one hand this means the necessity to learn from experience. On the other hand, due to reduced uncertainty and ambiguity, the organisation may be able to learn since it faces attributable consequences and since it has developed rather stable preferences during the decision making process (5.4).

5.2 External Decision Pressure: The Waste Policy at the State Level

I will begin with a sketch of the external decision pressure that was exerted mainly by the state government and the district administration. With the instrument of the waste management plan, the district administration tried to force Düren to build a waste incinerating plant on its territory. However, Düren developed a strong political resistance against the expectation to plan a waste incinerating plant. I will argue that the political pressure from the district administration failed to absorb uncertainty for the risky decisions to be taken by the community of Düren.

The behavioural expectations to build a waste incinerating plant in Düren were mainly put forward by the government of the state of Nordrhein-Westfalen. The policy of the SPD state minister of the environment, Klaus Matthiesen, was to implement the Technical Instruction for Household Waste faster than in other federal states. The core of this policy was the shortening of the transitory period of the technical instruction. Thus, in Nordrhein-Westfalen, the communities were supposed to incinerate their waste already by 1999, instead of 2005, as prescribed in the Technical Instruction for Household Waste.

This strict and demanding state policy was supported actively by the district administration of Cologne, which was also responsible for Düren. Due to his very adversarial style of decision making, the Administrative District Officer Antwerpes used the instrument of the waste management plan to prescribe the construction of several waste incinerating plants in the administrative district of Cologne. For the case of Düren, the proposed plants in Aachen and in Düren are of considerable importance. It is important to note that the project in Aachen was pushed forward parallel to the planning in Düren. Furthermore, three other waste incinerating plants in the Regierungsbezirk Cologne were in operation or were planned: Cologne, Bonn, and Leverkusen, all three in considerable proximity to Düren. The most important of these projects, Aachen, was located in a distance of only 12 kilometres from the proposed plant in Düren.

The project of a waste incinerating plant on the territory of Düren initially was pushed forward by the private runner of the proposed plant and by the political and administrative decision makers of Düren. The style of decision making was characterised by opaqueness and by efforts to keep the project secret as long as possible. When the project became public in 1988, the public resistance against the plant was organised very quickly (Herbold / Timmermeister / Vorwerk 1998). A citizens' action group was founded. Different from the usual strategy of comparable groups, the citizens' action group in Düren did not confine itself to the organising of public protest. Moreover, the citizens founded a political party that ran for the next election of the local parliament (Gemeinderat) in the respective municipality. The result of this election was the entry of this small party into the local parliament. This meant an important step towards the politicisation of the issue in the region (Herbold / Timmermeister / Vorwerk 1998).

The next important step into this direction was the local elections for Düren in 1989. Until then, the conservative party (CDU), that pursued the project of the waste incinerating plant very actively, held the majority. The election led to a loss of this majority and to a change to the social democrats (SPD). This loss of a political majority was attributed to the strong commitment of the CDU to the project of waste incineration. Together with the political success of the citizens' action group this was the beginning of a change in attitude towards waste incineration. The result of this process was a broad political consensus in Düren, supported by all political parties, to reject waste incineration (Interview Administration, October 1995).

This development towards a political consensus against the project corresponded with an increasing pressure exerted by the district administration. The first significant step in this direction was made by Administrative District Officer Antwerpes in September 1992. He increased the capacity of the incinerating plant from 274.000 tons to 640.000 tons per year. The justification for this measure was the need for incinerating capacities in the region. Furthermore, the Administrative District Officer demanded that besides Düren two other neighbour communities should incinerate their waste in the plant in Düren (Jülicher Volkszeitung, 3.9. 1992). This initiative to force the communities to build the plant and to fix the most important features of the plant (amount of waste) by hierarchical instruction was the first step that created political resistance in Düren. The attempt to force Düren to incinerate waste from other communities endangered the until then co-operative style of decision making in Düren.

Throughout the whole conflict, the issue of the expected amount of waste was the most contested one. By the beginning of 1993, the citizens' action groups of Düren presented an experts' report that claimed that the proposed incinerating plant was not necessary since even the existing plants in Nordrhein-Westfalen were not running to capacity (Jülicher Nachrichten, 18.2. 1993). The district administration ignored these emerging doubts about the necessity of the plant and in summer 1993 made another attempt to force Düren to construct the plant. The Administrative District Officer even set a deadline of September of that year for Düren to make the decision in favour of the plant. If this were not done, the district administration was going to take compulsory measures to implement the state policy in Düren (Jülicher Volkszeitung, 9.7. 1993; Jülicher Nachrichten, 5.8. 1993). This was a certain climax in the conflict and Düren decided to take legal proceedings against the pressure of the district administration. The verdict of the administrative court in Münster was not communicated before the summer of 1995. In the meantime, the conflict between Düren and its district administration continued.

An important event that weakened the position of the Administrative District Officer was the announcement of the state government in April 1994, that the planned incinerating plant in Düren would, in contrast to the initial plan, only be necessary for the incineration of household waste. The treatment of hazardous waste (Sondermüll) would not take place in this plant. A step into the same direction was the communication of the decision of the district administration two months later to build only 5 instead of 7 incinerating plants in the region (Jülicher Nachrichten, 14.4. 1994; Jülicher Volkszeitung, 20.4. 1994). At the same time, the beginning of the operation of all the plants in the region was fixed for the year 2000. This meant a relief of the initial plan to start incineration by 1998.

The message of both events for the political discussion in Düren was identical: the informational basis of the decision to build a waste incinerating plant in Düren seemde to be uncertain. The information that was necessary to decide on the technical features of the plant was obviously in constant movement; thus the attempts of the district administration to fix certain assumptions about this information lacked legitimacy. The uncertainty about the relevant information was further heightened in October 1994 by a second experts' report, presented by the municipality of Baesweiler, located closely to the plant. This report claimed that even without the incinerating plant in Düren, in the whole Regierungsbezirk there would be an extra capacity of incinerating plants of about 40% in the year 2005 (Jülicher Nachrichten, 12.10. 1994).

By the end of 1994, the district administration made a last attempt to legitimise the project even in the face of massive uncertainty. The Administrative District Officer communicated the instruction to incinerate the waste from a further community of the region (Mönchengladbach) in the Düren plant as well (Jülicher Volkszeitung, 16.9. 1994). However, this last step of the Administrative District Officer naturally did not not overcome the resistance in Düren.

The 'victory' of Düren was completed by the verdict of the administrative court in Münster in March 1995. The court stated that the state policy of Nordrhein-Westfalen to shorten the transitory period for the implementation of the Technical Instruction for Household Waste lacked a legal basis. The obligation for the communities to start waste incineration by 1999 was considered illegal. The court argued that the communities need room for discretionary planning. This room for discretion must not be reduced by hierarchical instructions from higher administrative levels (Jülicher Volkszeitung, 18.3. 1995).

As a result of this development, in June 1995, the project for the waste incinerating plant in Düren was cancelled (Jülicher Volkszeitung, 10.6. 1995). It had become clear that the basis for the decision to build the plant had diminished: there was not enough waste in the region. Furthermore, the active implementation strategy of the state and of the district administration was lacking the necessary legal basis. The political resistance of Düren had been successful.

This brief sketch of the development of the external decision pressure on the community of Düren demonstrates the following: the attempts of the district administration created a decision pressure on the community of Düren. However, these expectations to take action in favour of a waste incinerating plant in Düren were not sufficient to serve as decision premises for politics and administration in Düren. This is because of two main reasons.

First of all, the instructions of the district administration could not absorb the uncertainty connected with the decision about a waste incinerating plant, because the main features of the plant were changed throughout the whole planning process. Specifically the size of the plant and the question of which communities of the region were supposed to use it underwent constant changes by the district administration. This showed that the underlying assumptions were uncertain, that the necessity to build the plant could not be demonstrated.

Secondly, due to the legal situation in German waste management, the hierarchical instructions from higher political levels could not reallocate the responsibility for the achievement of the goal of disposal safety at the local level. This is especially true for the crucial point of waste charges. The construction of an ill-sized waste incinerating plant, although carried out on behalf of the district administration, would have led to higher waste charges and to ongoing political conflicts at the local level. The reference to the hierarchical instructions from the higher level would not have been able to pass the political responsibility for higher waste charges to the district administration.

In addition to these arguments, derived from a risk-sociological framework, the development in Düren shows how pressure from higher political levels can create a political consensus in a community. The adversarial style of decision making of the Administrative District Officer of Cologne reinforced the tendency in Düren to resist to the technology of waste incineration. This tendency had its starting point in the local elections of 1989 when the political party that argued in favour of the waste incineration project lost its majority. Although the following major party, the social democrats, initially were not clear opponents to the project, the political development in Düren step by step led to a broad consensus against waste incineration. Already in 1993 both parties argued in favour of a waste treatment concept without waste incineration. The local elections in 1994 saw a change in the chairmanship of the social democrats of Düren. The now leading person in the social democratic party was a clear opponent to waste incineration in Düren (Herbold / Timmermeister / Vorwerk 1998).

This step-by-step-development of a consensus against waste incineration in Düren was reinforced by a parallel development in the community. As a reaction to problems with the landfill site, the project of a bio-mechanical waste treatment plant emerged. Initially only a technical measure for the improvement of the technical standard of the landfill site, against the background of the conflicts about waste incineration this project became a technological alternative for the treatment of waste. Due to institutional peculiarities to be discussed below, this alternative had more uncertainty absorbing capacity. Furthermore, it reinforced the process of consensus building in Düren, since it offered a potential alternative to the course of action that all political parties rejected. The following section presents the development of this internal decision pressure.

5.3 The Internal Decision Pressure

The structural development at the community level, or the internal development of behavioural expectations, took technical problems with the landfill site of Düren as its starting point. The tackling of these problems led to the belief that in order to avoid future problems with the landfill site it would be necessary to treat the waste before depositing it. This led to the suggestion that the bio-mechanical waste treatment plant be constructed. The development of this decision will be sketched in this section.

By the beginning of the eighties, it turned out that the landfill site, then run by the community of Düren, caused serious problems of toxic emissions. Due to its location in a valley, right within a groundwater reservoir, the uncontrolled emissions of the landfill site polluted the groundwater seriously (Herbold / Timmermeister / Vorwerk 1998). It was therefore necessary to redevelop the landfill site and to equip it with the best available technology.

The necessity to redevelop the landfill site was obvious. However, it turned out that the costs of such a project would be excessive. Düren therefore decided to privatise the operation of the landfill site. After a formal invitation of tenders the task was passed to Trieneckens, a private company specialising in disposal technologies and services. This was the beginning of the co-operation between Düren and Trieneckens. The DDG (Dürener Deponiegesellschaft) was founded; this private company was a 100% subsidiary company of Trieneckens. The DDG was founded in 1984.

In order to carry out the costly project of redevelopment, Düren and the DDG contacted the German Federal Agency for the Environment (Umweltbundesamt, UBA). The UBA agreed to participate in the project and even to share the financial burden. The interest of the UBA was to demonstrate in a pilot scheme the solution of a very common problem in German waste management at that time: the redevelopment of technically out-dated landfill sites. The intention was to gain scientific information that could be useful in other similar projects.

The organisational constellation that approached the task of the redevelopment was thus the community of Düren, the runner of the landfill site, the DDG, and the UBA, which provided the necessary scientific and financial resources. The technical redevelopment of the landfill site turned out to be extremely costly and difficult. The costs were ca. 55 million DM; 20 million DM were contributed by the UBA. The project was only completed in the early 1990s.

By the end of the project, the scientific experts of the UBA argued that the costly and technically sophisticated redevelopment of the landfill site would only make sense in the long run, if the quality of the waste disposed would be improved. The argument was that without any measures to improve the quality of the waste, within 20 years the landfill site would be in a state similar to that of the middle of the eighties. Thus, it became clear that only with further investments in technology for waste separation and treatment could the technical standard of the landfill site be ensured.

These arguments were the beginning of the process that in the end led to the decision to build a bio-mechanical waste treatment plant. The first plans were directed towards a more intensive separation of the waste. However, against the background of the political discussions of the Technical Instruction for Household Waste by the beginning of the nineties, it became clear that such a solution would not be sufficient. In several conceptual steps, the decision makers came closer to the plan to build a bio-mechanical waste treatment plant.

Officials of Düren state that the community step by step slipped into this decision (Interview administration, October 1995). Although experts of the UBA and of Trieneckens considered carefully the technical details of the plant, the main question - to build the plant or not - was decided by the local politicians without any external expertise. The decision was made during a period of several years, and from the political side the construction of the plant was never questioned fundamentally.

Another important factor, besides the strong political will to build the plant, was the informal way of calculating the costs of the project. Since Trieneckens had strong interests in building the plant (because of the possibility to gain important technical experience) the sharing of the financial burdens of the project was not regulated clearly. The technical experts of Trieneckens did much of the work without charging all the services. Trieneckens thus took much of the financial and technical risks during the phase of development of the plant.

Members of the administration of Düren state very clearly that this proceeding would not have been possible with an external partner (Trieneckens was not considered an external partner). Thus, as one interviewee stated, Düren could only take the courageous decision to build the plant because of the close relationship with Trieneckens (Interview administration, November 1995). The willingness of Trieneckens to take much of the risks of developing the plant, and the strong political consent of the politicians in Düren, led to the absorption of much uncertainty in the decision process: Trieneckens took the responsibility for the technical layout of the plant and the political consensus allowed the legal demands to be ignored.

The combination of these two institutional mechanisms of uncertainty absorption - the political consensus and the co-operative relationship with a private partner - make the events right before the final decision to build the plant more comprehensible. The UBA, still participating in the project, had suggested financial aid be sought from the federal ministry of the environment. The interest of the UBA was to gain information with respect to the question of whether the bio-mechanical technology was able to comply with the requirements of the Technical Instruction for Household Waste. With this argument, the project in Düren became important for the federal environmental policy. In order to find out whether the federal government would support the project, Düren organised an experts' hearing in June 1993. The result of this hearing - with participants from the federal and the state government and from scientific institutions - was that there would be no financial support from the federal level.

Nevertheless, a few days later, on the 22nd of June 1993, the community of Düren made the decision to build the plant. Due to the institutional peculiarities of the decision network in Düren the decision was already pushed so far that the final information, that in the long run the plant would not be sufficient legally and there would be no financial support, was ignored. The formal permission was already made, and Trieneckens had already invested too much. It was not possible to stop the development towards the building of the bio-mechanical plant that had started many years ago.

The explanation of this irrational decision making must be an institutional one. The institutionalised co-operation between Düren and Trieneckens, that was rooted in the operation of the landfill site, provided a pattern of action that was matched with the new task, the planning of a waste treatment plant. The uncertainty absorbing capacity of this structural routine was so high that it enabled the political decision makers to ignore relevant information. Among this relevant information the most important aspect was the fact that the project was not sufficient with respect to the prescriptions of the Technical Instruction for Household Waste.

Summing up the arguments of sections 5.2 and 5.3, one can say that the community of Düren was subject to two different structural developments. Both put the decision makers under pressure to take action in important waste management issues. The *external* decision pressure was exerted by the district administration that tried to force the community of Düren to build a waste incinerating plant on its territory. The adversarial approach of the Administrative District Officer together with the obviously uncertain information basis of his instructions created a climate of resistance at the level of the community. The emerging political consensus in the community was reinforced when the *internal* structural development - the construction of a waste treatment facility to improve the technical quality of the landfill site - seemed to offer a considerable decision alternative. The decision to build this waste treatment plant was made on the basis of a co-operative relation to the DDG, the private company that runs the landfill site and which was also responsible for the planning of the bio-mechanical treatment plant. This relationship had developed during the running and redevelopment of the landfill site. Thus, the reliance on this known relation for the carrying out of a new decision can be considered a matching of an already existing decision routine with a new task. Since the private company had considerable interest in building the plant, the costs of the planning process were not clearly divided between the two partners. Thus, the following of the routine absorbed a considerable amount of uncertainty for the decision makers in Düren. Only against the background of the conflicts with the district administration, the bio-mechanical treatment plant appeared as a long-term alternative to waste incineration. The project to build this plant was initiated without this intention. Only the interplay of the step-by-step development of the plant with the political conflicts about waste incineration made the bio-mechanical plant a courageous decision. The result was that, after the decision, Düren found itself in conflict with the legal expectations and in a position of a political innovator.

In terms of uncertainty and responsibility, the two main aspects of organisational risks, the conclusion is the following. The *external* expectations to build a waste incinerating plant in Düren neither absorbed uncertainty nor did they relieve Düren of responsibility. During the conflict with the district administration the weak informational basis of the implementation strategy of the Administrative District Officer became evident. The uncertainty connected with the decision for a waste incinerating plant was thus always present. Furthermore, the political responsibility for an appropriately sized waste treatment plant was still with the community level. On the contrary, the *internal* institutional arrangement between Düren and its private partner Trieneckens absorbed uncertainty and reduced responsibility for the community. The reliance on the successful routine of passing waste management tasks to this private partner and the consensus of all political parties absorbed the uncertainty about the appropriateness of the bio-mechanical waste treatment plant. As regards responsibility, the strong commitment of Trieneckens during the development of the plant, together with the contract that allocated all financial liability for failures with the firm, led to a considerable relief of responsibility for the decision makers of Düren.

As we will see in the following section, the absorbed uncertainty returned after the decision in the form of negative legal, technical, and organisational consequences. These negative consequences put the community under new decision pressure, since it turned out that the decision strategy of Düren had to be adjusted in order to fulfil the legal and technical requirements of a waste management system that provides for long-term disposal safety. In other words, Düren is expected to learn. The following section will examine the possibilities and constraints for organisational learning from experience in Düren.

5.4 A Risky Decision and its Consequences

The innovative decision of Düren to build a bio-mechanical waste treatment plant is not the end of the decision making process about the waste treatment concept of this community. On the contrary, in certain respects this is only the starting point for further developments into the direction of a waste management system that fulfils the legal, technical and organisational requirements.

The construction of the bio-mechanical plant in Düren led to certain problematic consequences. The tackling of these new problems creates new action pressure for the community. In the following sections I will argue that the presence of these consequences put Düren under pressure to learn. Whether Düren will really be able to learn from its experiences is a difficult question to answer. There are however some hints that suggest that an intelligent adaptation as described in much of the literature on organisational learning (Argyris / Schon 1978; 1996; Dodgson 1993; Wiesenthal 1995) will not take place.

The most important consequences of the construction of the plant in Düren that create new decision pressure are the following. *Firstly*, it turned out that the bio-mechanical plant was ill-sized. Düren had not enough waste to make the plant run to capacity. This is the classical problem of communities that have built waste treatment plants; it creates the pressure to do something about it, because otherwise the community runs the risk of creating political conflicts by increasing the waste charges. In Düren the situation is mainly characterised by unclear responsibilities between the communtiy and the private runner of the plant (5.4.1). *Secondly*, as already mentioned several times, the present structure of the waste management system in Düren in the long run will not be sufficient to fulfil the requirements of the Technical Instruction for Household Waste. The several possibilities to tackle this problem will be discussed in section 5.4.2. *Thirdly*, due to the technical features of the plant, it is only possible to treat waste without any biological components in it. This means that Düren has to collect and treat biological waste separately because any pollution of the normal waste with biological ingredients creates serious technical problems in the treatment plant. Section 5.4.3 shows the organisational problems of this technical requirement.

The tackling of these newly emerged problems would necessitate a change in the course of action for Düren. Co-operation with other neighbouring communities would relieve Düren of many problems. From the decision making process observed so far, one can identify factors that might facilitate the adjustment of the chosen course of action as well as potential obstacles to learning from experience. Dürens adaptation might be facilitated by the fact that the strategy of co-operation, which might lead to a technically sound solution at the regional level, has already been outlined and prepared by the administration. Furthermore, one can hypothesise that, due to the decisions already made, a considerable amount of uncertainty and ambiguity of the decision situation is already reduced. The burdens in terms of risk for follow-up decisions might not be that high.

On the other hand, the possible obstacles to learning from experience in Düren are the following. Firstly, the political part of the organisation has committed itself to the rejection of waste incineration technology. This strong commitment, that initially concentrated on Düren itself, was reinforced during the decision making process and now applies to the use of this technology in general. A contract with the waste incinerating plant in Aachen, that would be part of any regional co-operation, would not fit with this political position. Secondly, since different political levels judge the results of Dürens decisions differently, the environmental feedback about success or failure is ambiguous. This does not allow a clear evaluation of the decision outcomes. Without an attribution of decision outcomes as failure, an important precondition of organisational learning is missing (March / Olsen 1995; Henrich 1998). The possibilities of Düren to learn from its experiences will be discussed in the conclusions of the present chapter.

5.4.1 An Ill-Sized Waste Treatment Plant

With its risk-taking strategy of building a waste treatment plant by ignoring much of the relevant information, the community of Düren ran into exactly the same problems that almost all administrative decision makers in German waste management try to avoid: they constructed a waste treatment plant that does not run to capacity. In general, there are two possibilities to tackle this problem: one can heighten the waste charges, or one can try to let other communities treat their waste in the respective plant.

The main reasons for this negative decision outcome are the following: First of all, like all other German communities Düren suffers the effects of the legal developments in waste management in recent years. The result of these efforts (described in detail in chapter 3) is the dramatic **decrease in the amount of waste that is to be treated and disposed of by the** communities. This general development could not be anticipated by the decision makers in Düren.

The second main reason for the ill-sized waste treatment plant is, however, specific to the situation in Düren. The institutional arrangement in which the development and construction of the treatment plant took place was characterised by unclear and ambiguous mechanisms of risk attribution. On the one hand, the DDG was fully responsible for the size of the plant (Interview administration, November 1995). This meant that the contract between the DDG and Düren contained a fixed price for the treatment of the waste. Due to this allocation of the risk with the DDG, the private enterprise took control over the planning process and relied on the expertise of an engineering office that is a subsidiary company of the same company as the DDG, Trieneckens. Politics and administration of Düren had thus no influence on the sizing of the plant.

However, in a parallel development, the community of Düren tried to gain more control over the processes and structures in the DDG (Interview administration, October 1995). The result of these efforts was the participation of Düren as a partner in the DDG. Düren now holds 25,1% of the DDG. This means that by now the community must also take care of the problem of the ill-sized waste treatment plant. The risk lies with the community as well. The tackling of this classical waste management problem creates conflicts in Düren. Particularly, between administration and politics there are different opinions about the appropriate reaction to the problem.

In order to avoid an increase of the local waste charges, the *administration* of Düren developed a strategy, that was supposed to allow other communities to use the waste treatment plant as well. The plan was to treat the waste of the neighbouring community of Heinsberg in the plant of Düren. Furthermore, the waste of Heinsberg and Düren was supposed to be incinerated after the bio-mechanical treatment in Düren. This incineration was supposed to take place in the incinerating plant of Aachen.

With this co-operative strategy, Düren would not only resolve its own problem of a waste treatment plant not running to capacity but also the other communities, especially Aachen, would achieve a technically more sound solution through a potential co-operation with Düren. Firstly, the incinerating plant in Aachen does not run to capacity either. Thus, the waste of Düren and Heinsberg would help Aachen to lower its waste charges or to avoid an increase of the charges. Secondly, the bio-mechanical pre-treatment of the waste increases its chemical quality and thus allows for better exploitation of the waste incineration technology (Interview administration, November 1995).

However, due to its inclusion of waste incineration, this proposed strategy of the administration is in conflict with the *political* consensus in Düren. This consensus was initially formed with respect to the project of a waste incinerating plant in Düren. However, during the process of decision making the consensus was reinforced and at the end applied to the use of the waste incineration technology in general. Thus, the political position of the community does not even allow the participation of Düren in the incinerating plant of a neighbouring community, as proposed by the administration (Herbold / Timmermeister / Vorwerk 1998).

The proposed strategy of the administration would also allow the problem that the current waste treatment system does not correspond to the legal requirements of the Technical Instruction for Household Waste to be tackled.

5.4.2 The Conflict with the Legal Requirements

With the decision to rely on the technology of bio-mechanical waste treatment, the community of Düren has placed itself in conflict with the present legal obligations regarding German waste management. The Technical Instruction for Household Waste requires waste incineration at the latest by the year 2005. Having ignored this requirement before the decision, Düren had to face it *after* the decision.

Generally speaking, Düren has two possibilities to achieve the legal appropriateness of its waste management system. The *first* possibility is the development of a co-operative approach together with other communities facing similar problems, as described in the previous section. The co-operation with neighbouring communities offers the possibility to develop a waste treatment concept that is sound and flexible at the regional level. The second possibility is created by political changes at higher political levels which may lead to a re-interpretation of the legal prescriptions.

Besides the political problems, the decisive question with the co-operative strategy is when the co-operation will start: before or after 2005. The beginning of the co-operation after 2005 would be politically more acceptable in Düren, since it would not imply an immediate participation in a waste incinerating plant. However, this approach would weaken the position of Düren because the potential partners by then will have different solutions to their problems. The strategy of co-operating before 2005 would thus be more sound technically, it creates however the political problems already described. Thus, the task for the administration is to balance the technical and political requirements of a possible co-operation with the neighbouring communities Heinsberg and Aachen.

Although the co-operation with neighbouring communities would not only solve the legal but also the financial problems Düren faces with its waste treatment plant (see above 5.4.1), due to surprising developments at higher political levels, another solution seems to be possible. By the beginning of 1998, the political change at the state level in 1995 begins to show effects on the waste policy of the state.

For the decision making process in Düren, this political change created an ambiguous situation. The technology of bio-mechanical waste treatment is strongly favoured by the green party in Germany. Therefore, the new green minister for the environment clearly supported the course of action chosen in Düren. However, the Administrative District Officer did not change his attitude and continued to put Düren under political pressure. Thus, the strange situation arose that the community was supported by the state government and attacked by the district administration (Interview administration, October 1995).

This ambiguous situation was more or less resolved in March 1998, when the environmental minister of Nordrhein-Westfalen published an official guideline for the interpretation of the Technical Instruction for Household Waste (MURL 1998). This guideline argued that the Technical Instruction as an administrative instruction has not the same strong binding effect as a legal act. Since the requirements of the technical instruction seriously affect the principle of local self-administration (cf. above, 3.2.1), the communities can choose freely how to fulfil the obligations of the instruction. In other words, it is not possible to prescribe the use of waste incineration technology with an administrative instruction. This argumentation leads the guideline of the minister to the conclusion that the bio-mechanical treatment of the waste can be sufficient and that waste incineration is not obligatory.

For Düren, this means that the chosen course of action may be sustainable in the long run. In its most recent Waste Management Concept (Abfallwirtschaftskonzept, Kreis Düren 1997), the community proposes the following strategy to minimise the conflict with the Technical Instruction for Household Waste. Düren wants to apply for a exceptional permission according to clause 2.4 of the Technical Instruction for Household Waste (cf. above 3.3.2). Due to the newly emerged political support from the state level, this strategy may lead to positive results.

Put in the context of the whole decision making process, this surprising possibility has advantages and disadvantages. On the one hand, the reliance on the political support from the state and the clause 2.4 of the Technical Instruction for Household Waste, allow Düren to solve the problem of legal inappropriateness without conflicts at the local level. The alternative, the initiation of a co-operation with the waste incinerating plant in Aachen, would be in conflict with the political consensus in the community. On the other hand, the strategy of co-operation seems to be technically very sound, since it would also resolve the problem that the plant in Düren is ill-sized. Furthermore, the co-operation of the communities of Heinsberg, Aachen, and Düren, described in section 5.4.1, would also contribute to an appropriate solution to the waste treatment problem at the regional level. The political signal from the state level, however, discourages the initiation of the co-operation. Düren now has political support for its strategy to treat the waste exclusively with bio-mechanical technology. This is likely to reinforce the commitment of the local politicians to this position. The adaptation of Düren to the technical requirements is therefore hindered by political factors, learning may not take place.

The conflict with the legal prescriptions of the Technical Instruction for Household Waste, one of the main consequences of the decisions made in Düren, seems to diminish by unforeseeable political developments at the state level. This means that the way of making the decisions in Düren, decision making by ignorance, may lead to a success in the long run. Although in this special case this new situation came about by chance, this is an interesting result. Due to the surprising political developments at the state level the unorthodox course of action of Düren seems to be rewarded.

5.4.3 Technical and Organisational Problems with Biological Waste

The operation of the bio-mechanical waste treatment plant in Düren causes further problems which are created by the technical features of the plant. In order to operate without technical disturbance, the plant can only treat waste without any biological or organic components. This means that the biological waste has to be collected and treated separately. Although in the long run this is a legal requirement for all communities in Germany, the pressure for Düren to achieve the goal of separate collection and treatment of biological waste is very high due to the technical problems in the bio-mechanical treatment plant. Moreover, the difficulties of tackling the problem have their roots in the organisational structure of waste management in Düren. The responsibility for the collection of biological waste does not lie with the community of Düren but with the municipalities. This means that the community has little influence on the effective collection of the biological waste (Herbold / Timmermeister / Vorwerk 1998).

The other problem is the construction of a composting plant in Düren. The community has difficulties in finding an appropriate location. Furthermore, there are conflicts with the DDG about the participation of the community in the planning and operation of the plant. The DDG wants to plan and to run the plant on its own, the community wants more influence in the decisive technical and economic features of the plant.

These organisational problems hinder the resolution of the technical problems of the bio-mechanical plant in Düren.

5.5 Risk and Routines: Conclusions

Some of the relevant theoretical conclusions from the case of Düren have already been sketched above. In the following sections I will discuss them in further detail. This will be done against the background of the important aspects of organisational decision making under risk: uncertainty, responsibility, and ambiguity. Furthermore, the case highlights some problems of organisational learning from experience.

First of all, the case of Düren shows a peculiar way of uncertainty absorption. It seems to be a classical case of matching an old routine with a new decision situation. In this case we see the importance of this way of decision making for the taking of risks (5.5.1). The institutional precondition that allowed Düren to absorb high loads of uncertainty - the close co-operation with Trieneckens - provided also for the allocation of responsibility in the process of risk taking (5.5.2). As regards the problem of ambiguity, I argue that the conflict between the community of Düren and the district administration has provided for a stable definition of the situation. The definition of the planning process as a conflict with a higher political level meant a further simplification of the decision making process. A second important aspect of this development was the formation of a political consensus in Düren that waste incineration would be unacceptable for the community (5.5.3). Since the risk taking strategy of Düren has led to negative decision outcomes, the community now is forced to adjust its course of action, to learn from experience. In section 5.5.4, I discuss the possibilities of Düren to learn from past experiences.

5.5.1 Absorption of Uncertainty

In the theoretical introduction of this study, I stressed the importance of uncertainty absorption as a precondition for organisational decision making under risk. If a decision is burdened with too much uncertainty, the decision itself has to absorb too much uncertainty. The burdening with too much uncertainty has been identified as one of the most crucial factors that can block the decision making process in an organisation (cf. above, chapter 2). Therefore the uncertainty has to be absorbed to a certain extent *before* the decision. This uncertainty absorption takes place by institutional mechanisms that have been called decision premises. For the case of Düren one can say that the organisation reacted to the uncertainty, imposed on it by external legal demands, by relying on established routines, that had been developed for different decision situations.

The argument that organisations act and decide according to established rules of appropriateness is right in the centre of institutional analyses of decision making in political organisations (March and Olsen 1989; 1995). However, this has not been interpreted as an organisational strategy of coping with problems of risk. The case of Düren shows how the matching of an existing decision making routine with a new and ambiguous situation can absorb uncertainty and thus allows the organisation to take a risk. This way of making a choice is in contradiction with the prescriptions of classical theories of rational decision making, since absorption of uncertainty in this case meant the ignoring of relevant and central information.

To put it briefly, Düren matched the old routine of constructing and running a landfill site to the new task of constructing a waste treatment plant. The landfill site of the community was run by the private company Trieneckens and for the planning of a waste treatment system, the decision makers relied on this established co-operation.

In this case the uncertainty was mainly absorbed by the fact that the project initially was only meant to improve the technical quality of the landfill site. Only step by step and against the background of the pressure exerted by the district administration, was the bio-mechanical waste treatment plant seen as a potential alternative to the technology of waste incineration. When the alternative had become clear, the project was already pushed so far that it was impossible to stop.

In fact, the decision making process in Düren shows some traits of the famous garbage can model developed by Cohen et al. (1972). In an ambiguous situation the organisation developed a technical solution, that at a certain point in time was matched with an emerging problem. Thus, we cannot observe a rational search for solution to an existing problem. Due to the partial irrationality of this decision making process, the organisation did not consider all relevant information for the task and was thus able to absorb uncertainty.

It is difficult to identify whether the reliance of Düren on the co-operation with Trieneckens was motivated by a real trust in the expertise of the company, or whether Düren does not have the resources to change the partner, i.e. whether Düren is in a relationship of dependence with Trieneckens. For the effect of this established relationship on the decision making process in Düren, this does not make a difference. What is important, is the fact that this stable partnership absorbed the main part of the uncertainty that is connected with a decision for a waste treatment plant.

The institutional absorption of uncertainty by co-operation is closely interconnected with a certain mode of allocating the responsibility between the two partners. In the next section, I argue that this allocation of responsibility was very important for the risk taking course of action of Düren.

5.5.2 The Allocation of Responsibility

Once Düren had relied on Trieneckens for the development of the bio-mechanical waste treatment plant, the planning process was pushed forward mainly by an engineering office which is a subsidiary of Trieneckens. It is quite obvious that this engineering office had a substantial interest in the development of the plant and in the collection of technical experience with this rather new technology.

Since Trieneckens and their engineering office had this strong interest in the development of the plant, the allocation of costs, and of accountability for failures, was not regulated very clearly. Trieneckens was willing to push forward the planning process without allocating all the financial burdens to the community. Trieneckens invested expertise and financial resources in this project in order to gain more technical experience in the technology of bio-mechanical waste treatment.

A second important aspect in this context was the contract between Düren and Trieneckens that allocated the responsibility for an ill-sized plant almost exclusively with Trieneckens. This meant that Düren was guaranteed a fixed price for the treatment of the waste. Thus, the community could be sure that any failure in the planning process would have no immediate effects on its charge budget.

The relieving effect of this mode of allocating the responsibility for failures was, however, slightly undermined by the efforts of the politicians of Düren to gain more control over the decision making processes of the DDG. In order to gain this control, the community demanded the possibility to become a partner in the DDG. Thus, Düren now holds 25.1% of the DDG. Düren is therefore burdened by the financial effects of the ill-sized waste treatment plant. However, when Düren gained access to the DDG, the decision to build the plant was already made. Therefore we can assume that the specific allocation of the responsibility to the private partner relieved the decision to build the plant significantly. Together with the uncertainty absorbing effect of relying on the technical expertise of Trieneckens described above, the main obstacles for organisational risk taking, uncertainty and responsibility, were reduced to a considerable degree. This can explain the taking of risk which can be observed in the case of Düren.

5.5.3 The Reduction of Ambiguity

For the community of Düren, as for all German communities that have to fulfil the task of establishing a waste management system, the decision situation was highly ambiguous. Due to some peculiar developments in Düren, this ambiguity was reduced. This led to a stable definition of the situation and of the role that Düren had to take in this situation. The reduction of the ambiguity was provided by the *consensus* at the community level and by the *conflict* with the higher political levels.

The first important aspect in this context is the political consensus that was formed in Düren. According to this consensus, all political parties rejected the option of waste incineration as a solution to the waste management problems of Düren. The starting point for the building of this consensus were the local elections in 1989. These elections led to the loss of the majority for the conservative party that had supported the project of waste incineration in Düren very actively. Thus, the loss of the majority was ascribed to the support of the waste incineration project. Step by step this led to the development of the consensus against any form of waste incineration in Düren.

The politicians of Düren thus had very clear preferences with respect to the question of waste treatment. For the administration of the community, this created contradictory demands. On the one hand, it was necessary to prepare the community for the possible necessity to incinerate its waste, i.e. to give in to the pressure from the district administration. On the other hand, any action in this direction was interpreted as administrative action without political mandate at the local level.

As already noted above, the political consensus at the local level was reinforced by the strong political pressure exerted by the higher political level, the district administration. The constant demands of the Administrative District Officer to participate in the regional planning process for waste incinerating plants met the emerging consensus at the local level and reinforced it. The reinforcement of group coherence by conflicts with external opponents is a well acknowledged fact of conflict sociology (Coser 1956). By the conflict with a higher administrative level the already emerged political consensus in Düren was reinforced and thus the decision to build a bio-mechanical waste treatment plant gained further support. The interpretation of the situation as a political conflict with the district administration was facilitated by the strong personal commitment of the Administrative District Officer.

The emergence of the strong conflict with the district administration had another relieving effect with respect to the decision situation. Luhmann (1988: 299) notes that conflicts can have the effect of reducing decision pressure. If decision makers find themselves in a situation with multiple behavioural expectations that exert contradictory action pressure, the decision makers can gain prestige and can simplify the situation by selecting conflicts: they decide against one expectation, create a conflict and thus make the other expectations less important - at least for external observers. This simplification of the situation by selecting one conflict can have a strong relieving effect in situations characterised by complex and multiple behavioural expectations.

Conflicts can reduce complex situations to a simple dual structure: The confrontation between the Administrative District Officer and the community led to the impression that the waste management policy of Düren only consisted in the conflict with the district administration. This reduced the ambiguity of the situation. General sociological theory points to this complexity reducing effect of conflicts. Conflicts can be interpreted as highly integrated social systems that reduce any action to a reaction towards the opponent. All other references of the action are cut. Conflicts are highly interdependent internally, and highly inconsiderate towards their environment (Luhmann 1995: 388pp.).

For the decision situation in Düren this had the implication that the alternatives were reduced significantly: the question was whether to give in or to resist. Thus, the situation was not burdened by complicated calculations about the necessity of a waste treatment plant and about its size. The Administrative District Officer prescribed all these decisive issues and it was easy to present experts' reports that proved the weakness of these prescriptions. The option of *concurring* behaviour was thus not very attractive. The consensus in Düren and the emerging decision alternative to rely exclusively on bio-mechanical waste treatment finally led to the choice of *deviant* behaviour and Düren decided to build a waste treatment plant on its own.

The reduction of the complex decision situation to a simple conflict was a major contribution to the decision making process in Düren. Together with the strong political consensus at the local level this led to a clear definition of the situation: the ambiguities about identity and preferences were reduced, the organisation was able to decide.

5.5.4 Learning from Experience

The fact that Düren, in its decision to build a waste treatment plant, did not consider all relevant information led to a decision outcome that was only provisional. It was clear that the solution in Düren would not be the final one. The decision to build the bio-mechanical waste treatment plant produced consequences that led to new decision pressure for the community. This decision pressure implies the expectation to learn from the results of past decisions. The literature on organisational learning describes the possibilities of adapting organisational courses of action in the face of negative decision outcomes. With the discrediting of anticipatory rationality, the requirement of adaptive rationality has become one of the most prominent topics in organisation theory, both as an analytical tool and as a normative prescription (Levitt / March 1988; March / Olsen 1995; Olsen / Peters 1995). Especially in the debate about organisational risk taking, the capabilities of organisations to learn from the consequences of risky decisions are of great interest (Morone / Woodhouse 1986; Japp 1992; Sagan 1993).

For the case of Düren, I identified three main consequences of the decision to build a bio-mechanical waste treatment plant (cf. above, 5.4): the plant does not run to capacity and thus is likely to create financial problems; whether the plant is sufficient with respect to the legal prescriptions is ambiguous; the plant creates technical and organisational problems since the separate collection and treatment of biological waste is the precondition for the sound functioning of the plant. Can Düren learn from these consequences?

Some features of the decision making process seem to hint at a capability to learn. Since the first decisions already absorbed a high amount of uncertainty, the follow-up decisions are not overburdened by uncertainty. The decision situation is characterised by less uncertainty and less ambiguity. Thus, the situation in Düren after the building of the bio-mechanical waste treatment plant shows some advantageous features. First of all, during the conflicts with the district administration Düren has formed a certain identity with respect to waste management issues. Düren has taken over the role of an innovator. The plant in Düren is at the centre of attention since it is one of the first bio-mechanical waste treatment plants in Germany. The identity and the interests of Düren were formed during the decision making process. The decision itself was made without any clear preferences. The decision makers of the community made a decision, observed the consequences and the reaction of other observers and then knew what they had done (cf. Weick 1979). Ambiguities with respect to their own preferences and external reactions to their decisions have been reduced. Düren has developed new routines and new assumptions about cause-and-effect-relationships and has thus improved its ability to make further uncertainty absorbing decisions.

These institutional results of the decision making process reduce the burdens of future decisions. Furthermore, the external consequences of the course of action in Düren lead to lower uncertainty. The community by now has clear tasks - the organising of the collection and treatment of biological waste, and the solution to the problem that the plant is ill-sized - that leave few alternatives. The uncertainty that has to be absorbed with future decisions is not as high as with the initial decisions.

On the other hand, there are prominent factors that inhibit the ability of the organisation to adjust its course of action. First of all, one of the most important preconditions for organisational learning is missing: there is no clear and unambiguous signal for a failure. This is true for the requirements to solve the financial and legal problems of the waste treatment plant. Due to the political changes at the state level some of the negative consequences - the lacking compliance with the legal requirements - seem to be re-evaluated. They might turn into positive consequences since the waste management concept of Düren - according to the new guideline of the minister of the environment of Nordrhein-Westfalen (MURL 1998) - fulfils the requirement of an ecological waste treatment. However, this political support does not guarantee the success of Düren, since it is unclear to which extent the implementation of the federal waste policy can be influenced by state governments. The ambiguity about the evaluation of the legal fit of the technical arrangement in Düren is heightened by the fact that the district administration, which is responsible for the permission of the waste management concept of Düren, continues to interpret the federal waste policy in a strict manner.

Thus, the evaluation of the legal consequences of the decisions of Düren is ambiguous. This might inhibit the capability of the organisation to solve the other problem of the waste treatment plant: The plant is not running to capacity. In order to avoid financial burdens for the citizens of the community, it would therefore be necessary to co-operate with neighbouring communities and to participate in the operation of the waste incinerating plant of Aachen. The probability that Düren will be willing to co-operate with Aachen is quite low, since the political part of the community has committed itself very clearly to the position of avoiding waste incineration in any form. This political commitment, which has been identified as one of the important institutional preconditions for the decision outcome in Düren, has been reinforced during the decision making process. This structure enabled Düren to make risky decisions, but at the same time might block the ability to learn. This effect would be in accordance with findings that decisions tend to be self-reinforcing (Japp 1992): The uncertainty absorbing premises a decision is based on immunise the decision against negative feedback.

These institutional obstacles to organisational learning in Düren may explain the fact that the community, despite the organisational problems caused by its decisions, shows tendencies of sticking to its chosen course of action. Düren therefore is trying to get an exceptional permission for its waste treatment concept according to clause 2.4 of the Technical Instruction for Household Waste. With this course of action, the probability of a regional co-operation, which would solve Düren's financial problems as well, is reduced. The lock-in effect of the institutional mode of uncertainty absorption seems to be too strong. Organisational learning becomes difficult under these conditions.

The case of Düren shows how an organisation absorbs uncertainty, re-allocates responsibility, and reduces ambiguity, by relying on institutionalised routines. This way of absorbing uncertainty does not only hinder the possibilities of anticipatory rationality *before* the decision. Additionally, the uncertainty absorption has effects on the period *after* the decision, when the organisation is expected to learn from the consequences of the decision. Learning in this case would mean the questioning of the taken-for-granted assumptions that were the basis for the decision. Especially in situations characterised by strong political conflicts, this questioning of one's own premises seems to be difficult.

6 Summary and Conclusions

The risk taking behaviour of organisations is a function of institutional preconditions. The institutional equipment of an organisation, introduced in the second chapter as decision premises, absorbs uncertainty and allocates responsibility, and thus is a major determinant of organisations' capability to handle risks. This is the result of the theoretical and empirical investigations of this study. The present chapter is dedicated to the concluding presentation of these results. Furthermore, I will try to connect the findings of the study to related problems. Firstly, from the conclusion that institutionalised routines govern the decision making, and thus risk taking behaviour of organisations, follows the question of how organisational routines are formed and changed. These problems are addressed in the literature on organisational learning. Secondly, the findings about the mechanisms of decision making under risk in organisations call for an analysis of the contribution of organisations to risk taking at the societal level.

This concluding chapter will be organised as follows. First, I will give a summary of the theoretical basis (6.1) and the empirical findings (6.2) of the study. Then I will outline the implications of the theoretical and empirical results for the question of how organisations can react to consequences of their own decisions. This will lead to conclusions about how organisations can achieve flexibility in decision making, and learning, under risk (6.3). Finally, I will sketch the implications of the findings about organisational decision making for processes of risk taking and avoiding at the societal level (6.4).

6.1 Risk, Decisions, and Organisations

The starting point for the theoretical considerations is the argument that concepts of risk that are rooted in economic theory cannot be a guide for empirical sociological research about risk taking behaviour. Knight (1921) defines risk as calculable uncertainty and thus distinguishes it from pure uncertainty which cannot be calculated by the decision maker. From a sociological perspective, the main criticism of this conceptualisation can be summarised as follows: First, if risk denotes decision situations in which the decision maker can work out probabilistic calculations about the occurrence of future events, almost no empirical situation fulfils the requirements of this definition. It would therefore be difficult to explain, why risk has become such a prominent topic in social and political conflicts. Second, the basic assumptions of a rational actor with preferences, who is facing alternatives, do not allow the analysis of the issues that would interest a sociological inquiry: how do situations of risk come about? Under which conditions will decision makers be confronted with the expectation to choose from alternatives and to do this in a rational, calculated manner?

Thus, a sociological analysis cannot depart from the economic tradition. The basis for a sociological concept of decision making under risk can be demonstrated by examining the two basic terms, decision making (6.1.1), and risk (6.1.2). In order to analyse organisational decision making under risk, these general concepts have to be applied to the specific structural conditions of organised social systems (6.1.3).

6.1.1 Decisions in a Sociological Perspective

The economic tradition argues that one can speak of a decision if an actor is equipped with preferences and faces a range of alternatives, out of which he chooses the one that serves his preferences best. The theory assumes that this is done by anticipatory calculation of the possible consequences of each alternative. The research question is then the degree of rationality - defined as the relation between the decision maker's preferences and the chosen alternative - that is achieved by the decision (cf. March 1994: 1pp.).

This concept has been questioned, particularly by empirical research on decision making processes in organisations. March and Simon (1958) argue that there are serious cognitive limits on rationality. Since the decision maker normally will not be able to consider all available alternatives and to estimate all consequences, one can only speak of bounded rationality instead of perfect rationality. The degree of rationality - which is still the centre of interest - can only be judged by the analysis of the structural context in which the decision takes place. These assumptions introduce some real world conditions into the economic theory of decision making. They are, however, still compatible with the economic model: A rational actor chooses alternatives according to his preferences.

March and Olsen (1976) take an important step further toward a sociological perspective on decision making. Their central argument is that decisions very often will take place under conditions of ambiguity. Ambiguity refers to incomplete knowledge of cause-and-effect relationships, unclear rules about the participation of decision makers in decisions, and unstable attention of decision makers to decisions. *Ambiguity de-couples decisions from preferences*: Since decisions take place without constant attention of individual decision makers, and since the decision makers do not know which actions lead to which outcomes, one cannot explain observable decisions by the calculation of consequences and their evaluation according to the decision maker's preferences.

Although March and Olsen de-construct the concept of preferences as the basic term of a decision theory, they do not offer a substitute. They formulate, however, requirements for a theory of decision making that is not based exclusively on preferences. March and Olsen (1976: 22) call for analyses of how organisations make choices even in cases of ambiguity; they state the necessity of analysing processes of allocation of attention; and they argue for a theory of learning, i.e. a theory of how decision makers develop stable causal assumptions about the organisation and its environment.

In later publications, March and Olsen (1989; 1995) argue that these preconditions for decisions are provided by institutions. Institutions - like organisational structures, procedures, role expectations, and rules of appropriateness - structure the decision situation for the decision maker, they allocate his attention, and enable him to learn from past decision outcomes (March / Olsen 1995). March and Olsen argue that decisions do not take place by calculating future consequences and evaluating them on the basis of preferences ('logic of consequences'). Instead, decisions are made according to a 'logic of appropriateness': Decision situations are matched with existing organisational rules and routines that are considered appropriate for the respective task. What is appropriate is determined by the institutions that structure the decision. Preferences are substituted by institutions as the basic concept of a theory of decision making.

If institutions are to substitute preferences in decision theory, their function must be *constitutive* instead of *regulatory* (Scott / Meyer 1994). In this perspective, institutions do not only provide the frame for actors and their preferences, but they *construct* the actors. This constitutive function of institutions can be conceptualised on the basis of a structure-event-theory of social systems (Allport 1962; Katz / Kahn 1966; Luhmann 1995).

In such a theory, actions are selective, time binding events that are connected by expectations (Luhmann 1981). If expectations are themselves expected, they can serve as a structure for action. On this basis, one can say that decisions are generated if an expectation is directed explicitly towards an action. If an action is observed as a reaction towards an expectation, the alternative of concurring or deviant behaviour occurs and a decision has to be made (Luhmann 1988). This situation is reinforced if several, and maybe contradictory, expectations have to be taken into account by the action.

Thus, decisions are no longer defined by the fact that they take place on the basis of preferences. One can speak of decisions, if actions refer explicitly to behavioural expectations. Within such a conception, one can account for decisions that take place without preferences, or even against given preferences. Furthermore, such a theory can analyse the often observed phenomenon that decisions are rationalised ex post, i.e. that the decision makers present preferences in order to justify their choice *after* the choice. Finally, within such a framework one can see how decisions are constructed afterwards.

The basic research question for a sociological theory of decision making can thus no longer be that of rationality. The basis for this question, the notion of preferences, is no longer in the central theoretical position. The first important question for an analysis working with the expectation-based concept of decision is: How do decision situations occur? By which structures is the decision pressure directed to the action? Furthermore, one must ask how the decision situation - in terms of the expectations to be fulfilled - can be characterised. For the decision maker, the main problem is not to choose the optimal or a satisfying alternative, but to get rid of the pressure, to be able to justify his behaviour as a decision (Luhmann 1988), and to keep his identity as a decision maker (March / Olsen 1995). Generally speaking, the problem is one of establishing expectational certainty under conditions of selectivity and contingency.

On the basis of these considerations concerning the general concept of decision, Luhmann (1990a; 1993a) has developed a theory of risk that accounts for the structural developments in society that lead to the occurrence of situations in which risky decisions have to be made.

6.1.2 Risk in a Sociological Perspective

Efforts to develop sociological theories of risk have been undertaken in order to explain the ongoing social conflicts that are centred around the potential hazards of complex technologies. The most prominent and important contributions have been made by Douglas and Wildavsky (1982) and Beck (1986). Another sociological suggestion for a theory of risk was put forward by Luhmann (1990a; 1993a). Luhmann starts with a definition of risk as a potential future damage that is attributed to a decision. Thus, risk is distinguished from danger, which refers to possible damages that are not perceived as consequences of one's own decisions. The *first* important effect of this approach is the abstraction from conflicts about risky technologies. Risk is something that is connected with decision making in general. *Second*, it becomes clear that risk is no objective fact, but something that is socially constructed by processes of attribution. *Third*, on the basis of the above sketched expectation-based concept of decision, one can analyse how situations of risk emerge. If decision makers are confronted with expectations of making decisions about the future, and if the outcomes of these decisions are uncertain, one can speak of risk.

The problem of risk thus consists in the necessity to commit oneself to a decision in the face of an uncertain future. This is considered a case of time binding, thus all the problems connected with time binding are relevant for risky decisions as well (cf. chapter 1). First, the commitment to a course of action is likely to lead to surprises, since the future cannot be anticipated and there are millions of parallel decisions happening. Second, risky decisions carry the message of contingency, since they are selections from alternatives. Thus, this selection can be questioned. This leads to problems of acceptance. These problems are reinforced by the *third* problem connected with time binding: risky decisions create people affected. The people affected by the potential consequences of risky decisions will conceive of these consequences in a different way than the decision makers, since they are not under the same decision pressure. To generate expectations of certainty under these conditions is the central problem in decision making under risk.

The most important issue for such a theory of risk is the emergence of risk situations. Why are surprising events attributed to decisions? For the societal level, Luhmann argues that due to the changing semantic of time in modern society the future is no longer determined by the past. The future can be shaped. This led to a semantic of progress, and then, in the face negative outcomes, to the semantic of risk. As a result, negative events in the present are ascribed to past decisions, and present decisions are expected to do something about it. They are supposed to bring about positive effects without too many negative side effects.

Organisations are right at the centre of this structural development. Organisations are the classical addressee for social expectations to make decisions and thus get under increasing decision pressure in the risk society. It is thus of crucial importance to get an idea of how the social expectations directed *towards* organisation are transformed into expectations *within* organisations. How are organisations structured in terms of behavioural expectations? What does their structure imply for their possibilities to handle risks? Answers to these questions will be discussed in the next section, that brings us directly to the main topic of this study, decision making under risk in organisations.

6.1.3 Organisational Decision Making under Risk

The arguments so far imply that decisions take place on the basis of behavioural expectations and that risk situations arise when future consequences are attributed to present decisions. In order to clarify how situations of risk in organisations come about, it is therefore necessary to apply these general concepts to organisations. This will be done with the concept of *decision premises*. Decision premises are the behavioural expectations that are relevant in organisations. They structure the organisational activities, they create situations of decision, they prescribe what has to be taken for granted in the decision, and they direct the organisational attention. The second important aspect of the framework is indicated by the notion of responsibility. The attribution of future events to present decisions takes place if an organisation is *responsible* for the bringing about of future consequences. Responsibility creates risks for organisations.

The central and basic notion of such a theory of organisations is that of *uncertainty absorption by decisions* (Luhmann 2000). The concept of uncertainty absorption goes back to March and Simon (1958). It refers to the connecting of decisions: A decision 'A' draws inferences from given information and communicates only this inference, instead of the underlying information. A decision 'B', that is made on the basis of 'A', takes this inference for granted and does not examine the correctness of the information processing that 'A' was based upon. By this mechanism, the uncertainty under which 'A' was made is *absorbed*. By absorbing uncertainty, the organisation constructs expectations of certainty in an uncertain world.

This function of uncertainty absorption can be fulfilled in a processual manner, by connecting decisions with decisions, or it can be fulfilled on a structural basis, by decision premises. Decision premises are the behavioural expectations that structure the decision making activity of organisations. Decision premises are behavioural expectations that are formalised, because their fulfilment is the precondition for getting and maintaining the membership in organisations. They are institutionalised, because it can be assumed that they are acknowledged throughout the organisation. Finally, they are generalised, because they are valid for more than one decision situation.

Luhmann (1976; 2000) distinguishes three types of decision premises: *Programmes* fix the conditions for correctness of a decision, for its success and failure. *Channels of communication* fix the rules of participation, i.e. which positions of the organisation have to contribute to the decision and with which competencies. The *personnel* as a decision premise provides for individual motivation and skills that are necessary to make organisational decisions. These premises thus provide the structural context for decisions, they fix what can be taken for granted, and what has to be questioned, when making a decision.

For risk problems, the programmes of the organisation play a crucial role. Programmes can take the form of conditional, or of goal programmes. If it is programmed on a *conditional* basis, the organisations has to apply given norms and rules to situations: *if* a certain situation is given, *then* a prescribed decision has to be made. A conditional programme does not impose risks on the organisation, because it is only responsible for the correct application rules, and not for the consequences. The responsibility for the consequences lies with the level that made the programme. A *goal* programme fixes a goal that has to be achieved by the decision. This way of programming a decision does create risks, because the organisation has to take responsibility for the occurrence of the desired consequences of the decision, and because this occurrence will normally be uncertain. This responsibility for the occurrence of uncertain future events is a risk as defined by the general sociological theory of the risk society: future events are attributed to decisions to be made in the present.

Thus, risks for organisations are created by programmes. The possibilities of organisations to handle these risks is restricted and made possible by all three types of decision premises. If the risks imposed on the organisation are too high in terms of uncertainty and responsibility, then uncertainty has to absorbed, and responsibility to be reduced, by the structure of the organisation. The external expectations directed to the organisation are transformed in internal premises that can structure the decision making behaviour of the organisation. The organisation develops rules of appropriateness that fix criteria of acceptable outcomes (programmes), it can reduce or extend the network of participating positions (channels of communication), or it can rely on personal skills and motivation for the absorption of uncertainty and the re-allocation of responsibility (personnel). Such structural responses to risks will also be necessary if the given decision premises are ambiguous and contradictory, i.e. if they do not impose clear expectations on the decision making behaviour of the organisation. In accordance with the general framework used here, these organisational reactions to ambiguous and contradictory expectations are seen as efforts to generate expectational certainty in the face of high decision pressure.

The institutional responses of organisations to situations that are characterised by uncertainty, responsibility, and ambiguity were to be analysed in this study. To address these issues, I conducted two qualitative case studies that examine planning processes of local administration bodies in Germany. The administrative decision makers in these cases were confronted with the task to plan and construct facilities for the treatment of household waste. In the following sections, I will summarise the results of the case studies. Section 6.2.1 will sketch the general structural context for the decision making processes at the local level, mainly provided by the German federal waste policy of recent years. The two case studies present two different ways of handling the risks connected with the implementation of this policy. The first case highlights opportunities and restrictions for a strategy that stresses citizens' participation and anticipatory analysis (6.2.2). The second case presents an organisation that relies on established rules of appropriateness to handle the new and ambiguous situation of planning a waste treatment plant (6.2.3).

6.2 Decision Making under Risk in Organisations: Empirical Findings

I will now turn to a brief summary of the empirical results of the study. The presentation of the case studies will be preceded by a summary of the decision situation in which local administrations in Germany find themselves. The federal waste policy creates a complicated mix of responsibilities, uncertainties, and ambiguities for the implementing organisations. These expectations directed towards local administration have to be outlined briefly before presenting the case studies.

6.2.1 The Structural Context: Waste Policy in Germany

The ecological dangers of household waste that call for political regulation start from the problems of depositing waste. Waste disposal sites are complicated bio-chemical systems, which cannot be predicted and analysed with known scientific methods. Their potential for chemical reactions is unpredictable because of their unknown composition; it changes over time; and every waste disposal site has its specific character. Thus, it is very difficult to control the gas and water emissions of waste disposal sites. The technical and organisational responses to these dangers are the following. Firstly, the technology for waste disposal sites becomes more sophisticated in order to minimise toxic emissions. Secondly, the waste is treated before it is deposited in order to reduce its potential chemical reactions. Finally, the different types of waste are collected separately and recycled in order to minimise the amount of waste that is to be deposited.

The German waste policy of recent years has concentrated on these issues. The diverse types of waste have to be collected separately and, if possible, recycled. The remaining waste has to be treated before it is put on the waste disposal sites. The waste disposal sites have to be equipped with the best available technology that minimises the risk of hazardous emissions. The responsibility for the effective implementation of all these requirements lies exclusively with the communities.

The important notion with respect to this responsibility is that of disposal safety (Entsorgungssicherheit). Disposal safety is achieved if the waste is collected, recycled, treated, and deposited according to the legal prescriptions. This requirement is a goal programme, since it can only be known in the future, whether the technical and organisational measures that have to be taken really lead to a waste management system that achieves disposal safety. A further heightening, or politicisation, of the responsibility for the communities is brought about by the prescription that all measures in waste management have to be financed by waste charges to be paid by the citizens of the respective community. This means that all failures in planning that result in higher costs lead to higher waste charges for the citizens and thus to intense political conflicts. Furthermore, this mode of financing counterbalances to a considerable extent the goal of disposal safety. Whereas long-term disposal safety suggests large waste treatment plants and disposal sites, the necessity of cost-efficiency requires plants and sites that run to capacity, since they create enormous fixed costs. Thus, to fulfil both goals, disposal safety and cost-efficiency, is extremely difficult. The communities are, however, *responsible* for the reaching of both.

For the correct sizing of plants and disposal sites, the decision makers need one central piece of information: How much waste will have to be treated? This information is highly uncertain, since due to the parallel efforts of avoiding and recycling waste, the amount of waste that is to be incinerated and deposited is in constant movement. Thus, the central information that is needed to fulfil the requirements of the goal programme 'disposal safety' is highly *uncertain*.

The central point for the decision making processes that have been analysed in this study is, however, the requirement to build waste incinerating plants. Household waste must be incinerated before it is deposited. This is a quite recent policy in Germany and puts the communities under pressure to make enormous long-term investments in high-tech waste treatment facilities. This has to take place under the above mentioned circumstances of responsibility and uncertainty. Further aspects of uncertainty and ambiguity are introduced by the special features of the policy that prescribes waste incineration.

Firstly, the technology of waste incineration suffers serious problems of acceptance in Germany. The risk of toxic emissions, the financial burdens that are created for the communities and their citizens, and its character as an end-of-pipe technology that hinders efforts to avoid and recycle waste, are the main arguments put forward against waste incineration. Thus the implementation of the federal waste policy leads to intensive political conflicts in the communities. Whether the decision makers manage to overcome the political and legal obstacles against planning processes for waste incinerating plants is *uncertain*. Secondly, the policy prescribing waste incineration contains elements of *ambiguity* concerning its implementation. The policy has to be implemented only by the year 2005, it contains the possibility of exceptions, and its interpretation differs between the political parties. A change in government at the state or federal level can lead to different requirements. This is of crucial importance, since the implementation period is very long. Thus, the policy imposes *ambiguous* demands on the local decision makers.

A final important point has to be made. The above mentioned requirements for local waste management have emerged only in recent years. The field of waste policy in Germany is characterised by rapidly growing complexity. As a result, many of the German communities do not have the experience necessary to fulfil the diverse, and partly contradictory, demands. In other words, they lack established routines that would allow them to transform the external expectations into internal decision premises that absorb uncertainty, re-allocate responsibility, and reduce ambiguity.

Put very briefly, these are the structural elements that provide the context for the case studies. The two cases show different approaches to handle these problems of responsibility, uncertainty, and ambiguity. The case studies focus on one decision problem: the planning of waste treatment plants. The other important aspects of establishing a functioning waste management system are left aside.

In the first case, the decision makers tried to analyse the situation and to reach consensus with the citizens about this analysis. This anticipatory analysis and consensus building was supposed to generate an institutional basis for the decisions about the waste treatment system in that region. By and large, these efforts failed. The second case presents a community that relied very much on its routines. An action pattern that had been developed for the planning of the waste disposal site was matched with the new task of constructing a waste treatment plant. The technical and legal results are not optimal. Thus, the question remains whether the decision makers in this case will be able to learn from experience.

6.2.2 Risk and Participation

The most striking characteristic of the first case examined is the almost complete lack of organisational routines that can be applied to the task of planning a waste treatment structure. Four communities initiated a co-operation to make this decision and founded a private company, with the four public authorities as exclusive partners. The four partners had different experiences in the field of waste management, and their co-operation was characterised by inconsistent expectations and interests. Since the organisation that was supposed to carry out the planning was a newly founded one, it suffered a lack of established routines that would have allowed it to absorb uncertainty and to come to feasible patterns of responsibility. The situation was ambiguous with respect to the organisation's premises and with respect to the connection between its own decisions and environmental events.

In this situation, characterised by high degrees of responsibility, uncertainty, and ambiguity, the respective organisation initiated a complex procedure of citizens' participation. The intention was to gain consensus with interest groups and citizens potentially affected about the following central points of the planning process: The expected amount of waste, the technology of waste treatment, and the location of the plant. These three issues were discussed in three phases of the participation. The result of each phase were the so-called citizens' reports, that were supposed to serve as a basis for the political decisions to be made. This means that there was no direct conflict resolution between decision makers and those affected, but the citizens took the role of advisors, thus being in direct competition with the technical experts that advised the decision makers as well.

The result of the participation was not very encouraging. The influence of the citizens' reports on the political decisions was ambiguous after each phase. This was mainly due to the fact that there were no real decisions made. No uncertainty was absorbed because the decision makers tried to keep open as many alternatives as possible. After the first phase, when the citizens' report had suggested a prognosis of the waste amount to be handled, which at that time seemed to be very optimistic, the political decision makers accepted this suggestion in their preliminary waste prognosis. However, this prognosis had to be changed afterwards, without reference to the contribution of the citizens. When the second citizens' report suggested, with a majority vote, the bio-mechanical treatment of the waste, whereas the minority of the participating interest groups voted in favour of waste incineration, the political decision was not to decide about this issue. After the last phase, the political decision departed very clearly from the report made by the citizens. This seemed to be comprehensible because in the meantime new information had appeared (a new technology of treating waste), that changed the basis for the decision. This new information could however not be taken into account by the citizens. And in the end, the political suggestion to share burdens between the four communities by relying on a combination of bio-mechanical treatment and waste incineration was not implemented and the regional co-operation ended: The newly founded private enterprise was broken up. The organisation did not survive its search for consensus and information. The four partners decided to look for solutions to the waste treatment problem on their own. This will very likely lead to contracts with existing waste incinerating plants, rather than to efforts to plan such facilities alone.

The conclusions from the theoretical perspective suggested in this study are the following. The methodological concept of the citizens' participation relied very much on anticipation, analysis, and consensus. The aim was to gain consensus about the central issues of the decision *before* the decision. The decision was supposed to be made on the basis of the consensus achieved, and the information collected. The participation thus did not only aim at more fairness in the procedure of decision making, but also at an improvement in the objective quality of the complex decision about a regional waste treatment concept. Fairness and competence was the goal (Renn et al. 1995).

This concept was based on the assumption that the problem for the decision was a lack of information. The events in the case show however, that available information was *ignored* on a regular basis. Rather, the problem consisted in the necessity to commit oneself to a course of action, although the relevant information was in constant movement. To make a decision under these circumstances means to assume certainty in an uncertain world. The ability to absorb uncertainty, and this is the lesson from the case, is not improved by procedural rationality.

Both my theoretical arguments and the sketch of the structural situation in German waste management suggest that the problems connected with the decision to be made were high loads of responsibility, massive uncertainty, and ambiguity about premises. My theoretical conclusion is therefore, that anticipatory analysis combined with the extended search for consensus, could not contribute to the solution to these problems. This can be explained in the context the three problems of the decision.

The *responsibility* connected with the decision could not be re-allocated. The main reason for this was the fact that the participating citizens' and interest group were pressure groups with a low degree of organisation and professionalisation. These groups rely, and depend, to a very large extent on the mobilisation of public opinion (Rucht 1994). Their capability to participate in political compromising - which would have been a precondition of taking a certain amount of responsibility - is rather restricted. By compromising these groups lose their clear media profile, which would lead to the loss of their main channel of political influence. On the side of the decision makers, the above mentioned fact that during the whole planning process no real decision was made led to the result that the responsibility could not be reduced step by step. The reference of the political decision makers to the contributions of the citizens' group was ambiguous throughout the period that has been analysed. Thus, a sharing of responsibility was not achieved.

The *uncertainty* about available alternatives and the occurrence of their consequences could not be absorbed. On the contrary, it was increased. This was due to the underlying concept of anticipation and analysis. The careful search for information and possible alternatives, together with the tendency of the decision makers to commit themselves to a choice as late as possible, led to a further burdening of the decision making process with uncertainty. The procedural rationality, that without any doubt was achieved by the citizens' participation, could not contribute to the solution to the uncertainty problem. Information increased uncertainty.

The *ambiguity* about premises could not be reduced. One aspect of the search for new information and the testing of new alternatives was the constant questioning of the premises of the decision, especially the Technical Instruction for Household Waste. There was dissent between the four partners about the goals of the decision (programmes), and the extension of the communication network by allowing for citizens' participation could not be established as stable way of communication within the organisation. Thus, the structural preconditions of the decision continued to be ambiguous, maybe the ambiguity was even increased by the complexity of the participation.

The main result of the first case study is thus the conclusion that concepts of anticipatory analysis and consensus building are not appropriate to the requirements of complex decisions under conditions of risk. The task of taking responsibility under ambiguous premises and in the face of uncertain information about the future, is not facilitated by more information. One could say that the organisation during the participatory procedure gained too realistic a picture of its environment, of the uncertainties, and the political resistance, connected with the decision. The organisation was too afraid of bad surprises. As a result, the decision makers expected failure, rather than success. This was no proper basis for the making of a risky decision.

6.2.3 Risk and Routines

Compared to the first case, the second one shows different institutional preconditions, and thus a different course of action, with different outcomes. The evaluation of success or failure of the decision makers in this case is not easy however. Since the organisation in the second case study made a decision, it was surprised by its consequences, and thus is subject to expectations to learn from its experiences, many important issues in organisational risk taking can be studied in this case.

To begin with, the community in the second case found itself in a different structural situation. This situation was mainly characterised by a close and successful partnership with a private disposal enterprise, and by the constant pressure exerted by the district administration to take action in favour of waste incineration.

The adversarial strategy of the district administration was part of a state policy that tried to implement federal waste policy very quickly. The core of this state policy was the shortening of the transitionary period for the implementation of waste incineration. Thus, the community was expected to construct a waste incinerating plant together with a private enterprise that was appointed by the district administration. The most important aspect to note in this context was the obvious uncertainty that was underlying these efforts to force the community to plan a waste incinerating plant. The district administration had to correct its waste prognosis very often. To counterbalance the uncertainties regarding this central information, the district administration proposed ever changing communities to participate in the planning of the facility. In sum, it became obvious that the information the hierarchical intervention was based upon was extremely uncertain. Since the community nevertheless would have had to take political responsibility for failures in the planning, the willingness to give in to the pressure from the district administration was very low. Finally, as an effect of the pressure from above and the political resistance in the community - that for the supporters of the project resulted in the loss of their political majority at the local level - the political parties in the community built a strong consensus against waste incineration as a solution to the problem of treating waste.

The refusal to decide in favour of the risky project of a waste incinerating plant was reinforced by the second important structural development in the community. Technical problems with the local landfill site had led to a project to redevelop it. With the financial resources of a private partner, and the scientific input of the Federal Agency for the Environment (Umweltbundesamt, UBA), the community redeveloped its landfill site. At the end of the project, it was clear that in order to keep the technical standard of the landfill site, the community had to treat the waste before depositing it. Step by step, it was then decided to build a bio-mechanical waste treatment plant. Against the background of the political and legal pressures exerted from the district administration, this suggestion became an alternative to the option of waste incineration. The community then relied on the expertise of its private partner, that already ran the landfill site, to plan and construct the waste treatment plant.

The uncertainty absorbing capacity of this institutional arrangement between the community and its private partner consisted of the following aspects. *First* of all, and most importantly, the decision to build the plant developed step by step and initially was not seen as an alternative to waste incineration. Thus, at the time when the important steps towards this decision were made, it was not connected with too many risks. It was seen as a technological completion of the landfill site. When the alternative arose to choose between the option of waste incineration and the bio-mechanical plant, the decision had already been taken very far. Uncertainties had already been absorbed, the last step was easy to make. *Second*, the responsibility for failures in the planning, especially in the sizing of the plant, were allocated with the private operator of the landfill site. The contract between the two partners contained a fixed price that the community had to pay for the treatment of its waste. Thus, for the political decision makers the main risk of the decision was allocated with the private partner. The operator of the landfill site was willing to take this risk because he had strong interests in the development of, and learning about, the bio-mechanical technology. *Finally*, the discussions about waste incineration had led to a definition of the situation as a sharp conflict between the community and the district administration. The reduction of the complexity and uncertainty of a planning process to a simple conflict relieved the community of expectations to calculate the decision. The public and political attention was absorbed by the conflicts with the district administration.

In this case, we see the steady interplay of uncertainty absorption and surprise: After having absorbed the risks of the decision by institutional mechanisms, the community had to face surprising consequences of the decision. The legal requirements were not met (although this was no surprise), the plant did not run to capacity, and the technical features of the plant require the separate collection and treatment of biological waste - an organisational precondition which causes many problems for the community. The interesting question is therefore, how the community can handle the surprising consequences of its own actions.

The possibility to adjust the chosen course of action in order to relieve the community of at least some of the negative consequences was identified by the administration of the community: it would be necessary and promising to initiate co-operation with neighbouring communities. This co-operation would imply the bio-mechanical treatment of the other communities' waste in the ill-sized plant, and the incineration of the pre-treated waste in an incinerating plant of another neighbouring community. This would not only make the bio-mechanical plant run to capacity, but it would also lead to the fulfilment of the legal obligation not to deposit waste without first incinerating it.

The obstacle for this possible adjustment is the strong political commitment in the community against any use of the waste incineration technology. This commitment has been a major factor in the process of deciding in favour of the bio-mechanical option. It enabled the community to make a risky decision. After the decision, it seems to block the organisation in its efforts to learn. Although the administration is strongly in favour of the co-operative strategy, the political part of the organisation is not willing to question its premises.

Furthermore, due to political changes at the state level, the signal about success or failure with respect to the legal appropriateness of the bio-mechanical plant is highly ambiguous. The new state government encourages solutions to the waste treatment problem without waste incineration. Although this attitude is in conflict with the federal policy and the position of the district administration, the signal for the local level does not allow the exact evaluation whether the chosen course of action is a success or a failure. An important precondition for learning is thus missing. This is a peculiarity of the case which hinders the ability of the scientific observer to study learning from experience. The interesting question would therefore be, how the community would behave after a clear feedback saying that the waste treatment concept is not legally appropriate.

The events after the decision in favour of the bio-mechanical plant suggest that the organisation will stick to its course of action. The community has asked for an exceptional permission for its waste treatment concept. This would lead to it being legally acceptable, but it would not resolve the technical and organisational problems of the plant. This would only be possible in co-operation with other communities, which, however, is in conflict with the political commitment of the organisation.

The case shows how structural uncertainty absorption works. By institutional arrangements that allowed important information to be neglected and responsibility to be re-allocated, the organisation was able to take a risk. The organisation was not afraid of bad surprises. However, it seems that the institutional features hinder the organisation to learn from experience. Learning in this case would require to question the premises that had been taken for granted *before* the decision. This requires more complex organisational preconditions.

The two case studies show that the crucial requirement in decision making under risk is the achievement of flexibility. In the first case, the decision makers tried to achieve this flexibility by not committing themselves to a decision too early. They looked for information, consensus, and for the right point in time in order to make the optimal decision. The second case shows an organisation that committed itself to a risky course of action and faced surprising consequences after this decision. The organisation has however difficulties to adjust its course of action to the new requirements.

What can we learn from these observations with respect to the general problem of organisational flexibility in the face of risk? The decision making literature offers models for the solution to this problem. The next section will be dedicated to the discussion of such models against the background of the empirical findings of this study.

6.3 Organisational Flexibility: Uncertainty Absorption and Learning

Social scientific inquiries of risk taking behaviour regularly lead to the issues of learning and flexibility: How do individuals and organisations react to negative consequences of their own actions? Are they able to learn? Are there structural possibilities to ensure this flexibility? The problem of achieving flexibility in the handling of risky situations has been identified in many studies of risk (Japp 1992; Krücken 1997b; Morone / Woodhouse 1986; Wiesenthal 1994; Wildavsky 1988). The ability to learn is stated as one of the main requirements for the risk society (Ladeur 1995).

6.3.1 Learning and Flexibility: Empirical Findings

The empirical results of the present study point to exactly the same problems of learning and flexibility in the face of risks. The decision makers in the two case studies were very aware of the necessity of flexibility in making their decisions. However, the problem was tackled in different ways.

In the first case, the organisation tried to stay flexible by not deciding, by searching for information, and by looking for the right point in time to make the decision. This organisation relied on analysis. This approach shows traits of models that suggest procedural rationality in order to keep open as many alternatives as possible. This is supposed to lead to flexibility (Ladeur 1992). At least one important argument against such an approach can be derived from the theoretical and empirical investigations of the present study: Decision making processes can be blocked if they are burdened with too much uncertainty (cf. above chapter 2). This theoretical argument was confirmed by the events in the first case study: The procedural rationality that was achieved during the decision making process generated too much information and thus uncertainty. The selectivity of a decision becomes too obvious if a rational procedure is used (Brunsson 1985). Instead of achieving flexibility, the organisation becomes subject to external developments outside its control because in the meantime, things go on and create structural pressures (Luhmann 1993a; chapter 4, above).

The second case shows how an organisation becomes aware of the demand for flexibility only after the decision. The risky decision about a waste treatment plant was made by neglecting important information. The absorbed uncertainty returned after the decision in the form of negative consequences. The organisation now would have to question the assumptions that had been taken for granted: the premise for the decision was the unacceptability of waste incineration, whereas a solution to the newly arisen problems would consist of co-operation with an existing waste incinerating plant. This questioning of something that has been taken for granted does not seem to be possible in this case. The political commitment to the avoidance of any use of the waste incineration technology seems to be strong. The case thus shows traits of escalating commitment to an ineffective course of action (Brockner et al. 1986), a well-documented phenomenon in the literature on organisational decision making (Janis 1972; Hart 1990; Japp 1992). Flexibility is blocked by the inability to question one's own premises.

The empirical observations of problems in achieving flexibility are in accordance with the theoretical framework employed in this study. In this perspective, the precondition for taking risks is a strong mechanism of structural uncertainty absorption. The organisation must, to a certain degree, be able to neglect the uncertainties connected with the decisions. In the case of too much procedural rationality (case 1), the organisation undermines this structural precondition of action and cannot make the decision. If the organisation manages to ignore information (case 2), the same institutional preconditions that enable the decision makers to make the decision, hinder them from learning from consequences. Thus, the challenge for organisations seeking to achieve flexibility is to organise the interplay of the two contrasting mechanisms of uncertainty absorption, and of learning. On the one hand, without prior uncertainty absorption the organisation does not face consequences to learn from. On the other hand, once it *has* absorbed uncertainty, it is very likely that it is unable to reintroduce uncertainty and thus to learn.

6.3.2 Learning and Flexibility: Theoretical Discussion

Although none of the cases studied here can be evaluated positively with respect to the achievement of flexibility, they can - in combination with some theoretical suggestions from the literature - give hints for the solution to this problem. Much of the literature on effective decision making strategies works with models that suggest combinations of at least two mechanisms of decision making.

Etzioni (1968) calls his suggestion for effective political decision making 'mixed scanning'. The term refers to a mixture of models of anticipatory and incremental decision making (cf. also Dror 1983; Morone / Woodhouse 1986 for similar concepts). According to Etzioni's suggestion successful decision making processes are divided into two different modes: contextual decision making and incremental decision making. Contextual decisions set the goals and criteria for success, incremental decisions (Lindblom 1965) are dedicated to the more detailed problems that are connected with the consequences of the contextuating decisions. At first sight, this model seems to fit the findings of the second case study reported here. There was a contextuating decision that was carried by the strong commitment against waste incineration and the follow-up decisions have to tackle the legal, financial and technical problems that arise from this commitment. However, the effective solution to these problems (co-operation with neighbouring communities) would touch the premises under which the contextuating decision has been made since this solution would make necessary the participation in waste incineration. This feedback of incremental on the premises of the contextuating decisions is not contained in Etzioni's model. The concept of mixed scanning does not offer a solution to the problems of flexibility observed in this study.

Another suggestion for effective organisational action by balancing two modes of decision making has been made by Weick (1979). The concept of the 'split decisions' assumes that organisations act on the basis of their memory, i.e. on the basis of their routines. Organisations then have two possibilities to handle their memories in inducing action: they can believe in their experience or they can discredit it. In order to combine effective functioning in the present with the ability to react to changing circumstances in the future, the organisation has to combine crediting and discrediting:

> If words and deeds are contradictory and if one perpetuates past wisdom and the other discredits past wisdom, then current functioning should be effective and future adaptation to changed contingencies should be possible. (Weick 1979: 222)

If we apply this model to the requirements of the second case study, the following conclusions arise with respect to the achievement of flexibility. The interplay of crediting and discrediting would take place if the organisation, after committing itself against waste incineration, would initiate co-operation with neighbouring communities which do incinerate waste. This would mean a discrediting of past wisdom, as Weick would put it, that has been perpetuated by previous actions. However, the administrative part of the organisation follows the political commitment to past wisdom. The organisation fails to adapt to changing circumstances.

The ability to do contradictory things is achieved, as is well documented in organisation theory, by structural differentiation. The most pronounced statement in this direction has been Brunssons idea of loosely coupled talk and action segments (Brunsson 1989). Brunsson stresses the importance of this structural differentiation for buffering the action part of the organisation against fast changing environmental demands (cf. Thompson 1967; Meyer / Rowan 1977). In the empirical context of the present study, and with the help of Weick's concept of split decisions, we see the contribution of this differentiation for the achievement of organisational flexibility.

The conclusion with respect to the second case study is thus that the organisation lacked a sufficient structural differentiation between talk and action, between politics and administration. The action in this case is blocked by the talk. Although the administration had already prepared a strategy to evade the negative decision consequences, the commitment of the political segment of the organisation overrules this adjustment. The organisation lacks the structural ability to make split decisions because the coupling between politics and administration is too tight.

With the help of the distinction between talk and action we can also shed further light on the events in the first case study. The concepts of Brunsson and Weick suggest that the clear differentiation and loose coupling between these two segments is a precondition for the achievement of effective action in the present and adaptability in the future. The first case shows an organisation that concentrated on talk (public participation, information gathering) and was not able to take action. The organisation was lacking routines, and the exercise in participation and rationality did not contribute to the formation of such routines. There was thus no basis for action. In the end, the organisation did not survive the amount of uncertainty that was generated by its talk, since uncertainty absorbing action was missing. The interplay of talk and action did not work.

The general conclusion with respect to flexibility is the following. Flexibility is *not* achieved by the careful collection of information and by efforts to find the right point in time to make the optimal decision. Such an approach burdens the decision making process with too much uncertainty as the organisation is blocked and then suffers effects of events that have happened in its environment in the meantime.

Since organisational action is based on routines, flexibility is achieved by the formation of multiple routines and by the ability to retrieve these routines if necessary. The *first* requirement are thus multiple organisational routines. On the other hand, routines are formed on the basis of past experiences. Here we see the fundamental interplay between action and structure, between decision and expectation that has been introduced in the first chapter of this study. Thus, the organisation has to act, maybe to experiment, in order to gain a 'structural repertoire' (Clark / Staunton 1989). The *second* precondition for flexibility, the ability to retrieve different routines, is achieved by differentiation and loose coupling of talk and action. Only on this structural basis, the organisation can make split decisions.

None of the case studies examined here meets the requirements of this model of organisational flexibility. The organisation in the first case could not take action because of lacking routines. The talk could not produce routines and generated too much uncertainty. The organisation did not survive in the face of the arising decision pressure, it lost its identity in a very fundamental way. The second organisation did take action by matching an old routine to the new situation. The assumption that this routine was appropriate allowed the decision makers to neglect much of the uncertainty. However, the organisation shows difficulties in adapting its course of action to the requirements that arose out of the consequences of its own decisions. This is due to the inability of the organisation to question the things that have been taken for granted. The differentiation between talk and action was not sufficient.

Thus, the findings of the present study about decision making and learning under risk at the organisational level are rather pessimistic. In the next section, I will discuss some aspects of the question of how organisations contribute to *societal* processes of risk taking and learning. Since this will be done on the basis of my empirical findings, the results will only be preliminary. However, if one observes the interplay of uncertainty absorption and learning between the organisational and the societal level, the picture becomes more optimistic.

6.4 The Risk Society and its Organisations

One of the intentions of the present study was to supplement analyses of risk handling in the modern society (Douglas / Wildavsky 1982; Luhmann 1993a; Japp 1996; Krücken 1997a; Schmidt 1997) by an organisational analysis of risk taking and avoiding. The assumption was that knowledge about organisational mechanisms of decision making under risk will contribute to our understanding of the structural possibilities and constraints of the risk society. With the example of the issue of learning and flexibility, discussed in the previous section, I will try to give some hints in this direction. This will lead to a contribution to the question of how to conceive of the modern society as a system that learns by experimentation (Krohn / Weyer 1989; Krohn 1997; Wildavsky 1988).

Although the level of analysis is now society instead of organisations, the basic concepts used in this study can be applied here as well. In the face of an uncertain future, the society has to absorb uncertainty, to form certain expectations (Bonß 1995), in order to take action. On the other hand, in the face of negative consequences of past decisions, the society may have to learn, i.e. to question the certain expectations that were the basis for past actions. Organisations can contribute to this interplay of societal uncertainty absorption and learning. In order to develop this idea with the help of the material presented in this study, we will have to take a brief look at the general features of German waste policy (cf. above, chapter 3).

German waste policy, the implementation of which was in the focus of my analysis, is characterised by the strong commitment to one option for the solution to the waste problem: By relying on waste incineration, the main problems of this policy field are supposed to be solved. Waste incineration reduces the volume of the waste, thus reducing the requirements for large landfill sites. It reduces the potential for biochemical reactions in the waste, thus providing for a waste disposal without aftercare. And its toxic emissions are controllable due to modern filter technology and due to strict emission standards in German environmental law. These are at least the assumptions of certainty underlying this policy (cf. SRU 1998: 174ff.). By taking these assumptions for granted, uncertainties about appropriate disposal methods were absorbed, and waste incineration was prescribed as obligatory for communities responsible for disposal safety. This is a clear political decision, that however suffers the same problems as all risky decisions.

First of all, there is the general problem that by this policy a political decision is made about an issue that is highly contested scientifically and in social conflicts. Legal prescriptions are, however, inappropriate for the generation of certain expectations in risk conflicts (Luhmann 1993). The legal obligation to plan waste incinerating plants is one of the main factors causing organisational risks and uncertainties at the local level. Second, and more important in the context of this study, the absorbed uncertainty can return in the form of negative ecological effects. For the future, one could think of several developments that could question the strict reliance on waste incineration in German waste policy. For example, it is possible that refined methods of scientific analysis discover that waste incineration does not lead to disposal without aftercare. It may be discovered that the emission standards are not sufficient from a scientific point of view. Or one may discover that, due to the emission-oriented approach in the German Nuisance Act (cf. Héritier et al. 1996), even the strictest emission standards cannot control pollution in regions with a high concentration of industrial and waste incinerating plants (SRU 1998). If only one of these speculations became reality, then a properly and effectively implemented waste policy relying exclusively on waste incineration would turn out to be a grave mistake. Adjustments would be very costly and time-intensive since experiences with different technological methods for treating waste would not be available. The reliance on waste incineration would have led to loss of experiences with other technological options (cf. MacKenzie / Spinardi 1995). Societal learning would be difficult.

If this argument is correct, then the problems of local politics and administration in implementing federal waste policy immediately are an important contribution to societal flexibility in the face of ecological risks. The hesitation of many local authorities to take the risk of planning waste incinerating plants, and efforts of many decision makers to push ahead the technology of bio-mechanical waste treatment (cf. Herbold / Timmermeister / Vorwerk 1998), contributes to the formation of a structural repertoire of the society for the handling of the waste problem. Experiences with alternative technologies are made, thus complementing the broad technical knowledge about waste incineration. This comes close to Thompson's suggestion of a multi-cultural approach to the 'waste crisis' (Thompson 1998).

In the case of bad surprises with the use of waste incineration as the final solution to the waste problem, this increased structural repertoire will allow new challenges to be reacted to. The requirement for societal flexibility is thus the same as on the organisational level: it is important to have multiple routines available. The *organisational* problems to take the risk of implementation contribute to *societal* flexibility. By the help of its organisations, the society learns. The picture is thus one of a perfect and smoothly working differentiation of talk ('The waste crisis is solved') and action ('Things are not that simple'). German waste policy of recent years shows traits of a split decision and thus promises to be successful also in the long run.

Analysing German waste policy, one can thus collect arguments for the position that ineffective policy implementation leads to increased societal flexibility in the handling of technological and environmental risks. Whether this point is a general one cannot be addressed here. The claim is however that the framework of risk sociology allows such new perspectives on familiar phenomena to be developed.

Concluding Remarks

Risk sociology assumes that the social production of, and reaction to, risks is determined by social structures. This argument has been elaborated with respect to general cultural patterns (Douglas / Wildavsky 1982) and with the argument that modern society is differentiated in functional subsystems and that this structure is crucial for the understanding of the risk society (Luhmann 1993a). The present study argued that this perspective has to be complemented by a perspective on organisations. The perspective of risk sociology suggests that an understanding of social structures is crucial for an analysis of decision making under risk. For organisations, these enabling and constraining structures have been identified as institutionalised decision premises that determine what is taken for granted in risky decisions, and what can be neglected. They do this by absorbing uncertainty about, and allocating responsibility for, future events. Generally speaking, structures connect future events with present decisions. This is true both for the societal and the organisational level.

Bibliography

Allport, F.H. (1940), 'An Event-System Theory of Collective Action', *The Journal of Social Psychology*, vol. 11, pp. 417-445.
Allport, F.H. (1954), 'The Structuring of Events: Outline of a General Theory with Applications to Psychology', *Psychological Review*, vol. 61, pp. 281-303.
Allport, F.H. (1955), *Theories of Perception and the Concept of Structure*, Wiley, New York.
Allport, F.H. (1962), 'A Structuronomic Conception of Behavior: Individual and Collective', *Journal of Abnormal and Social Psychology*, vol. 64, pp. 3-30.
Anand, P. (1993), *Foundations of Rational Choice under Risk*, Clarendon Press, Oxford.
Argyris, C. and Schon, D. (1978), *Organizational Learning*, Addison-Wesley, Reading.
Argyris, C. and Schon, D. (1996), *Organizational Learning II*, Addison-Wesley, Reading.
Arrow, K.J. (1970), *Essays in the Theory of Risk-Bearing*, North-Holland, Amsterdam.
Baecker, D. (1993), *Die Form des Unternehmens*, Suhrkamp, Frankfurt.
Baier, V.E., March, J.G. and Sætren, H. (1988), 'Implementation and Ambiguity' in J.G. March, *Decisions and Organizations*, Blackwell, Oxford, pp. 150-164.
Barnard, C. (1938), *The Functions of the Executive*, Harvard University Press, Cambridge.
Battis, U. (1988), 'Das Planfeststellungsverfahren nach dem Verwaltungsverfahrensgesetz', *Die Verwaltung*, vol. 21, pp. 23-41.
Bechmann, G. (1993), 'Risiko - ein neues Forschungsfeld?' In G. Bechmann (ed.), *Risiko und Gesellschaft*, Westdeutscher Verlag, Opladen, pp. VII-XXIX.
Beck, U. (1986), *Risikogesellschaft: Auf dem Weg in eine andere Moderne*, Suhrkamp, Frankfurt.
Becker, U. (1970), 'Zur Veränderung der Struktur der Verwaltung', *Die Verwaltung*, vol. 3, pp. 389-420.
Beckmann, M., Appold, W. and Kuhlmann, E.-M. (1998), 'Zur gerichtlichen Kontrolle abfallrechtlicher Planfeststellungen', *Deutsches Verwaltungsblatt*, vol. 103, pp. 1002-1012.
Berger, U. and Bernhard-Mehlich, I. (1993), 'Die verhaltenswissenschaftliche Entscheidungstheorie', in A. Kieser (ed.), *Organisationstheorien*, Kohlhammer, Stuttgart, pp. 127-159.
Bienroth, S., Fischer, K.-J. and Praetzel, R. (1995), 'Die Gebühren für Müll und Abfall in Baden-Württemberg', *Müll und Abfall*, vol. 27, pp. 685-691.

Bingham, G. (1986), *Resolving Environmental Dispute: A Decade of Experience*, Washington.

Böhret, C. (1982), 'Reformfähigkeit und Anpassungsflexibilität der öffentlichen Verwaltung', in J.J. Hesse (ed.), *Politikwissenschaft und Verwaltungswissenschaft*, Westdeutscher Verlag, Opladen, pp. 134-150.

Bonß, W. (1995), *Vom Risiko. Unsicherheit und Ungewißheit in der Moderne*, Hamburger Edition, Hamburg.

Brockner, J. et al. (1986), 'Escalation of Commitment to an Ineffective Course of Action: The Effect of Feedback Having Negative Implications for Self-Identity', *Administrative Science Quarterly*, vol. 31, pp. 109-126.

Brückner, C. and Wiechers, G. (1985), 'Umweltschutz und Ressourcenschonung durch eine ökologische Abfallwirtschaft', *Zeitschrift für Umweltpolitik und Umweltrecht*, vol. 8., pp. 153-180.

Brunsson, N. (1985), *The Irrational Organization: Irrationality as a Basis for Organizational Action and Change*, Wiley, Chichester.

Brunsson, N. (1989), *The Organization of Hypocrisy. Talk, Decisions, and Actions in Organizations*, Wiley, Chichester.

Burns, T. and Stalker, G.M. (1961), *The Management of Innovation*, Tavistock, London.

Cichonski, P. and Heinrichs, D. (1995), 'Die GmbH - zeitgemäße Organisationsform für Entsorgungsbetriebe?' *Müll und Abfall*, vol. 27, pp. 490-498.

Clark, P. and Staunton, N. (1989), *Innovation in Technology and Organization*, Routledge, London.

Clarke, L. (1989), *Acceptable Risk? Making Decisions in a Toxic Environment*, University of California Press, Berkeley.

Cohen, I.J. (1989), *Structuration Theory. Anthony Giddens and the Constitution of Life*, MacMillan, London.

Cohen, M.D., March, J.G. and Olsen, J.P. (1972), 'A Garbage Can Model of Organizational Choice', *Administrative Science Quarterly*, vol. 17, pp. 1-25.

Cord-Landwehr, K. (1994), *Einführung in die Abfallwirtschaft*, Teubner, Stuttgart.

Coser, L. (1956), *The Functions of Social Conflict*, The Free Press, New York.

Coyle, D.J. (1997), 'A Cultural Theory of Organisations', in R.J. Ellis and M. Thompson (eds), *Culture Matters. Essays in Honor of Aaron Wildavsky*, Westview Press, Boulder, pp. 59-78.

Cyert, R.M. and March, J.G. (1963), *A Behavioral Theory of the Firm*, 2nd edition 1992, Blackwell, Oxford.

Daft, R.L. and Weick, K.E. (1994), 'Toward a Model of Organizations as Interpretation Systems', in H. Tsoukas (ed.), *New Thinking in Organizational Behaviour. From Social Engineering to Reflexive Action*, Butterworth Heinemann, Oxford, pp. 70-89.

Dally, A., Weidner, H. and Fietkau, H.-J. (eds) (1994), *Mediation als politischer und sozialer Prozeß*, Evangelische Akademie, Rehburg-Loccum.

Dean, M. (1998), 'Risk, Calculable and Incalculable', *Soziale Welt*, vol. 49, pp.25-42.

Dickinson, D.G., Driscoll, M.J. and Sen, S. (eds) (1994), *Risk and Uncertainty in Economics*, Elgar, Aldershot.

Dienel, P. (1992), *Die Planungszelle*, Westdeutscher Verlag, Opladen.

Dodgson, M. (1993), 'Organizational Learning: A Review of Some Literatures', *Organization Studies*, vol. 14, pp. 375-394.

Douglas, M. (1966), *Purity and Danger. An Analysis of Concepts of Pollution and Taboo*, Routlegde & Kegan Paul, London.

Douglas, M. (1985), *Risk Acceptability According to the Social Sciences*, Routledge & Kegan Paul, London.

Douglas, M. (1992), *Risk and Blame. Essays in Cultural Theory*, Routledge, London.

Douglas, M. and Widlavsky, A. (1982), *Risk and Culture. An Essay on the Selection of Technological and Environmental Dangers*, University of California Press, Berkeley.

Dowding, K.M. (1991), *Rational Choice and Political Power*, Elgar, Aldershot.

Dowding, K.M. (1994), 'The Compatibility of Behaviouralism, Rational Choice, and New Institutionalism', *Journal of Theoretical Politics*, vol. 6, pp. 105-117.

Dowding, K.M. and King, D. (1995), 'Introduction', in K.M. Dowding and D. King (eds), *Preferences, Institutions, and Rational Choice*, Clarendon Press, Oxford, pp. 1-19.

Dror, Y. (1983), *Public Policy Making - Reexamined*, 2nd edition, Transaction Books, New Brunswick.

Eckhoff, T. and Jacobsen, K.D. (1960), *Rationality and Responsibility in Administrative and Judicial Decision-Making*, Munksgaard, Copenhagen.

Edelman, M. (1967), *The Symbolic Uses of Politics*, University of Illinois Press, Urbana.

Elster, J. (1989), 'When Rationality Fails', in J. Elster, *Solomonic Judgements. Studies in the Limitation of Rationality*, Cambridge University Press, Cambridge, pp. 1-35.

Etzioni, A. (1968), *The Active Society. A Theory of Societal and Political Processes*, The Free Press, New York.

Feldman, M.S. and March, J.G. (1981), 'Information in Organizations as Signal and Symbol', *Administrative Science Quarterly*, vol. 26, pp. 171-186.

Fietkau, H.-J. and Weidner, H. (1994), *Umweltmediation. Das Mediationsverfahren zum Abfallwirtschaftskonzept im Kreis Neuss*, WZB, Berlin.

Fonteyn, R. and Pfänder, P. (1988), 'Kommunale Computer-Abfallberatung - ein Weg zum vorsorgenden Umweltschutz', *Zeitschrift für angewandte Umweltforschung*, vol. 1, pp. 391-397.

Foschi, M. (1972), 'On the Concept of Expectations', *Acta Sociologica*, vol. 15, pp. 124-131.

Fricke, W. and Zink, U. (1996), 'Einführung eines Controlling der Abfallwirtschaft beim Kreis Aachen', *Müll und Abfall*, vol. 28, pp. 727-732.

Fröhlich, W. (1994), 'Schwierigkeiten mit dem Erleichterungsgesetz. Neue Zulassungsverfahren für Abfallentsorgungsanlagen', *Zeitschrift für Umweltrecht*, vol. 6, pp. 126-129.

Galbraith, J. (1973), *Designing Complex Organizations*, Addison-Wesley, Reading.

Galtung, J. (1959), 'Expectations and Interaction Processes', *Inquiry*, vol. 2, pp. 213-234.

Gans, B. (1994), *Mediation: Ein Weg des Umgangs mit Konflikten in der räumlichen Planung?*, Munich.

Gaßner, H., Holznagel, B. and Lahl U. (1992), *Mediation. Verhandlungen als Mittel der Konsensfindung bei Umweltstreitigkeiten*, Bonn.

Gaßner, H. and Siederer, W. (1997), 'Anspruch und Wirklichkeit. Über dem Streit zur Müllverbrennung darf die Vorbehandlung nicht auf der Strecke bleiben', *Müllmagazin*, vol. 10, pp. 35-37.

Giddens, A. (1984), *The Constitution of Society*, University of California Press, Berkeley.

Greve, H.R. (1998), 'Performance, Aspirations, and Risky Organizational Change', *Administrative Science Quarterly*, vol. 43, pp. 58-86.

Gusy, C. (1990), 'Verwaltung durch Verhandlung und Vermittlung', *Zeitschrift für Umweltpolitik und Umweltrecht*, vol. 13, pp. 353-363.

Haber, W., Halbritter, G. and Krieger, S. (1991), 'Von der Abfallbeseitigung zur Abfallwirtschaft - das Abfallwirtschaftsgutachten des Rates von Sachverständigen für Umweltfragen', *Zeitschrift für angewandte Umweltforschung*, vol. 4, pp. 22-35.

Habermas, J. (1981), *Theorie des kommunikativen Handelns*, Suhrkamp, Frankfurt.

Haltiner, E.W. (1993), 'Dioxine: Fakten statt Polemik', *Müll und Abfall*, vol. 25, pp. 641-643.

Hannan, M.T. (1992), 'Rationality and Robustness in Multilevel Systems', in J.S. Coleman and T.J. Fararo (eds), *Rational Choice: Advocacy and Critique*, Sage, Newbury Park, pp. 120-136.

Harrison, J.R. and March, J.G. (1988), 'Decision-Making and Postdecision Surprises', in J.G. March, *Decisions and Organizations*, Blackwell, Oxford, pp. 228-249.

Hart, P.'t (1990), *Groupthink in Government. A Study of Small Groups and Policy Failure*, Swets & Zeitlinger, Amsterdam.

Hasse, R. and Japp, K.P. (1997), 'Dynamik symbolischer Organisationspolitik. Umwelt- und Selbstanpassung als Folgewirkung ökologischer Leistungserwartungen', in M. Birke, C. Burschel and M. Schwarz (eds), *Handbuch Umweltschutz und Organisation*, Oldenbourg, München, pp. 134-162.

Hasse, R. and Krücken, G. (1996), 'Was leistet der organisationssoziologische Neo-Institutionalismus?', *Soziale Systeme*, vol. 2, pp. 91-112.

Hechter, M. (1987), *Principles of Group Solidarity*, University of California Press, Berkeley.

Hechter, M., Opp, K.-D. and Wippler, R. (1990), 'Introduction', in M. Hechter, K.-D. Opp and R. Wippler (eds), *Social Institutions: Their Emergence, Maintenance, and Effects*, de Gruyter, Berlin / New York, pp. 1-9.

Herbold, R., Kämper, E., Krohn, W. and Vorwerk, V. (1997), 'Innovation in partizipativen Akteurkonfigurationen. Abfallwirtschaft im Spannungsfeld von Technik, normung und Akzeptanz', in M. Birke, C. Burschel and M. Schwarz (eds), *Handbuch Umweltschutz und Organisation*, Oldenbourg, München, pp. 434-464.

Herbold, R. and Timmermeister, M. (1997), 'Parteipolitischer Konsens bei Entscheidungen unter Risiko. Zur abfallpolitischen Innovationsfähogkeit kommunaler Entsorgungsnetze', in R. Herbold, M. Timmermeister and V. Vorwerk (eds), *Unterwegs zur Kreislaufwirtschaft. Interdisziplinäre Beiträge*, Institute for Science and Technology Studies, Bielefeld, pp. 79-95.

Herbold, R., Timmermeister, M. and Vorwerk, V. (1998), *Regionalstudie Kreis Düren*, Institute for Science and Technology Studies, Bielefeld.

Herbold, R. and Vorwerk, V. (1993), 'Die Entwicklung der Abfallwissenschaft: Deponiesickerwasser als Risiko und die Entstehung einer neuen Disziplin', *Müll und Abfall*, vol. 25, pp. 355-364.

Herbold, R. and Wienken R. (1993), *Experimentelle Technikgestaltung und offene Planung. Strategien zur sozialen Bewältigung von Unsicherheit am Beispiel der Abfallbeseitigung*, Kleine, Bielefeld.

Héritier, A., Knill, C. and Mingers, S. (1996), *Ringing the Changes in Europe: Regulatory Competition and the Transformation of the State*, de Gruyter, Berlin / New York.

Hermann, T. et al. (1997), *Einführung in die Abfallwirtschaft. Technik, Recht und Politik*, 2nd edition, Deutsch, Thun / Frankfurt.

Hey, J.D. (ed.) (1997), *The Economics of Uncertainty. Vol 1: Risk*, Elgar, Cheltenham.

Hiller, P. (1993), *Der Zeitkonflikt in der Risikogesellschaft. Risiko und Zeitorientierung in rechtsförmigen Verwaltungsentscheidungen*, Duncker & Humblot, Berlin.

Hoffmann-Hoeppel, J. (1994), 'Beschleunigung des Fachplanungsrechts. Erfahrungen aus der abfallrechtlichen Zulassungspraxis', *Die Verwaltung*, vol. 27, pp. 391-412.

Hoffmann-Riem, W. and Schmidt-Aßmann, E. (eds) (1990), *Konfliktbewältigung durch Verhandlungen*, Nomos, Baden-Baden.

Hölscher, F. (1995), 'Öffentliche und private Abfallentsorgung: Ihre Stellung nach dem Abfallgesetz und dem Kreislaufwirtschaftsgesetz', *Zeitschrift für Umweltrecht*, vol. 7, pp. 176-182.

Holznagel, B. (1990), 'Verhandlungslösungen als Mittel der Konfliktbewältigung bei der Ansiedlung von Sonderabfallanlagen in den USA und in der Bundesrepublik', *Zeitschrift für angewandte Umweltforschung*, vol. 3, pp. 405-417.

Ihmels, K. (1993), 'Wider die Illusion der Müllvermeidung durch

Gebührenanreize', *Müll und Abfall*, vol. 25, pp. 434-438.
Janis, I.L. (1972), *Victims of Groupthink*, Houghton Mifflin, Boston.
Jansen, C. (1989), 'Stoffliche Abfallverwertung - getrennte Sammlung, Vermarktung, Bioabfall', *Zeitschrift für angewandte Umweltforschung*, vol. 2, pp. 92-93.
Jansen, D. (1997), 'Das Problem der Akteurqualität korporativer Akteure', in A. Benz and W. Seibel (eds), *Theorieentwicklung in der Politikwissenschaft - eine Zwischenbilanz*, Nomos, Baden-Baden, pp. 193-235.
Japp, K.P. (1992), 'Selbstverstärkungseffekte riskanter Entscheidungen. Zur Unterscheidung von Rationalität und Risiko', *Zeitschrift für Soziologie*, vol. 21, pp. 31-48.
Japp, K.P. (1994), 'Verwaltung und Rationalität', in K. Dammann, D. Grunow and K.P. Japp (eds), *Die Verwaltung des politischen Systems*, Westdeutscher Verlag, Opladen, pp. 126-141.
Japp, K.P. (1996), *Soziologische Risikotheorie*, Juventa, Weinheim / München.
Jones, E.E., Kanouse, D.E., Kelley, H.H., Nisbett, R.E., Valins, S. and Weiner, B., (1987), *Attribution: Perceiving the Causes of Behaviour*, Erlbaum, London.
Jungermann, H. and Slovic, P. (1993), 'Die Psychologie der Kognition und Evaluation von Risiko', in G. Bechmann (ed.), *Risiko und Gesellschaft*, Westdeutscher Verlag, Opladen, pp. 167-207.
Kämper, E. and Vorwerk, V. (1996), *Evaluation der 1. und 2. Phase des Bürgerbeteiligungsverfahrens in der Region Nordschwarzwald*, Centre for Technology Assessment, Stuttgart.
Kappelhoff, P. (1997), 'Rational Choice, Macht und die korporative Organisation der Gesellschaft', in G. Ortmann, J. Sydow and K. Türk (eds), *Theorien der Organisation: Die Rückkehr der Gesellschaft*, Westdeutscher Verlag, Opladen, pp. 218-258.
Katz, D. and Kahn, R.L. (1966), *The Social Psychology of Organizations*, Wiley, New York.
Kaube, J. (1996), 'Rationales Handeln - Probleme seiner Theorie', *Soziale Systeme*, vol. 2, pp. 137-152.
Keeney, R., Renn, O., v.Winterfeldt, D. and Kotte, E. (1984), *Die Wertbaumanalyse. Entscheidungshilfe für die Politik*, München.
Kelly, G.A. (1955), *The Psychology of Personal Constructs*, Norton, New York.
Klockow, S. (1995), 'Steigerung der Akzeptanz von Abfallentsorgungsanlagen durch Maßnahmen zum Lastenausgleich?', *Müll und Abfall*, vol. 27, pp. 90-96.
Knight, F.H. (1921), *Risk, Uncertainty, and Profit*, 2nd edition 1965, University of Chicago Press, Chicago.
Koch, R. (1992), 'Entscheidungsverhalten und Entscheidungsunterstützung höherer Verwaltungsbediensteter: Zur Weiterentwicklung des Führungs- und Entscheidungsinstrumentariums öffentlicher Verwaltungen', *Verwaltungsarchiv*, vol. 83, pp. 26-52.
Kopp, F. (1987), 'Zehn Jahre Verwaltungsverfahrensgesetz. Anspruch und Wirklichkeit - eine Bilanz', *Die Verwaltung*, vol. 20, pp. 1-28.

Kreis Düren (1997), *Abfallwirtschaftskonzept für den Kreis Düren*, Düren.
Kremer, P. (1994), 'Die Technische Anleitung Siedlungsabfall: Zwang zur Müllverbrennung?', Kommunale Briefe für Ökologie, vol. 21, pp. 14-21.
Krohn, W. (1997), 'Rekursive Lernprozesse: Experimentelle Praktiken in der Gesellschaft. Das Beispiel der Abfallwirtschaft', in: W. Rammert and G. Bechmann (eds), *Jahrbuch Technik und Gesellschaft 9*, Campus, Frankfurt / New York, pp. 65-89.
Krohn, W. and Krücken, G. (1993), 'Risiko als Konstruktion und Wirklichkeit', in W. Krohn and G. Krücken (eds), *Riskante Technologien: Reflexion und Regulation*, Suhrkamp, Frankfurt, pp. 9-44.
Krohn, W. and Weyer, J. (1989), 'Die Gesellschaft als Labor. Die Erzeugung sozialer Risiken durch experimentelle Forschung', *Soziale Welt*, vol. 40, pp. 349-373.
Krücken, G. (1997a), *Risikotransformation: Die politische Regulierung technisch-ökologischer Gefahren in der Risikogesellschaft*, Westdeutscher Verlag, Opladen.
Krücken, G. (1997b), 'Risikotransformation: Voraussetzungen, Strukturen und Folgen der politischen Regulierung von Arzneimittelgefahren', in P. Hiller and G. Krücken (eds), *Risiko und Regulierung*, Suhrkamp, Frankfurt, pp. 116-146.
Ladeur, K.-H. (1992), *Postmoderne Rechtstheorie. Selbstreferenz - Selbstorganisation - Proceduralisierung*, Duncker & Humblot, Berlin.
Ladeur, K.-H. (1995), *Das Umweltrecht der Wissensgesellschaft. Von der Gefahrenabwehr zum Risikomanagement*, Duncker & Humblot, Berlin.
Lawrence, P.R. and Lorsch, J.W. (1967), *Organization and Environment*, Harvard Business School Press, Boston.
Lemser, B., Maselli, J. and Tillmann, A. (1998), 'Betriebswirtschaftliche Beurteilung alternativer Entsorgungspfade aus der Sicht einer entsorgungspflichtigen Körperschaft', *Müll und Abfall*, vol. 30, pp. 4-10.
Lemser, B. and Tillmann, A. (1996), Zur Bildung von Abfallgebühren und zur Kosten- und Leistungsrechnung in der öffentlichen Abfallentsorgung aus betriebswirtschaftlicher Sicht', *Müll und Abfall*, vol. 28, pp. 64-71.
Leporn, P. and Henschel, P. (1993), 'Verfahren zur Charakterisierung des biologisch abbaubaren Anteils der organischen Substanz', *Müll und Abfall*, vol. 25, pp. 530-537.
Levin, M.A. and Singer, M.B. (1994), *Making Government Work. How Entrepreneurial Executives Turn Bright Ideas into Real Results*, Jossey-Bass, San Francisco.
Levitt, B. and March, J.G. (1988), 'Organizational Learning', *Annual Review of Sociology*, vol. 14, pp. 319-349.
Lindblom, C.E. (1965), *The Intelligence of Democracy. Decision Making Through Mutual Adjustment*, The Free Press, New York.
Lübbe, W. (ed.) (1994), *Kausalität und Zurechnung. Über Verantwortung in komplexen kulturellen Prozessen*, de Gruyter, Berlin / New York.
Luhmann, N. (1964), *Funktionen und Folgen formaler Organisation*, Duncker &

Humblot, Berlin.
Luhmann, N. (1965), *Grundrechte als Institution*, Duncker & Humblot, Berlin.
Luhmann, N. (1970), 'Institutionalisierung - Funktion und Mechanismus im sozialen System der Gesellschaft', in H. Schelsky (ed.), *Zur Theorie der Institution*, Bertelsmann, Düsseldorf, pp. 27-42.
Luhmann, N. (1971), 'Lob der Routine', in N. Luhmann, *Politische Planung*, Westdeutscher Verlag, Opladen, pp. 113-142.
Luhmann, N. (1976), 'A General Theory of Organized Social Systems', in G. Hofstede and M.S. Kassem (eds), *European Contributions to Organization Theory*, Van Gorcum, Assen, pp. 96-113.
Luhmann, N. (1981), *Soziologische Aufklärung 3*, Westdeutscher Verlag, Opladen.
Luhmann, N. (1982), 'Interaction, Organization, and Society', in N. Luhmann, *The Differentiation of Society*, Columbia University Press, New York, pp. 69-89.
Luhmann, N. (1983), *Legitimation durch Verfahren*, Suhrkamp, Frankfurt.
Luhmann, N. (1987), *Rechtssoziologie*, 3rd edition, Westdeutscher Verlag, Opladen.
Luhmann, N. (1988), 'Soziologische Aspekte des Entscheidungsverhaltens', in N. Luhmann, *Die Wirtschaft der Gesellschaft*, Suhrkamp, Frankfurt, pp. 272-301.
Luhmann, N. (1990a), 'Risiko und Gefahr', in N. Luhmann, *Soziologische Aufklärung 5*, Westdeutscher Verlag, Opladen, pp. 131-170.
Luhmann, N. (1990b), *Political Theory in the Welfare State*, de Gruyter, Berlin / New York.
Luhmann, N. (1993a), *Risk: A Sociological Theory*, de Gruyter, Berlin / New York.
Luhmann, N. (1993b), 'Die Paradoxie des Entscheidens', *Verwaltungsarchiv*, vol. 84, pp. 287-310.
Luhmann, N. (1995), *Social Systems*, Stanford University Press, Stanford.
Luhmann, N. (2000), *Organisation und Entscheidung*, Westdeutscher Verlag, Opladen.
MacCorquodale, K. and Mehl, P.E. (1953), 'Preliminary Suggestions as to a Formalization of Expectancy Theory', *Psychological Review*, vol. 60, pp. 55-63.
MacKenzie, D. and Spinardi, G. (1995), 'Tacit Knowledge, Weapons Design, and the Uninvention of Nuclear Weapons', *American Journal of Sociology*, vol. 101, pp. 44-99.
Mayer, F., Ilbher, P., Holtwick, A. and Kreiser, H. (1994), 'Genehmigungsverfahren: Planfeststellung für die Schwel-Brenn-Anlage in Fürth', *Müll und Abfall*, vol. 26, pp. 121-130.
March, J.G. (1988), *Decisions and Organizations*, Blackwell, Oxford.
March, J.G. (1994), *A Primer on Decision Making. How Decisions Happen*, The Free Press, New York.
March, J.G. and Olsen, J.P. (1976), *Ambiguity and Choice in Organizations*, Universitetsforlaget, Bergen.
March, J.G. and Olsen, J.P. (1989), *Rediscovering Institutions*, The Free Press,

New York.
March, J.G. and Olsen, J.P. (1995), *Democratic Governance*, The Free Press, New York.
March, J.G. and Shapira, Z. (1988), 'Managerial Perspectives on Risk and Risk-Taking', in J.G. March, *Decisions and Organizations*, Blackwell, Oxford, pp. 76-97.
March, J.G. and Simon, H.A. (1958), *Organizations*, 2nd edition 1993, Blackwell, Oxford.
Martens, J. (1990), 'Deponiegas - Grundlage für ein weitreichendes Reststoffminimierungsverfahren auf Deponien', *Müll und Abfall*, vol. 22, pp. 76-79.
Mayntz, R. (ed.) (1980), *Implementation politischer Programme*, Hain, Königsstein.
Mayntz, R. (1985), *Soziologie der öffentlichen Verwaltung*, Müller, Heidelberg.
Mayntz, R. and Scharpf, F.W. (1995), *Gesellschaftliche Selbstregelung und politische Steuerung*, Campus, Frankfurt.
Meyer, J.W., Rowan, B. (1977), 'Institutionalized Organizations: Formal Structure as Myth and Ceremony', *American Journal of Sociology*, vol. 83, pp. 340-363.
Meyer, J.W., Boli, J. and Thomas, G.M. (1994), 'Ontology and Rationalization in the Western Cultural Account', in W.R. Scott, J.W. Meyer and Associates, *Institutional Environments and Organizations. Structural Complexitiy and Individualism*, Sage, Thousand Oaks, pp. 9-27.
Meyer, U., Schneider, T. and Weigel, U. (1996), 'Auswahlprozeß für eine Restabfallbehandlung am Beispiel der Landeshauptstadt Hannover', *Müll und Abfall*, vol. 28, pp. 519-529.
Michael, D.N. (1993), 'Governing by Learning: Boundaries, Myths, and Metaphors', *Futures*, vol. 25, pp. 81-89.
Morone, J.G. and Woodhouse, E.J. (1986), *Averting Catastrophe*, University of California Press, Berkeley.
Müllmann, C. (1993), 'Die Zulassung von Abfallbehandlungsanlagen nach dem Investititionserleichterungs- und Wohnbaulandgesetz', *Müll und Abfall*, vol. 25, pp. 645-654.
MURL (Ministry of the Environment of Northrhine-Westfalia) (1998), *Leitfaden für die Integration der mechanisch-biologischen Restabfallbehandlung in ein kommunales Abfallwirtschaftskonzept*, MURL, Düsseldorf.
Muth, J.F. (1961), 'Rational Expectations and the Theory of Price Movements', *Econometrica*, vol. 29, pp. 315-335.
Oechler, A. (1993), 'Müllmengenorientierte Gebührensysteme. Neuorientierung in der kommunalen Abfallentsorgung', *Müll und Abfall*, vol. 25, pp. 312-316.
Offe, C. (1974), 'Rationalitätskriterien und Funktionsprobleme politisch-administrativen Handelns', *Leviathan*, vol. 2, pp. 333-345.
Olsen, J.P. and Peters, B.G. (eds) (1995), *Lessons from Experience. Experiential Learning in Administrative Reforms in Eight Democracies*, Scandinavian University Press, Oslo.

Otway, H. and Wynne, B. (1989),' Risk Communication: Paradigm and Paradox', *Risk Analysis*, vol. 9, pp. 141-145.

Paetow, S. (1991), 'Zur Struktur der abfallrechtlichen Planfeststellung', in E. Franßen et al. (eds), *Bürger - Richter - Staat*, Beck, München, pp. 425-442.

Parsons, T. (1951), *The Social System*, Routledge & Kegan Paul.

Parsons, T. et al. (1951), 'Some Fundamental Categories of the Theory of Action: A General Statement', in T. Parsons and E.A. Shils (eds), *Toward a General Theory of Action. Theoretical Foundations for the Social Sciences*, Harvard University Press, Harvard, pp. 3-29.

Perrow, C. (1984), *Normal Accidents: Living with High-Risk Technologies*, Basic Books, New York.

Petter, U. (1994), 'Rechtsfragen bei der Standortbestimmung für Abfallentsorgungsanlagen', *Müll und Abfall*, vol. 26, pp. 749-753.

Powell, W.W. and DiMaggio, P.J. (eds) (1991), *The New Institutionalism in Organizational Analysis*, Chicago University Press, Chicago.

Pressman, J.L. and Wildavsky, A. (1973), *Implementation*, University of California Press, Berkeley.

Rahner, T. (1993), 'Investitionserleichterung durch Deregulierung des Abfall- und Immissionsschutzrechts?', *Zeitschrift für Umweltrecht*, vol. 5, pp. 200-203.

Rehmann-Sutter, C., Vatter, A. and Seiler, H. (1998), *Partizipative Risikopolitik*, Westdeutscher Verlag, Opladen.

Renn, O. (1992), 'Concepts of Risk: A Classification', in S. Krimsky and D. Golding (eds), *Social Theories of Risk*, Praeger, London, pp. 53-79.

Renn, O. and Webler, T. (1994), 'Konfliktbewältigung durch Kooperation in der Umweltpolitik. Theoretische Grundlagen und Handlungsvorschläge', in oikos (ed.), *Kooperation für die Umwelt. Im Dialog zum Handeln*, Rüegger, Zürich, pp. 11-52.

Renn, O., Webler, T. and Wiedemann, P. (eds) (1995), *Fairness and Competence in Citizen Participation*, Kluwer, Dordrecht.

Rucht, D. (1994), 'Öffentlichkeit als Mobilisierungsfaktor für soziale Bewegungen', in F. Neidhardt (ed.), *Öffentlichkeit, Öffentliche Meinung, Soziale Bewegungen*, Westdeutscher Verlag, Opladen, pp. 337-358.

Sagan, S.D. (1993), *The Limits of Safety: Organizations, Accidents, and Nuclear Weapons*, Princeton University Press, Princeton.

Scharpf, F.W. (1997), *Games Real Actors Play: Actor-Centered Institutionalism in Policy Research*, Westview Press, Boulder.

Scheffold, K. (1995), 'Bioabfall eine relevante Gebührengröße', *Müll und Abfall*, vol. 27, pp. 217-224.

Schimank, U. (1992), 'Erwartungssicherheit und Zielverfolgung. Sozialität zwischen Prisoner's Dilemma und Battle of the Sexes', *Soziale Welt*, vol. 43, pp. 182-200.

Schink, A. (1994), 'Organisationsformen für die kommunale Abfallwirtschaft', *Verwaltungsarchiv*, vol. 85, pp. 251-280.

Schmidt, J.F.K. (1997), 'Politische Risikoregulierung als Risikoerzeugung? Zur

Bedeutung von Gefährdungshaftung und Versicherung im Rahmen gesellschaftlicher Risikobearbeitung', in P. Hiller and G. Krücken (eds), *Risiko und Regulierung*, Suhrkamp, Frankfurt, pp. 279-312.

Schneider, V. (1997), 'Zwischen Beschränkung und Ermöglichung: Strukturalistische Erklärungen in der Politikanalyse', in A. Benz and W. Seibel (eds), *Theorieentwicklung in der Politikwissenschaft - eine Zwischenbilanz*, Nomos, Baden-Baden, pp. 165-190.

Scott, W.R. and Meyer, J.W. (1994), 'Developments in Institutional Theory', in W.R. Scott, J.W. Meyer and Associates, *Institutional Environments and Organizations. Structural Complexity and Individualism*, Sage, Thousand Oaks, pp. 1-8.

Short, J.F. (1984), 'The Social Fabric at Risk: Toward the Social Transformation of Risk Analysis', *American Sociological Review*, vol. 49, pp. 711-725.

Short, J.F. (1989), 'Toward a Sociolegal Paradigm of Risk', *Law and Policy*, vol. 11, pp. 241-252.

Siekmann, H. (1994), 'Rechtsprobleme umweltorientierter kommunaler Benutzungsgebühren', *Zeitschrift für angewandte Umweltforschung*, vol. 7, pp. 441-447.

Shackle. G.L.S. (1949), *Expectations in Economics*, Cambridge University Press, Cambridge.

Simon, H.A. (1957), *Administrative Behavior*, 2nd edition, The Free Press, New York.

Simon, H.A. (1960), *The New Science of Management Decision*, Harper & Row, New York.

Simon, H.A. (1965), 'Administrative Decision Making', *Public Administration Review*, vol. 25, pp. 31-37.

Simon, H.A. (1967), 'The Changing Theory and Changing Practice of Public Administration', in Ithiel de Sola Pool (ed.), *Contemporary Political Science*, McGraw-Hill, New York, pp. 86-120.

Simon, H.A. (1981), *The Sciences of the Artificial*, 2nd edition, The MIT Press, Cambridge.

Smelser, N.J. (1992), 'The Rational Choice Perspective', Rationality and Society, vol. 4, pp. 381-410.

SRU (Sachverständigenrat für Umweltfragen) (1991), *Abfallwirtschaft. Sondergutachten September 1990*, Metzler-Poeschel, Stuttgart.

SRU (Sachverständigenrat für Umweltfragen) (1998), *Umweltgutachten 1998*, Metzler-Poeschel, Stuttgart.

Stichweh, R. (1995), 'Systemtheorie und Rational Choice Theorie', *Zeitschrift für Soziologie*, vol. 24, pp. 395-406.

Stinchcombe, A.L. (1990), *Information and Organizations*, University of California Press, Berkeley.

Stogdill, R.M. (1959), *Individual Behavior and Group Achievement*, Oxford University Press, New York.

Thompson, J.D. (1967), *Organizations in Action*, McGraw-Hill, New York.

Thompson, M. (1998), 'Waste and Fairness', *Social Research*, vol. 65, pp. 55-73.
Thompson,, M., Ellis, R. and Wildavsky, A. (1990), *Cultural Theory*, Westview Press, Boulder.
Vorwerk, V., Timmermeister, M. and Brandt, A. (1997), *Die politische Umsetzung einer Bürgerbeteiligung*, Institute for Science and Technnology Studies, Bielefeld.
Wagner, R. (1996), 'Die Misere der aktuellen Abfallwirtschaftspolitik am Beispiel der Region Hamm-Unna', *Zeitschrift für angewandte Umweltforschung*, vol. 9, pp. 565-572.
Weick, K.E. (1979), *The Social Psychology of Organizing*, Addison-Wesley, Reading.
Weick, K.E. (1995), *Sensemaking in Organizations*, Sage, Thousand Oaks.
Werner, F. (1971), 'Jurist und Techniker', in F. Werner, *Recht und Gericht in unserer Zeit*, Heymanns, Cologne, pp. 379-389.
Wiemer, K. et al. (1995a), 'Kohlenstoff als Ressource', *Müll und Abfall*, vol. 27, pp. 403-415.
Wiemer, K. et al. (1995b), 'Das Trockenstabilatverfahren', *Müll und Abfall*, vol. 27, pp. 769-777.
Wienhöfer, E. (ed.) (1996), *Bürgerforen als Verfahren der Technikfolgenbewertung*, Centre for Technology Assessment, Stuttgart.
Wiesenthal, H. (1987), 'Rational Choice. Ein Überblick über Grundlinien, Theorefelder, und neuere Themenakquisition eines sozialwissenschaftlichen Paradigmas', *Zeitschrift für Soziologie*, vol. 16, pp. 434-449.
Wiesenthal, H. (1994), Lernchancen der Risikogesellschaft. Über gesellschaftliche Innovationspotentiale und die Grenzen der Risikosoziologie, *Leviathan*, vol. 22, pp. 135-159.
Wiesenthal, H. (1995), 'Konventionelles und unkonventionelles Organisationslernen: Literaturreport und Ergänzungsvorschlag', *Zeitschrift für Soziologie*, vol. 24, pp. 137-155.
Wildavsky, A. (1988), *Searching for Safety*, Transaction Books, New Brunswick.
White, H.C. (1992), *Identity and Control: A Structural Theory of Social Action*, Princeton University Press, Princeton.
Wynne, B. (1987), *Risk Management and Hazardous Waste. Implementation and the Dialectics of Credibility*, Springer, Berlin.
Wynne, B. (1992), 'Risk and Social Learning: Reification to Engagement', in S. Krimsky and D. Golding (eds), *Social Theories of Risk*, Praeger, London, pp. 275-297.
Zieschank, R. (1991), 'Mediationsverfahren als Gegenstand sozialwissenschaftlicher Forschung', Zeitschrift für Umweltpolitik und Umweltrecht, vol. 14, pp. 27-51.
Zwehl, W. and Kaufmann, M. (1994), 'Ökologisierung kommunaler Gebührenpolitik aus betriebswirtschaftlicher Sicht', *Zeitschrift für angewandte Umweltforschung*, vol. 7, pp. 447-453.